PRAISE FOR DAWAYNE WILLIAMS'
REPUTATIONS

"Dawayne Williams is a brilliant storyteller. In his memoirs, Dawayne places you in the middle of DC's crime zone where a young man's survival is a number's game. This colorful true tale details Dawayne's many near death experiences as he is shot, stabbed, left to die and spiritually awakened amidst his cousin's murder mission and the city's drug wars. *Reputations Fade Away* is a deliberate page-turner...every chapter implores you to discover what's next."

—Yvonne Rose, Associate Publisher
Amber Communications Group, Inc.

"Gird yourselves for a titanic ride of laughter, harsh adversity, cruel truth, family betrayal and warfare that leaves echoes in the soul! Yet through it all Dawayne Williams is everything opposite society claims a Black Man will be that wore his shoes! He is victorious, relevant and a "CLASS ACT" for every youth that has had a hard knocks life to emulate after! *Reputations Fade Away* must make it to the Silver Screen!"

—Virgie Lindsey, Author-Gospel
Artist-Philanthropist-Promoter

"Dawayne Williams' book, *Reputations Fade Away* is the story of a generation of young DC men, some who ended up dead or in jail. He was one of the luckier ones who seem to have escaped the worst. He did not escape the pain. His book is a voice from the streets that describes life on the edge in DC, where his love affairs with women are in many ways more vicious to him than his violent conflicts with other men. His book is a revelation to all."

—Sam Ford, ABC 7 & News Channel 8,
Washington, DC

"Williams has the good instincts of a story-teller, and his memoir is an important document in the tradition of Marc Levin's eye-opening 1999 HBO documentary "Thug Life in D.C." If we want our city's longstanding reputations for violence to fade away soon, some in our government—and definitely some who run our schools—will need to reckon with the challenges Williams' book describes."
—Jim Myers, *Jill Rag Newspaper*

"*Reputations Fade Away* is the true-life story of a former Drug dealer. Today Williams is reaching out to kids and telling them there is more to life than crime."
—Mark Segraves, WTOP Radio

"*Reputations Fade Away* is compelling reading, troubled, challenging and a survivor's story."
—Bruce DePuyt, News Talk host
Channel 8, Washington DC

"Powerful message in Dawayne Williams' book *Reputations Fade Away!*"
—Nancy Yamada, News host
Channel 9, Washington, DC

6,591 Murders In Washington, DC

Reputations Fade Away

The Memoir Of Dawayne Williams

By Dawayne Williams

Kojack Enterprises
Washington DC

To: "Marquis"

Thanks for your Support

God Bless

Remember Purpose

Dawayne Williams

Reputations Fade Away
The Memoir of Dawayne Williams

By Dawayne Williams

Published by:
Kojack Enterprise
P.O. Box 91733
Washington, DC 20090
Kojackkmw@aol.com
www.Reputationsfadeaway.com

Dawayne Williams, Publisher
Yvonne Rose / Quality Press, Editorial & Project Consultant
The Printed Page, Interior Design / Cover Layout
Cover Photo and Design by Kevin Dickerson, www.kevindickinson.com

All Bible verses are taken from King James Versions of the Bible

ISBN 13: 978-0-9786547-2-6
ISBN 10: 0-9786547-2-2

Dedication

This book is dedicated to my grandmother Beatrice, my mother Joyce and my beautiful beloved daughter Khari. No one else could have given me the love that God has placed in you three. Thanks for being my angels.

Reputations Fade Away

Acknowledgements

Thank you Lord God for your only begotten Son Jesus Christ and the testimony you allowed me to write under your grace, will, power and spirit. And I overcame them by the blood of the Lamb, and by the word of my testimony. (Revelation 12:11)

Mom, I thank you for all the memories, tears, and prayers. Besides God, you're my hero because you've been there through all the hardship and pain I've suffered in life. I know I went left when you told me to go right but I thank you for staying on me and never giving up on your son. In all essence, I've realized the true appreciation of life because of you. Everything I've ever tried to do, you believed in me and I will never forget that. NEVER! I love you Mom.

SPECIAL, SPECIAL thanks to: Lee's Barber Shop, Chanel Wilson, Daniel Jones, Roger & Lynz Richardson and family, John Lewis, Irish Ross, Labonita Graves, Tyrone Dancy, Regina L. Martin, Bennisha Lucas, Lamont Walker, Javiar Pelham, Jonathan Ingram, Sir Rodney, Terrace Dior Thomas, Friendship House, Russell Wester, Yvonne Rose, Amber Books/Quality Press and the entire Washington Wizards Basketball Operations. Without your support and encouragement I would've given up. Thank you all for being there for me.

….And thanks to all of you who were key to this project in ways you can't imagine: "Jim Myers" writer of the "Hill Rag Newspaper." My niece Kimmiko, my cousin Tilly Willy Wilson, Sharon Barnes, Ms.

Simpson, Mr. Scott, Antwone Fisher (Antwone, your movie inspired me to write my story, because of God and your movie "Reputations Fade Away" is now a book and not a thought), Rubin "Hurricane" Carter & Lazarus ("Behold a son that is risen from the dead" quoted from the movie "Hurricane"), Muhammad Ali (The Champ is Here, The Champ is Here), Dr. Martin Luther King, Jr., Michael Jordan, T.D. Jakes, Pastor C.E. Pointer, DC Bookman & Tish Short, Vickie Stringer, Nathan McCall, Sister Souljah, Rick Warren, Steve Fuller, William "SunnyBoy" Thompson, My Pastor Betty Peoples & Joe Peoples…for encouraging me every Sunday and pushing me towards my goals and dreams.

Contents

Contents

As I reached to put the car in gear to drive off, this nigga pulled out his gun. I froze and looked him dead in his eyes. The thought ran across my mind, "I know this nigga isn't about to shoot me," but before I could finish my thoughts my sentence was interrupted by ten bullets sending me into total shock. The first two bullets swiftly greeted my back, resting directly on my spinal cord; the other eight anonymous bullets demolished my mother's car. I couldn't move or yell for help! All I could whisper was, "Nigga I'ma get chu"!

Chapter 1

Congress Park S. E.

October 1984, my family moved to Congress Park Projects located in the South East section of Washington, D.C.

Congress Park Projects is a 380-unit complex, which covers Savannah Street, Congress Street, 14th Place, Savannah Place, Alabama Avenue and 13th Place. My family moved into 3402 13th Place. At that time, my family consisted of my mother, London and my brother, Wylie. I'm two years older than my brother Wylie and I had celebrated my ninth birthday three months prior. The playground is three blocks away on the school grounds of Malcolm X Elementary, and we were anxious to go outside and play.

Before Wylie and I could go outside London laid down the rules of our new neighborhood. She said, "The both of you better listen to every word I say. This neighborhood isn't like our old neighborhood. If either of you get into a fight, jump them. I don't care whether they're young or old. If you're out-numbered, pick up something and bust'em in their head. No going over any friend's house without my permission. No talking to any strangers, no selling drugs or using them. Am I understood?" We replied, "Yes mamma." Wylie and I knew if we didn't obey London, we had a butt whippen coming.

We had to adapt to our environment quickly. Wherever I went Wylie was right beside me. When London transferred us to the neighborhood school Malcolm X Elementary, we were exposed as the new kids on the block. Kids in my class walked up to me and asked, "where you from?" I said, "Congress Park." Once I said Congress Park I was introduced to other kids who lived in the neighborhood. What Wylie and I didn't know was that Congress Park had a crew. They called themselves "The Young-Young Crew". The Young-Young crew is a vicious circle of teenagers and youngsters who controlled our entire neighborhood and school. They would jump, rob, kill and steal from you in a heartbeat...especially if you had a bike, skateboard, pair of new kicks or jewelry like a silver or gold chain.

Most of them carried knives, guns and baseball bats for protection. Wylie and I never pledged to join the Young-Young crew, but we became friends instantly with all of them to protect ourselves. We figured if you can't beat them you might as well be friends with them. Many of the members lived in our neighborhood and in the surrounding areas like Parkland, Garfield, 10th place and 15th place. In the 1980's D.C. had a crew in every section of the city, such as: Gangster Chronicles Crew, 8th and H crew, Young Jaw Breakers, A Team, Hill Boys and Minnesota Avenue Crew.

We had to prove to the kids in the other projects that we were just as bad as they were. We did all sorts of things from busting out windows to stealing. Every male in the projects got tested by another male to see if he had the heart to fight. Wylie and I passed that test. We wanted to come outside and play everyday; so, we fought whoever came our way whenever we had to. If anyone messed with either one of us, they had to deal with the other. We knew enough people in our neighborhood to be considered cool, and because we lived in Congress Park we got respect.

Crack came onto the drug scene in 1983, a year before we moved into the projects. Our neighborhood went from bad to worse; and even to this day Congress Park is still infested with drugs.

The difference between cocaine and crack is that cocaine lingers for a while before the high is felt, but crack gives a rush that hits immediately. James Brown made a song called "King Heroin" that spoke the truth about the King of the street (Heroin). Well, crack had become the Queen of the streets…. it took over Congress Park.

Some Miami and New York niggas moved into our neighborhood to set up their operations. The key to selling drugs and making big profit is the location. McDonalds, Wendy's and Popeye's can be placed anywhere, but only the ones in the right location makes a profit. So that's why out-of-towners like the New York and Miami niggas targeted Congress Park projects in 1987, but a year later they started getting killed and robbed. In fact, the death toll in D.C. roared from 145 to 369 murders a year between 1985 and 1988. The killing and the beefs increased when the out-of-town niggas tried to take over the streets of D.C. with guns and drugs. The local news called it "the war on drugs." Many people believed that only D.C. niggas were being killed, but that wasn't the case.

There were shooting's going on twenty-four seven in my neighborhood. London constantly reminded Wylie and me, "If they start shooting get on the ground first. Check yourself to see if you've been hit, and once the shooting stops come in the house immediately."

The police were scared to come into our neighborhood, unless they had backup. When they came to Congress Park there would be five to ten squad cars with four officers to a car. They would set up roadblocks to check for I.D.'s and registrations. There were at least three incidents in which I've witnessed a police officer being beaten with his own baton and having his gun confiscated. So, for precautionary reasons, police officers always brought a lot of backup. The police who wore uniforms and drove squad cars set up the roadblocks. The "jump-outs" were officers who dressed like everyday people and the cars they drove were unmarked…they only came on the first and fifteenth of the month when welfare checks where cashed.

Some mothers paid their rent for the month, bought food and other necessities; but there were other mothers who had only one thing on their mind—to get high. They couldn't wait to receive their check so they could pay off a drug advance. Many of those mothers were so addicted that their kids didn't eat and none of their bills got paid. Most of those kids had to take the responsibility of making sure that there was food and clothes, and the rent was paid before their mother got high.

The jump-outs were slick when they came. The hustlers stood on the corner all day and night selling drugs. Sometimes I would be sitting in front of my building and then, all of sudden, there would be cars coming at full speed hitting their brakes inches before stopping at the sidewalk. The police would jump out with their guns drawn saying, "get on the ground" and if you didn't move fast enough they would kick and punch you until you fell, covering yourself up like Rodney King. The jump-outs soon became corrupted and just as violent as the hustlers. Some jump-outs started taking money and drugs from the hustlers and then let them go. There were also many incidents when the jump-outs were shot and killed.

Behind all the drugs and money there was rivalry from other neighborhoods, schools and personal rival within your own

4

neighborhood. There were a few hustlers who concealed guns while they sold drugs. Some hustlers couldn't tell whether the jump-outs were their enemies or if they were Stick up Boyz.

London didn't want the streets and crime to take Wylie and me. She made sure we attended Malcolm X Elementary School every day. At lunchtime we would sneak off the school grounds to purchase some candy from the shopping mall three blocks away. We knew if we got caught we'd get suspended from school and whipped by London.

Everyday after school we'd buy even more candy from the ice cream truck, which was always parked in front of our building. We would buy candy like: Johnny Apple Treats, Alexander Grapes, Jingles, Cherry Chains, Boston Baked Beans, Sugar Daddy, Honey Buns, Big Bubble, Jaw Breakers and Bomb Pops. London always gave us spending money to buy junk food that wasn't good for our teeth. After getting our junk food we'd rush up the stairs full speed, banging on the door and calling London as if it were an emergency. After London opened the door we'd run past her to watch cartoons…we did our homework while we watched T.V. We watched cartoons like Fat Albert, G.I. Joe, Thunder Cats, Superfriends and Batman from the time we entered the door until they went off. Then, after looking at cartoons we'd watch all the sitcoms like Sanford and Son, 227, Facts of Life, Good Times, What's Happening, Give me a Break, Different Strokes, The Jefferson's, The Cosby Show, Dynasty, Dallas and Knots Landing.

Friday night was the best night to watch T.V. From eleven thirty to one o'clock in the morning, Wylie and I watched Friday night videos, like Music Video's Connection with Candy Shannon. Then, after the videos went off, we watched Benny Hill who was a freaky old man running around looking up women's dresses. When Benny went off, I tried moving the antenna from side to side, and if that didn't work I'd placed aluminum foil around the antenna. I tried hard as I could to get Super T.V. on channel 50 to come in clearly so that I could see the naked women, but it never worked. The T.V. would only clear up for a second then the screen would become bleary. On Saturday mornings Wylie and I watched cartoons, wrestling and Bruce Lee until noon. Then we'd go outside and play for the rest of day. London kept us looking clean and nice all the time. We had two sets of clothes—outside and school. If London caught us playing in our school clothes, we got a whippen.

London made sure we kept fresh haircuts. Everybody in my neighborhood called me, "Kojack". I had gotten the Kojack look when I was about nine months old after London ordered some hair grease out of a true stories magazine. The grease was supposed to make my hair grow in five days…guaranteed. London applied the grease as instructed and all my hair fell out.

She wanted my hair to grow long enough so she could braid it, something she wasn't able to do for two more years. London's girl friend Diane saw my head and said, "girl he looks just like Kojak" and they started laughing. From that day, the name Kojack stuck to me like super glue. "Kojak" is a detective played by Telly Savalas from the 1970's T.V. show called "Kojak".

Because London couldn't afford to get Wylie and me haircuts on a bi-weekly basis, she purchased a pair of clippers and cut our hair herself. I hated when London cut my hair because she could only cut a baldhead. Bald heads attracted too much attention. All the older guys smacked our heads as if we were a set of congas, the niggas made up excuses to smack our heads… excuses like, "my fault I thought you were somebody else." When they smacked my head, I would be thinking to myself, "I'ma kill all these niggas when I get older."

I had to do something to stop London from cutting my hair because I was starting to get fingerprints on my head. So, I started doing the cut and run. I'd go into any barbershop without money and tell the barber I wanted a taper. A taper is a haircut that left some hair on the top of the head and the side of your head bald. After my hair was cut the barber waited for my approval. I always said, "good" even if they took my shape up too far back.

After the barber brushed me off, I'd get up calm and cool, look in the mirror on the wall and wait for the opportunity to escape. One thing I noticed was that all barbers get distracted at least for a second or two. When they turned their heads the other way I'd run as fast as I could, like a speeding bullet. I wouldn't stop running until I felt safe and away from harm. I never got caught doing the cut and run because I went to different barbershops. What also made me so successful was I always went to the barbers next to the door... that made my escape easier. I always lied to London when she asked me, "How did you get your hair cut?" I'd say, "I found the money or my father gave me some money." After a while, she didn't bother asking me again.

I felt sorry for Wylie because he had a peanut head. Everybody loved smacking his head, even his father smacked his head for fun. One day I smacked his head while he was asleep. Wylie woke up and threw a glass ashtray at me, busting the side of my leg wide open. I had to get seven stitches. I knew I could beat Wylie, but that didn't stop him from challenging me. There were times I had to beat him up; then I would buy him candy or do his chores for him because I was afraid he'd tell London, and we both would get a whippen.

I loved hanging with the older teenagers in the hood, guys like Baby Brother, Freaky, and Daddy-O. On Thursday nights Baby Brother would gather all the niggas in the neighborhood who were brave enough to walk down to Martin Luther King Avenue. We'd go down to MLK and jump anybody that Baby Brother told us to jump. Baby Brother would knockout drunks and St. Elizabeth patients; then before leaving the avenue, everybody would rush into the High's corner store, grab whatever we could and run all the way home.

Wylie hung out with the younger guys in the neighborhood. They went to the creek to catch snakes, frogs, tadpoles, crayfish and rabbits. Every dog Wylie saw was a Pit-Bull to him. No one could tell him different. The dog could've been a Germen Shepherd... but the way Wylie looked at it, if a dog could bark it was a Pit Bull. Wylie had a love for animals that I didn't have, especially dogs.

Every day that we lived in the projects was an adventure. A fight could simply start by stepping on a person's shoes or looking at a person the wrong way; and it was automatic if you intentionally bumped into a nigga. With all the frustration, attitudes, jealousy, gossip and drugs, the projects taught me how to be a quick thinker and I learned that I couldn't show a sign of weakness.

Society labels anyone from the projects—male or female—as a drug dealer, user, robber, thief, prostitute, and uneducated. I learned the mindset of the projects that helped me with everyday life, and that was how to survive. Because tomorrow isn't promised, the reality of it all is that the projects can become too much for any person to handle. We had our ups and we had our downs, but we did what we had to do to survive. London tolerated four years of fighting, shooting and gambling in the projects. In 1988, after London got off welfare she got a good government job and we moved out of the projects...something that her girlfriends said she would never do. But, by getting a job and working hard instead of sitting home collecting a welfare check London proved to them that it could be done.

Chapter 2

Beatrice

Whenever London wanted to go out on the weekend, she sent Wylie and me to my grandmother Beatrice's house. Beatrice showed no favoritism toward us. She hugged and kissed both of us a lot, telling us she loved us. I laughed at Beatrice at times when Wylie and I got into trouble, because I knew she didn't want to beat us. She had an old white belt that couldn't kill a fly. Beatrice didn't like to see us cry. Even when London beat us, Beatrice would rescue us by either picking us up or telling London not to beat us anymore...we knew Beatrice's word stood.

Friday nights were the highlight of the week. Everybody knew that Beatrice's house was the place to be. She always invited her girlfriends and they would in turn invite more friends. The party started at seven every week and the music didn't stop playing until four in the morning. They listened to music by the Temptations, Marvin Gaye, Sam Cooke, the Supremes and Otis Redding. Beatrice wouldn't allow Wylie and me to be in her presence. We were only allowed to say, "hi" to everyone then, we had to go back into the bedroom to look at T.V., only coming out to use the bathroom.

One of Beatrice favorite songs was by Otis Redding, "Sitting on the Dock of the Bay." It seemed whenever this song played the dancing stopped...as if they all were sitting side by side on a real dock...the drinking increased and the mood swing became relaxed. Everyone seemed to be reflecting on their past failures, pain and struggles with life.

I had a tendency to wake up after Beatrice and her friends went to sleep. There would be cans of beer and large quantities of liquor on the table. I would sneak into the front room to sample every-thing…cigarettes, Budweiser, vodka and Hennessey. Once I felt the buzz from drinking, there was no telling what I was going to get into.

All kinds of thoughts would rush to my mind, then I would act on them…. thoughts like turning on all the water faucets in the house and letting them run, striking some matches and watching them burn, opening up all the windows and doors, and getting on top of Angela who was one of Beatrice's friends. Angela was big and fat like a buffalo and she looked like a moose. Being intoxicated made me think I could have sex with a lady that was old enough to be my mother.

After I got into bed with Angela I lifted up her dress, then I slowly pulled her underwear down. Angela felt her underwear moving so I tried to play it off as if I were asleep. But she woke up looking around and that's when I knew I was caught. Angela got up from Beatrice's bed and headed towards the front room, screaming at the top of her lungs panicking, "Bea, please wake up, wake up now!"

Beatrice was one of the hardest persons I ever attempted to wake up in my life…when I say hard, I mean hard. There were times I turned the T.V. up as loud as I could, jumped on her bed, slammed doors, let the phone ring for as long as it could… she slept through it all. When it came to waking her up, I had to be creative. One time I threw a shoe at Bea and I blackened her eye. She even slept through that until her eye swelled up.

Angela screamed even louder, waking up everyone in the house. "Bea, please wake up, your house is flooded with water!" Beatrice immediately woke up, looking around in amazement. Bea and her friends cleaned up everything and shut all the windows, including the balcony door, and cut off all the water faucets. I got whipped for everything I did that night. Because Angela was fat, all of Beatrice's friends started calling me "Fat booty." The rumor quickly got around the family that I liked fat booty women…. I hated that name with a passion.

Beatrice's neighborhood had a lot of kids. On Saturday everybody met at the playground. I became well known for fighting all the time and was considered crazy for my age. I did things the other kids were afraid to do. They were amazed at how foul my mouth was; every other word was a cuss word. If they didn't share their toys and bikes with Wylie and me, we beat them up and then took their bikes and toys. We'd play with them until their parents chased us into the house for roughing up their children.

Those kids were considered middle class because of the neighborhood. They didn't have to fight every day like we did to protect ourselves in the projects. They could walk and play freely without a care in the world. They didn't have a neighborhood bully until Wylie and I came over on the weekend to terrorize the neighborhood. Some kids didn't come out of their house on weekends, knowing we were outside.

At the time, Sunnyboy and his brother Fathead lived with Beatrice. They both were always out in the streets or working. Sunnyboy and I became real close…he became a mentor to me. I observed everything Sunny did and imitated him because he was respected by the youngin and the hustlers in the neighborhood.

Sunnyboy was a boxer…he trained four days out of the week. If he wasn't training at the Boys' Club, he'd train in the house for hours. Because of Sunnyboy, I learned how to fight and keep niggas off me.

In the 80's you had to fight… a good fighter was well respected by everybody, I mean everybody. Fighting symbolized manhood, bravery and heart. If I wasn't a fighter I would've been another kid with a toy that someone would've taken away from me. If I didn't stand up for myself, I would've been bullied for the rest of my life. I learned how to fight because I wanted the respect and praise that I had seen other niggas get. The older hustlers didn't believe that a little nigga like me could blacken another kid's eye. Once my reputation grew, money and respect gave me a little power. I was admired for fighting and I knew I had to keep on fighting to keep my fame. I was encouraged by a lot of older hustlers to knock out a kid they didn't like or who got smart with them.

The hustlers would tell a kid, "Wait until Kojack come around here. I'ma get him to stomp you out." Sometimes the kid would cuss both of us out, without me being present to defend myself. Hearing this made me want to go out and kill the kid. But, Sunnyboy would step in and say, "Kojack ain't fighting nobody, if he isn't getting paid." Sunny would collect the money then I'd go and crush the kid once I laid my eyes on him. I was paid anywhere from 20 to 50 dollars a fight. When I made fifty dollars I would try to beat the black off a kid. Every time I fought there would be crowds of people watching and instigating.

Sunnyboy taught me how to fight, lift weights and jog when I was seven years old. Whenever I didn't do what Sunny told me to do, he'd punch me in my stomach. When he punched me, he always knocked the wind out of me. I'd be laying on the floor gasping for air and Sunny would say, "Get up nigga." I hated Sunny for knocking the wind out of me but by learning from a person who was ten years older than me, how could I go wrong. He taught me different fighting techniques that saved me from being punked. Sunny always said, "don't go for a nigga's head all the time, hit'um with body punches too. Headshots are good, but nobody expects you to hit them in the stomach, ribs or chest. Most niggas don't even work on their body condition and that's why I have you doing push up's and sit up's to tighten your stomach muscles."

On Sundays Beatrice cooked a big meal for our family. Her two-bedroom apartment would be crowded from wall to wall. Family and friends would sit in places like the hallway, balcony, laundry room and some sat out on the playground…just to eat a good home-cooked meal. Beatrice was a very good hostess and her soul food cooking was the bomb. She'd cook food like: collard greens, candied yams, corn bread, coconut cake, sweet potato pie, turkey, stuffing, fried chicken, BBQ chicken, fish, pig's feet, chitlins, ham, lima beans and macaroni and cheese. I could eat everything Beatrice cooked, except pig's feet and chitlins…their smell made me nauseous. One time London tried to make me eat some chitlins and I wouldn't put the spoon near my mouth. Beatrice had to stop London from beating me, and that made me hate chitlins and pig's feet even more.

Those good Sunday dinners came to a halt. After Beatrice became aware of her illness, she gave up the negative aspects of her life. She was no longer drinking and smoking, but instead she was praying. She knew that God was her only salvation. After she schooled herself about cancer, she informed London. No matter how strong Beatrice tried to disguise the fear of death with happiness, we all knew that her death was inevitable. In the 1980's, there weren't elaborate treatments for cancer, there was nothing to prolong your life, so you simply had to embrace your last moments.

When London became fully aware of Beatrice's illness, she took a leave from her job. She realized that it was now time to take care of the woman who has always supported her. London cooked, cleaned and did the laundry; she also received help from family members. Everyone found time to fit Beatrice into his or her schedule. Beatrice's symptoms began to show. Her bones had begun to deteriorate. Her skin was thin and she lost a lot of her hair. Beatrice seemed to have gotten weaker with every minute and yet she still found the strength to laugh and smile in her pain. Beatrice knew that she was going to heaven.

She said to me one day, "Lamont, believe in God and in His Son Jesus Christ; and if you believe in Him, when you die you will go to Heaven." Lamont is the name she gave me from Sanford and Son. "Lamont, grandma is going to die, but I'll be waiting in Heaven for you. Okay?"

I dropped my head and my eyes filled with tears, not understanding why she had to die. Beatrice knew that I was too young to fully comprehend those statements, but little did she know, those statements would be carved into my heart forever.

In the winter of 1986, God sent angels down and gave Beatrice her wings. For sixteen years, Beatrice had worked at NASA Space Flight Center. All Beatrice's earnings from her previous occupation— insurance money, stocks and bonds—and her car were left to London.

Before Beatrice passed away she warned London, "Be careful of my family. There's money involved. All of my family members aren't for you and most of them are jealous of you. You're my child, my only child. I wouldn't tell you anything wrong, take the money I left for you, buy yourself a house and invest the rest in your children's future."

London didn't take Beatrice's last words to heart. She was blindsided by the anguish and misery she felt. She became the target of manipulation. Everyone needed money for whatever reason. It got to the point where my family wouldn't baby-sit Wylie and me on the weekend like they did before Beatrice's death, because they weren't getting paid to watch us.

There were a lot of gimmicks to rob London blind. At my Aunt Eve's house, things would get mysteriously broken. London rarely refused to give my family money, because that's the kind of person she was. She gave from her heart; she loved to share, so she embraced her mischievous family during the time of her emotional need. She would always endure loans, favors and borrowers because, at the time, it eased her sorrow.

To say the least, London was the backbone of my family, financially. Beatrice's death was definitely stressful for her. She had to take the bitter with the sweet. London found her strength in God. She knew she had to be a living example for Wylie and me. Through her weakness, I gained strength. I learned how to guard myself from pain. I hid my feelings for a long time, because I feared being hurt. During that time, God used my heart as a dwelling place. Sometimes at night while in bed, I would open up and talk to God...I questioned Him about a lot of things I didn't understand about life and death.

Chapter 3
Cousins

London and Faith became, Bonnie and Clyde. They did everything together from borrowing each other's clothes to getting their butts whipped. They couldn't tolerate not being around each other. Faith was like a big sister to London. She looked out for her, making sure she didn't do drugs or anything harmful. They made a childhood promise to each other stating that no matter what happened, their children would be in good hands if one of them died. If Faith died before London, London promised to look after Tyson (Faith's son) and vice versa for Wylie and me.

Unfortunately in August 1984, Faith was the first to die. She overdosed on rat poisoning, causing London to go into shock. What was London to do without her cousin, sister, best friend and confidante? London pushed through Faith's death the same way she overcame Beatrice's death two years later by turning to God for guidance.

London became Tyson's godmother. She kept her promise and was there for Tyson whenever he needed her. There were times London bought Tyson clothes and shoes before she bought them for Wylie and me.

Tyson lived with my Aunt Eve, who was his grandmother and Faith's mother. She took custody of Tyson after Faith's death. Eve lived on Constitution Avenue near the R.F.K. Stadium where the Redskins used to play before they moved out to Landover, Maryland.

After Beatrice passed away, London resorted to Aunt Eve to baby-sit for Wylie and me on the weekends. While in Aunt Eve's care, Wylie and I knew we were in a strict environment. She always had a full house consisting of her five children, two of her sister's children, and four grandchildren.... all of these people lived in a five-bedroom house.

When Eve whipped one, she whipped all. There were times when we had just gotten to Eve's house and we got a whippen, even though we weren't guilty of anything. Eve's children always lied or exaggerated situations. They would never be honest and accept the fact that they were wrong, because of their fear of Eve. And, Eve didn't like us telling on each other...to her it showed a sign of weakness, but when it came down to whippens it was her way of catching the right person. Eve would say "everybody go upstairs to the back porch now." While Eve went looking for her ironing cord, everybody started putting on extra clothes to protect us from welts that popped up on our skin like the letter "U".

Martin, Eve's only son and the comedian of our family, would always laugh at how we cried, what we said, or how we reacted to our whippen. Everybody would be crying and boo-hooing, then Martin would crack a joke and everybody would start laughing to ease the pain.

On Friday nights we had dancing contests to see who was the best dancer. We would do dances like the cabbage patch, Pee Wee Herman, the pop, break dancing, happy feet, prat, Elf, Smurfs and the snake. Martin was the best dancer out of all of us. We'd dance to songs like Run DMC's "Walk this Way," Salt-N-Pepa's "My Mic Sounds Nice," Doug E. Fresh's "The Show" and UTFO's "Roxanne, Roxanne." Our favorite movies every weekend were Breakin, Beat Street, Krush Groove and every movie Richard Pryor starred in.

When it was time for us to go to bed we had shoe fights. We would throw boots, high heels, tennis shoes and dress shoes at each other.

To make it more exciting we would turn the lights out so the room would be pitch black. Somebody would cry if they got hit. We'd sit up until three in the morning and joned on each other's mothers. Martin and Caesar joned on London's Jeri Curl and I joned on Eve's batman glasses. We would laugh so hard until our stomachs ached.

I never could out-jone Martin, none of us could. Nobody wanted to be the first to fall asleep and the last to wake up because we'd line up and fart in each other's faces. Farting would lead to fights, so I made sure that I was one of the ones to fall asleep last and the first to wake up.

Saturday morning, cleaning up the house was priority after breakfast. Everyone was assigned a cleaning duty. After we watched cartoons, we went to the Boys and Girls Club. At the club we'd swim, play basketball, and chase girls up and down the steps all day, until I got tired; then I would go to see Chicago on 15th Street.

Just blocks away from our Nation's Capitol, there's a world of drugs, winos, and prostitution....a world of vicious killers that our city newspaper (The Washington Post) has written many stories about. Fifteenth Street is the hangout spot for junkies, hustlers, thieves and killers. The convenience, Chinese, cleaners and liquor stores are all located on 15th Street. When Eve sent us to the store she timed us. If we didn't come back in twenty minutes, we got a whippen.

I always made up reasons and excuses to go to 15th Street to see my father. This was the only way I got to see him, so I risked getting a whippen from Eve. London and my father broke up when she was only two months pregnant with me. The first time London had sex she got pregnant by Chicago. Chicago wanted London to have an abortion but London told him, "I'm not having an abortion and that's final." Chicago replied, "Well, I already have a son and another child on the way. I can't afford to take care of three children."

I was born at 7 pounds and 14 ounces. When London looked at me she said, "Lord have mercy, if this boy don't look like Chicago."

Then Beatrice replied, "London, for those who disown their kids or don't acknowledge them, the child comes out looking just like their father." When I was three years old London took me to see Chicago in jail. Chicago asked me, "What do you want for Christmas?" I told him, "I want a green machine and a big wheel." "Well I'll see that you get one of them, okay?" "Okay." I kept on playing around like a normal kid would, not paying him any attention. Chicago got out of D.C. jail in 1982 and he automatically went back to doing what he does best, selling drugs. He wasn't into selling marijuana, crack, or cocaine...he sold heroin.

On 15th Street, Chicago is a legend; he was also well known throughout the city by the hustlers and junkies. His reputation spoke for itself.... niggas knew he carried a gun and had flunkies watching his back.

Whenever I approached Chicago on 15th Street, all his friends looked at me in amazement. His friends would say things like, "Man that's your son? Oh my God he looks just like you. Chicago, man you spit that boy out. If you disown him they need to lock you up and throw away the key." Chicago pulled me to the side and said, "what are you doing up here? Didn't I warn you before not to come up here? You don't belong up here...you're too young to be in this type of environment."

"I know that but I need some money?" Then he'd go into his pocket and pull out a big bankroll of money. That would make me say, "wow" in my thoughts. "Here, here's twenty dollars, call me on my car phone if you need me. Now I better not catch you back up here." "Okay, thanks Dad." Many times I walked away smiling because I got some money. But, still I felt empty inside because I really wanted us to have a father and son relationship. I wanted Chicago to know I valued him more than money. I needed what money couldn't buy and that was his time.

Wylie, Martin, and Tyson would be waiting for me a block away on 14th Street. They all would ask me, "Man did you get some money?" "Yeah, let's go to the candy store." I always treated them when I had money. But sometimes Tyson and Martin would tell Eve that I got some money from Chicago. Then she would ask me for the money and she'd tell London that she used it to buy food. After they snitched on me a couple of times, I stopped telling them when I had money.

In 1986, Chicago got busted driving in his Cadillac with a gun and a small amount of drugs. Chicago told me he believed somebody called the police on him. While Chicago was out on bail he sold his Jaguar, Honda Civic and his Saab. When he got sentenced he left his apartment to his wife. In the hustling game, if you're on top for a while, niggas get jealous. In Chicago's case they didn't kill or rob him because he was hard to get to because of his reputation and his connections. So, someone took the easy route and called the police on him, knowing he had his pistol under his car seat.

He left his wife his apartment and enough cash to pay the bills while he did his thirty-six months in jail. Eventually she got on drugs and was evicted from the apartment because she had fallen behind in the rent. With nine months to go, Chicago was ferocious when he found out his wife had spent all the money he left her and that she was about to be evicted. To avoid his wife getting evicted from the apartment, he came up with his only plan, and that was to escape from Lorton Correctional Facilities in Virginia. The U.S. Marshals were on Chicago's coattail, but because he was so slick and hard to pinpoint in his old man disguise, he slipped right through their fingers. Chicago even knew how to talk in codes over the phone and disguise his voice.

Chicago caused the Marshals to place him on "America's Most Wanted." One time they pulled up on me, thinking I was Chicago. They even followed me around on the streets and while I was in school, hoping that I could lead them to him. I hated the fact that my father was AMW because our phone lines were tapped. All the girls' numbers I had started with 5, and 5 was the number we couldn't dial out on our phone. I had to wait until I got to Eve's house on the weekend to catch up on my phone calls. After a year on the run, the police caught up with Chicago. I guess he got tired of running and gave up.

When I went to visit Chicago he told me he only escaped because he had $200,000 stashed in the floor of his apartment under his carpet. But before he could get to the apartment he found out that the police and U.S. Marshals were staking out at his place. Chicago said, "Man I couldn't tell my wife about the money because she already spent the money I left her. Just imagine if she would've gotten her hands on the two hundred I had stashed. I would've gone crazy, but I still lost it... so what the hell."

In June 1988, I graduated from Malcolm X elementary school. All my friends were going to Johnson Junior High in September. London had already made it clear that I was going to her old junior high school, Kelly Miler. She wanted me to go there because of how disciplined the principal was when she attended. The same principal has been there since London graduated back in the 70s.

The summer of 1988 was crazy and dangerous. Wylie, Omar, Jason and I spent the summer at Eve's house. With Tyson and Martin we took over the neighborhood as young hoodlums. We jumped all the youngins in the neighborhood. Any nigga who rebelled got whipped. When they saw us coming niggas started running. Wherever we went, we took over. We won the respect of the older hustlers and the youngins in the neighborhood. We fought against the youngins from Potomac Gardens and Kentucky Courts projects. They became our rivalry and the fighting went back and fourth to protect the neighborhood.

Potomac Gardens and 15th Street are the cornerstones of the neighborhood. Kentucky Courts and Potomac Gardens projects consider each other as family. They were one, whereas 15th Street stood alone. There was respect and love amongst the older hustlers from each crew. But the beefing was between youngins of my generation.

The only time we saw Potomac Gardens and Kentucky Courts' niggas was when they came to see the band that played in the neighborhood. Junkyard Band would play at Holy Comforter School just blocks away from Eve's house on East Capitol Street. They outnumbered us five to one, but I wouldn't let anyone from my crew get discouraged. Most of the youngins in this neighborhood were scared of Potomac Garden and Kentucky Courts' niggas. So, on Saturday everybody would team up with us so we could look like a real crew. Either we jumped, chased or took something from all the youngins who teamed up with us. But now, we had to make a name for ourselves. So, we pulled together and called ourselves "the 15th Street Crew." Fifteenth Street was the most popular street in the neighborhood and we knew that word would get out quicker that 15th Street was our turf.

One night we were at the Boys Club on 17th and Massachusetts Avenue where the 3rd Dimension band and show was performing. Martin overheard Carr saying that he and his crew were going to jump my crew after the go-go. After hearing Martin tell me the 411, I told my crew, "Follow me." With my crew behind me, fifteen of us, I walked up to Carr; and without questioning him, I punched him in his face causing him to hit the floor. Before you knew it, we were all fighting. The older hustlers from Carr's crew, Potomac Garden and Kentucky courts jumped in. Plus the older hustlers from my crew, 15th Street jumped in and they all broke up the fight.

From that night, it was World War III between Carr and I. Every time we saw each other, we fought. Even when it seemed like the beef was squashed, we kept attacking each other until someone broke up the fight. After each fight, the older hustlers would make us squash the beef. But we both knew that we'd be fighting the next time we saw each other.

When I started getting the best of Carr, his older brother stepped in. One day, I was standing on the corner of 15th and Independence Avenue. I was slap boxing with Chop and Tyson. A car rolled up on us with three niggas in it. It was Truck Carr's older brother...he and his two hit men jumped out of the car.

Truck walked up to me and smacked the daylight out of me. My face filled up with blood and his handprint was left on my cheek-bone. After nearly falling to the ground, I caught my balance. I stood up and threw up my guards ready to fight. As I was getting ready to swing, my eyes lit up like 1000-watt bulbs. Truck had a gun, a Mack—11, in his jacket. He grabbed hold of the gun, pulling it out; but his hitman grabbed him, "Truck don't kill that youngin." Truck's hitman convinced him to get into the car and they drove off.

Whenever I got into a situation I couldn't handle or a youngin went to get his father or older brother, I had to track down Bishop... he was the baddest nigga in the neighborhood and...he didn't let any-body bother me, even if I was wrong. Bishop was crazy and was known to put a bullet in a nigga. His father and Chicago grew up together and they considered each other family. Bishop also consid-ered me family, and he looked out for my cousins and me.

Bishop is the light-skinned version of the boxer Mike Tyson. If he looked at you, it was as if you looked into the eyes of a lion. Because of his reputation, fear automatically overcame you. When most guys saw him coming they would go the other way. Bishop made it known to everybody that he was not to be messed with. If Bishop walked up on a crap game, niggas would walk away leaving their money for him to pocket. Bishop tracked down Truck and Carr, and we all had a sit down and squashed the beef. Bishop didn't believe in talking, but we were all from the same neighborhood.

After that, the beef between our crews was squashed. Carr and I became good friends. From that beef, people that didn't know me, started asking, "Who's Kojack? Who's he kin to? That young nigga can fight." When they found out that I was Chicago's son my reputation grew. At the age of twelve, I was looked upon as a young hustler. Whatever the hustlers wore, I wore ...expensive clothes, shoes and jewelry. I stood out in the crowd of my cousins and Chop because I had material things they didn't have. The way I dressed amazed a lot of people, because only a few youngins my age dressed like hustlers.

I got my expensive taste from Chicago....everything he bought me was brand name and expensive. One time, in 1985, Chicago took Country, Syrup and me shopping for Christmas....Country is my older brother on my father's side and Syrup is my Uncle Junior's son. There was a big brown bag full of money on the back seat. Chicago told us to open it...we were all amazed to be counting three thousand dollars in ones. Chicago spent a thousand dollars on each of us.

On days we didn't have enough money to go see Junkyard Band, everybody would put me up to ask one of the hustlers for some money. They knew the hustlers would give it to me out of respect for Chicago. One night, when I couldn't borrow enough money to pay everybody's way to see the band, Jason came up with a plan. Whenever we got into a jam, Jason would always come up with something crazy... he's the daredevil type. The idea Jason had in mind was to cut up some soap and sell it as crack, to crack heads. Everybody agreed and we cut up some dial soap and Jason sold a $150 dollars worth. I was able to keep forty of the eighty dollars I borrowed. We all knew that we had an 8:00 PM curfew, so we told everybody else to meet us there later.

The band wouldn't start playing until 11:00 PM and the party was over at 2:00 AM. We'd eat dinner and then clean the house until it was spotless. We did that so Eve would relax and go to sleep, knowing that we ate and the house was clean. We planned to sneak out of the house no later than 11:30 PM. There had been times when Eve came and pulled us all out of a party and whipped us all. She got tired because we did it every week, so she saved her energy until we snuck back into the house and went to sleep, then she would tear us up with the ironing cord.

Since Jason had a little money left over from selling the soap, the next day he went downtown to purchase a starter pistol. I thought it was a real (duce duce) 22. Jason was in the alley just shooting away with the gun. Then he came up with another crazy idea, "Man I bet anyone of you that I could rob a nigga with this gun." Chop, Wylie, Omar, Tyson, and Martin all said, "Man a nigga is going to kill you once they see that's a starter pistol." I didn't bother to get into the conversation between them… I just stood there listening. Jason said, "Well the only way to know is to do it." Jason walked up to this old head coming out of the liquor store. And said, "Nigga, give me all your money." The old head got paranoid and said, "Please don't shoot me, please, please don't kill me." The rest of us were standing far off looking as if this nigga Jason was crazy.

The old head emptied everything from his pockets and even gave up his bottle of Hennessey. But Jason wasn't satisfied, "Nigga, get on the ground." The old head dropped to his knees and started begging Jason to spare his life. Jason looked him dead in his eyes and said, "I'm not going to kill you." The old head replied, "Thank you sir thank you." Jason pulled the trigger shooting all six rounds at the guy. "Pow, Pow, Pow, Pow, Pow, Pow, Pow". We started laughing because we knew he had a starter's pistol.

The old head started screaming loud at the top of us lungs, "I'm shot, I'm shot somebody please call the police, I'm shot." After Jason shot the rounds out he took off running. None of us could run even if we wanted to because we were laughing so hard. A few minutes later the police and ambulance came rushing to the scene.

The old head was still screaming, "I been shot." The paramedics tried to calm him down, but he was too overwhelmed with fear.

Once they calmed him down the paramedic repeated, "Sir you're not shot." He didn't believe the lady. She repeated again, "Sir wherever you're shot, I want you to touch yourself in that area." He did as he was told then he realized he was not shot. We met Jason back at the house and told him everything. We laughed. Jason said, "Man I told you that this blank gun would work."

Two weeks before school opened, all I could think about was going to a new school. I thought of meeting new people, new teachers and some nice looking females. I couldn't think nor imagine what junior high school would be like. Interrupting my thoughts, I was told by Tyson that Chop had gotten into a beef with an old head on 15th Street. I can't remember what the beef was over, but Chop came and got me.

Jason had stolen a 22 long gun from a guy he watched stash it in a bush. The gun was loaded with bullets and ready to be fired. Chop asked Jason if he could see the gun to handle this beef he got into on 15th Street. Jason told Chop, "Man, look it's loaded, so be careful how you hold it." Chop became a part of our crew because he lived across the street from Eve. He was bigger than the rest of us and he had heart. Chop talked a lot, but he backed it up. Out of the entire neighborhood he was the only one who loved fighting more than me. On days that I just wanted to chase girls and rap on the phone, Chop would create a fight or a beef with anybody, then he'd come and get me.

The corner of 15th Street was packed with niggas. We stood in the alley watching everybody's moves, like we had them under surveillance. Chop spotted the nigga, then pulled the gun from his waistband. The nigga he was about to shoot was standing in the crowd on the corner. I asked Chop, "Man do you want to do this?"

Chop shot into the crowd, which dispersed like roaches once the lights were turned on. He shot the gun three times, and then gave the gun to me. I marveled at the gun for a second because of its size and features. The most feared man on the streets is a nigga with a gun…a person who's standing behind a gun has the power of death in his hands.

Fear automatically comes to anyone who's even close to hearing a gun shot. So, when Chop handed me the gun he said, "Go head Kojack shoot the joint." With the power at my fingertips I squeezed the last three bullets out… an adrenaline rush came over me. There was one guy who slipped and fell while he was trying to get away with the crowd. I aimed the gun at him and shot him, then we all took off running.

I've never in my life felt the fear I was feeling after I shot that gun. My mind wasn't prepared to handle jail or the nigga coming back to kill me. I knew I was in a world of trouble… fear had come over me like never before. My conscience wouldn't let me sleep. I wanted to go home, but London told me to wait until Sunday. It was a Friday night when I called. I had to do something to feel free again, like I should have felt at the age of thirteen.

The next day early that morning I was at Bishop's door telling him what happened. "Bishop man, I don't know who I shot I just wanted to see what it felt like. It happened so quick I just got excited and fired the gun." Bishop told me to calm down and lay low until he found out whom it was I shot. Bishop said, "Stay off the streets until I come to get you." Bishop found out whom I had shot, then he came to get me from Eve's house. The old head I shot only had a leg wound that wasn't serious. Bishop set the meeting up between the old head and me. Bishop stood there with his gun in his waistband.

I thought Bishop was going to talk, but he let me talk for myself. The beef was squashed. I apologized. We shook hands; then we parted. Bishop warned me to stay away from guns, I wish I had listened.

Chapter 4

School Daze

My aunt Sara lived four blocks away from Kelly Miller Junior High School where I attended. After the first month of catching the bus back and forth from southeast to the northeast, I moved in with my aunt Sara and would occasionally go home to stay for the weekend.

After Beatrice passed away, Sunnyboy moved in with Sara. Her neighborhood was quiet and peaceful. The only thing I had to worry about was all the dogs... I got chased by dogs going and coming from school everyday. To save myself from getting bitten by a dog I had to jump on or over fences, cars, and trucks... and sometimes climb trees. But once I figured out that most of the dogs were mutts, I picked up rocks and threw it at them frightening them away so I could walk down the streets without being chased.

Lincoln Heights projects lies on the opposite side of Kelly Miller. The niggas from Lincoln Heights controlled Kelly Miller...they had power over anyone who entered their territory. Once you came into their territory willingly, you crossed enemy lines. It was just like giving them the right to jump, punk or make you their flunky.

Miller's environment held tension everyday, but one particular day, for some peculiar reason I felt it was my day to get tested. Something was about to happen, but like most things. I couldn't put my finger on it. Everyday was usually the same old immature games at lunch…like cold cocking, back of the head smacking, and punching someone in the nuts for fun. But these games frequently resulted in fights, so of course I didn't get involved. The bell rang signaling the end of recess and everyone had to line up against the wall…girls on one side and boys on the other. In line, the games started…usually with the person in the back.

That day, smacking was the game and the domino affect continued until I got smacked. I told the nigga behind me, "Don't smack my head." He smacked my head anyway. When I turned around, I punched the nigga so hard one of his teeth fell out. I made an example of him to show the other niggas that I wasn't meant to be messed with. But before I knew it, the nigga and I were going blow for blow. Everybody crowded around us; the teachers and security guards had to fight their way through the crowd to stop the fight. Consequently, I ended up in the principal's office explaining the situation. I told him that the other guy hit me first and after I warned him not to hit me he did it anyway; this was self-defense. I was given two weeks of detention and the guy I hit was suspended.

A lot of guys figured that if they couldn't beat the Lincoln Heights crew, they would join them. I looked at it from a different perspective. Either you're going to stand up for something or fall for anything and become a flunky. Word got around that I could fight. The whole idea of my reputation brought me more than expected. Fighting was cool but the only thing I feared was getting jumped. I had witnessed a lot of dudes dying from the injuries of a jump. My greatest fear was getting beat to death. So, I carried a "Rambo" knife just like the one in the movie to school everyday for protection. The upper classmen (eighth and ninth graders) tried to bully my homeroom. This beef started over girls liking a classmate of mine named Pops. Niggas envied him because of his looks and all the girls loved him, even the women teachers flirted with Pops. His rap game was strong, and for a seventh grader, he was the man. Pops is the light-skinned version of the rapper "Special Ed." His hair was real curly and his smile was worth a million dollars. I hung around Pops because I wanted to get noticed by the fly girls. Plus, Pops wasn't a punk…he carried a 38 long to school everyday and niggas respected him for the simple fact that he lived in East Gate Projects. I had a four-man crew—Pops, Wood, Shorty and me. Wood was the basketball star and Shorty just chilled and soaked up the attention from honeys.

Now I was envied because Pops and I were tight and I could jone good. My first month of school I was joned on by classmates because of how I combed my hair. I had a head full of waves with a part in the middle. My classmates would say, "Did Moses part your sea?" I was humiliated in front of everyone, and after years of combing my hair like Chicago, I started brushing my hair straight on top. Most of the guys and girls who laughed at me were now at my mercy.

With a chip on my shoulder, I joned on everyone who laughed at me the day before. The main guys were Ralph, Ronald and Shine; they would team up on me, and one by one, I would shut them all up. To take the focus off of them they would jone on someone else who was dirty or ugly, but I would keep the focus on them. This became an everyday session at lunchtime when crowds of people would surround us. Once I got heated up, I couldn't stop… people would be laughing so hard their stomachs ached.

One thing I could do, and do well, was keep people laughing. I could make this noise that sounded loud like a pig. The sound was annoying, but everyone loved to hear it. I would wait until the hallways were clear and everyone was in their classrooms. Then, I would ask my teacher if I could go to the bathroom. I made my rounds to certain classes of teachers I didn't like or classes of females I liked. If the door was closed, I would open it without being seen and make the noise real loud and run back to my class. All the students would laugh out loud.

When assemblies came around twice a month, the pressure would be on me. Everybody wanted me to perform the noise and they wouldn't stop asking me until I gave in. I waited until there was silence so the noise wouldn't be drowned out by anything else. Once the moment of silence struck, I made the noise.

My Principal said, "When I find out who made that noise that person will be suspended for a month." I was bold, so I did it again just to get on his nerves. My Principal replied, "I can't wait until I catch whoever it is. Teachers start walking around to see if we can catch this fool." Everyone in the assembly was laughing, even Ms. Barnes, my homeroom and English teacher. She never snitched on me. After the word got around that it was me, I had to make the pig sound as often as I was asked.

Seventh grade year I was crowned the class clown. I was so caught up in acting a fool that I lost focus of what I was really in school for...to get educated. While everyone else was learning, studying and doing homework, I played. When report cards came out my Grade Point Average was 1.7. Pops, Wood, and Shorty all made the honor roll and their GPA was well over 3.0. I couldn't understand how they made the honor roll when we all played and joked in class all day long. London was called to the school for a parent-teachers conference.

Ms. Barnes told London about my behavior and London ended the conversion with, "If you have anymore problems out of him call me on my job. I'll leave work, and he knows if I leave work then I'm bringing my ironing cord with me, and I have no problem embarrassing him in front of his classmates." I was punished for a month—no T.V., no outside, and London made me come home everyday and stopped me from going to Sara's house until my grades improved. I took London seriously, and I slowly cut back on joking in class. After that, I only played and joked during recess, or when we had a substitute teacher.

One day in class, I was reading the encyclopedia and found a very interesting thing talking about males reaching their puberty stage. The book stated that a male reaches puberty between 11-14 years old. I was now 13 and shooting blanks; I was desperate to have my anointing like my male classmates. The book went even further to say if a male allowed his feet to stick out from under the covers while sleeping, that he could possibly reach puberty... I tried it and it worked.

When I woke up in the morning, I thought I had peed in the bed, but there was no urine smell. I checked myself and then I screamed in the bathroom, "I can make babies now!" London overheard me and said, "What did you say?" "Nothing Ma." I lowered my voice and repeated to myself, "I can make babies."

After reaching puberty, I became extremely horny. Blood would rush to my penis without notifying me. I was caught off guard in class when Ms. Barnes asked me to come to the chalkboard to solve a problem. I had to lie and tell her, "My stomach hurts." To control my hormones, I masturbated.

One night, while London and Wylie were asleep, I woke up around 12 AM. The urge came stronger than ever before... and I couldn't resist my thoughts of masturbating. So, I closed my bedroom door and slipped the movie "Coffy" into the VCR, with the sound down where only I could hear it. I was caught up in my fantasy of Pam Grier, the main actress of the movie, in ways I never knew was possible. Ready to explode I heard the door crack open, it was London. "Boy what's wrong with you?" I was too embarrassed and humiliated to say anything, but London demanded that I answer her. "What are you doing watching T.V. at 1 AM in the morning, especially on a school night. What is wrong with you and why are you hiding yourself from me?"

I replied, "Ma, my ding-ding hurts." I was hoping London would leave well enough alone, but she insisted that we go to the doctor in the morning to see what was wrong with me. London thought I may have had an STD, so she told the doctor to check me out. The doctor asked me all kinds of questions like, "Am I having sex? Have I had a wet dream? Have I seen anything red or white come out the tip of my penis?"

I told him no to everything except the sperm. But that didn't stop him from sticking a Q-tip in my penis to check for any STDs. In my mind I wished that I told London that I was really wacking off so I wouldn't have to go through all that. I knew all along the doctor wouldn't find anything wrong with me. I overheard him telling London, "Your son has reached his puberty stage and most young men masturbate very frequently at his age. It's probable that he was masturbating when you walked in on him because there's nothing wrong with him." London laughed….I guess she figured out that I was masturbating.

Chapter 5
Enemy Of...

Enemy of my enemy is my enemy. I couldn't understand this riddle until the first day of my eighth grade year. Ms. Barnes said, "Dawayne Williams I'm not going through what I went through with you last year." She gave me an alternative ...either I would make the honor roll or she was going to kick me out of her homeroom and second period English class. By the end of my seventh grade year, I was able to make a little improvement on my grades, raising my GPA from 1.7 to a 2.3. Ms. Barnes had offered me a challenge I couldn't refuse. She told me if I made the honor roll she would pay me $50 dollars for each semester; but, if I failed to maintain a 3.0 she was going to ship me to another classroom, no exceptions.

With that challenge, I put forth my best effort to prove to Ms. Barnes that I wasn't a dummy. Plus with the bond Pops, Shorty, Wood and I had, I couldn't see myself going to another homeroom. I worked hard in school by completing my class work and my homework assignments; and to soften my workload, I did half of my homework during lunchtime, so I could watch cartoons after school.

My hard work did payoff and I continued to collect my $50 from Ms. Barnes every semester. My GPA improved to a 3.2; and by the end of the school year my GPA won me the most improved student award.

Honestly, I have to admit if it wasn't for Ms. Barnes tutoring me after school, I probably would be illiterate. In the seventh grade my reading skills were on a third grade level. I was able to get to Junior high school because teachers liked me. But, Ms. Barnes saw something in me—a weakness—and she helped me with that weakness, until I was comfortable enough to read in front my classmates. Once Ms. Barnes built my confidence, my grades improved.

Walking across the school stage to receive my award, I heard all kinds of things said about me. I paid none of them any mind, but in the back of my mind, I knew I was hated....hated because I was light skinned....hated because I wasn't a punk....hated for the simple fact that girls liked me.

Pops and I were in a homeroom rivalry that turned into a civil war. One day, while I was walking down the hallway to the water fountain in between classes, one of Ned's boys crossed the hallway from my right side and bumped into me, causing me to lose my balance. Once I caught my balance I punched the nigga in his face. With the teacher's standing guard to make sure everyone made it to their class on time, the fight was broken up; and I received detention for the brawl.

I traded in my knife for a weapon with more efficient results. I needed a weapon that would offer me guarantees....something I could depend on; so I got myself a gun.

In "1990" the death toll was 474 murders in D.C., the highest it's ever been. Not only black males between the ages of 18 and 24 were dying, but teenagers between the ages of 12 and 17 were also dying at a rapid rate. Fist fighting became ridiculous, no one wanted to fight anymore. Fighting was always optional for me. Everybody wanted a gun. Guns were like trendsetters....they were always in season. Death was like a new designer; and only the boldest nigga had his business card (a gun) and was willing to use it. A gun could make or break your reputation. Only a nigga with heart... or a nigga perpetrating that he had heart... had a gun.

Wood and Shorty weren't targeted with Pops and me because they lived in Lincoln Heights and were friends with Ned and his crew. Our homeroom was 8-301 and our rivalry homeroom was 9-300. These guys were punks, wannabe gangsters and fake lover boyz. They didn't have the slightest idea of what it took to stand up for themselves. The bad niggas in school were in 9-300 and they intimidated everyone else, except Pops and me. Ned Fred was the ringleader of 9-300 and the main instigator of everything that took place, from fights down to robberies on the school campus. With his crew running the school, Pops and I had to call in back up. He called in his crew from East Gate projects and I called Tyson and Chop.

Tyson and Chop couldn't turn down a favor from me; I was their backbone. Routinely on Fridays, I would skip school at sixth period in order to handle whatever they needed done. They would meet me at the Stadium Armory metro station at 2:45 PM, then we'd walk down to Elliot Junior high (only three blocks away) where they both attended school. Once the clock struck 3 o'clock they would point out any nigga that gave them a problem and I solved it by beating him unconscious with my fist. Week after week Tyson and Chop depended on my fighting skills, which caused niggas at Elliot to fear me, but not them.

Tyson carried a pump and Chop carried a .38 long to school for protection. Once Pops and I brought in reinforcement things changed instantly. At 3 o'clock Tyson, Chops and Pop's boyz (East Gate crew) were posted up together waiting for Pops and me to exit the building. For all the threats we received in school that day, we were ready to battle. Pops was packing a .38 and I was packing a

.25-caliber automatic that Tyson had let me borrow. It fit in the palm of my hand, unnoticed by everyone except me.

Pops and I walked out of the school building and stepped across the street with our eyes searching the crowd for Ned and his boyz. There was no sign of them. DGS is a small grocery store on 49th and Central Avenue where everybody hangs out before and after school, which is two blocks away. Pops and I led our crews down to DGS on foot. We spotted Ned's crew standing outside, chilling... but Ned was nowhere to be found. Unnoticed, we bum-rushed them. A few of them ran; but we beat the hell out of the ones we caught and we escaped before the police arrived.

Tyson and Chop ran towards the Benning Road subway station, and Pops and I ran in the opposite direction. Pop's crew vanished once they heard the sirens. Four blocks away, Pops and I caught another nigga and we beat and pistol-whipped him.

For two weeks, Pops and I were on a rampage. With a lot of brainstorming, Pops and I came up with ambushes that worked to perfection. One by one we caught Ned's crew and jumped them before and after school. Ned was slick and seemed to be a step ahead of us, but we were on his track. After we sent our message that we weren't playing, we returned to school like everything was normal.

Pops and I were harassed by the police, the school security guards, the Principal and teachers. Someone from Ned's crew had informed the police and the police inform the school that Pops and I carried guns. Our lockers were searched and we were searched everyday for weapons. The police increased their presence inside and outside the school because Ned and his boyz feared us. Pops and I had girls we trusted to hold our weapons in their lockers, and after school we retrieved them. The searchers and harassments continued until the end of our eighth grade school year.

Just before school let out, Ned had enough balls to approach Pops and me, trying to provoke us in front of the police and teachers during lunch. We ignored him...until Ned spoke the words of death to us, saying he was going to kill both of us. With those threats, Pops and I knew we had to kill the nigga, and we attempted that day. But as usual, Ned left the school grounds early.

The next day in school, during our 12 o'clock lunch break, unbeknownst to me, Pops was on his way to school with a Mack-11 fully loaded... with enough ammunition to wipeout half the school body. By 2:30 PM, the rumor had spread that Pops was arrested with the gun and two extra clips. The police had noticed Pops wearing a trench coat in 90-degree weather and that's how he was arrested. With only three weeks to go in school, I thugged my way through. Ned and his bandwagon graduated and moved onto high school.

With Pops still in jail serving a 3-year sentence, ninth grade year was awkward for me. I had no sidekick...no one to watch my back...so, I had to stand alone. Shorty, Wood and I were cool, but Pops and I had an eye to eye understanding. We saw things differently and our relationship made me feel like we were brothers.

I was finally relaxed, and after 14 years of fighting, I was now able to mack...with no more worries of a beef kicking off with anyone. Peace abounded in school, now that the bullies were gone. The only thing I had to watch out for was girls. During my first two years of school, I got negative attention from being a bad boy. All the females I tried to talk to shot me down, and I got the leftovers that I really didn't want. But now, the attention I was getting was positive. The girls I wanted, wanted me sexually... and I took full advantage of it.

Girls became a sport to me, and I played to win. Wood and I were on the same page and we played hooky over his house on days we were gonna bone a broad. I don't know how Wood did it, but he was able to get girls to do us both. Wood was a sex fanatic and every Friday he had something set up over his house. Both of his parents worked and we had access to the house until 6 o'clock in the afternoon during the weekdays.

From time to time, Wood would set up gangbangs with girls of my choosing… the petite ones. One time, Wood had this fat girl over the house…she was about 240 pounds. We left school at lunchtime and returned back at sixth period; by seventh period the rumor was around the school that we slept with the fattest girl in school.

"Twinky" had taken on eight guys, except me…I just couldn't do it. She was too big for me and I wasn't used to girls her size. Wood invited a few other classmates over and they got down. I only got into the mix when the female was down with it. Most of the girls we had, already experienced gangbangs before we got to them. I never went first, and if there were five of us, I always went last or next to last. While the others were having sex, I was afraid that the girl would call rape on us; so, when I walked into the room I made sure that we had an understanding that we both agreed to have sex.

After the girls got banged out they kept coming back for more and more. In my heart, I felt sympathy for the females we gangbanged, wondering, "how did they get this way? What happened in their lives that caused them to do this on a regular?" Somewhere in their lives, their self-esteem had been taken, and I played my role by sticking my hands into the cookie jar. I didn't like having sex that way…honestly, it really freaked me out. It was fun until after I had sex, then reality set in on me. Being a part of something like that played on my mind and made me think about what could happen if I had a daughter one day.

Learning the ropes from Wood on how to persuade a female into a gangbang, I used it on the weekends when I hung out with Tyson. Somehow or another, Tyson became obsessed with girls we banged and he wanted them all to himself. He would steal numbers off my pager and then perpetrate like he was me. On the weekends, when I wasn't home, London would let Tyson into the house and he would steal phone numbers off my cardboard Rolodex. I wasn't aware of this until a classmate who I was talking to told everyone in school that I was wearing Tyson's clothes and shoes.

Apparently, Tyson had looked into my closet and told her that everything from my used jeans down to my Guess jeans and shoes were his. I couldn't believe that Tyson had told Bia a lie to get with her. I should've addressed it when it happened, but I thought it was childish to approach Tyson when I knew I had owned and purchased my own clothes and shoes from working hard at my school recreation center in the afternoons. I didn't say anything to Tyson…if he was happy with getting my leftovers then so be it. I wasn't going to fight him over a female. I didn't believe in fighting over a female unless I was totally disrespected verbally or physically by a man…then it was on. The rule I lived by was no female would ever come between my family, friends and myself, but this rule was shattered like glass.

I met a female named Kacey at Eastern High school homecoming. I gave her my pager number and she called me a few days later. I had fallen asleep on my Aunt Sara's couch, and when I woke up I caught Tyson scrolling through my pager. I asked him, "What the hell are you doing with my pager?"

He said it went off and he was checking the number. He gave me my pager and I called the number back. It was Kacey…the call I'd been waiting for…for 96 hours. I took a deep breath as the phone rang, then Kacey answered, "Hello!" "Did someone page Kojack?" "Yeah, this is Kacey what's up?" After a few words were exchanged between us she said I sounded different over the phone, as if she'd spoken with me before. Several times throughout our conversation I had to convince Kacey that I was myself.

This conversation took place on January 5, 1991. It was Saturday evening and after 45 minutes on the phone, Kacey told me I was welcome to visit her later on that night after her grandmother went to work at 10 PM. Knowing South East like the back of my hand, I decided to take Tyson and Syrup with me for protection. We carried knives, because I didn't feel the need to bring a gun.

Tyson had tossed the .25 and the pump when he was running from the police, so we took knives for protection now that we were demoted from guns to knives. Once Kacey gave me the okay, we caught the W-4 bus from Benning Road over to Brothers Place S.E. where she lived. Her neighborhood was clear of present danger and we walked safely to her door from the bus stop. Kacey came to the door wearing a sexy nightgown with a pair of sexy shoes that showed her pedicure.

Tyson, Syrup and I sat down on the couch. My mind was blown when Kacey asked Tyson to come upstairs to the bedroom. She grabbed Tyson's hand and said, "Kojack come with me." Kacey continued up the stairs, letting Tyson's hand go. I thought maybe she had Tyson and I mixed up because we're both light-skinned and this was just our second time meeting. So I said, "I'm Kojack and he's Tyson." Tyson looked over at me as if I was skunking him and said in a low tone of voice. "We can run GB on Kacey, if you shut up. I was over here last night trying to break her in… she's a virgin. Just play along so we all can get some."

Tyson walked up the stairs to her room and closed the door. I stood there thinking to myself why does Tyson have to act like he's me to get some? I couldn't believe he stole Kacey's number off my pager. This wasn't the first time Tyson opened the back door and walked in on one of my girls. Now, I had no choice but to deal with Tyson. Avoiding a man-to-man talk would only cause a volcano to build up in me and the eruption would cause a beef between us. But this wasn't the time or place to address this issue. So, when Tyson came downstairs, I went up and after I came down, Syrup went up the stairs to Kacey's room.

At 6:30 in the morning Tyson, Syrup and I rode the W-4 bus back to Sara's house. After we got off the bus, we stopped at the nearby 7-Eleven. I purchased $10 worth of junk food—potato chips, cookies, juice, candy bars—and a box of doughnuts. When I walked through the door, Sunnyboy was awake. Before I went to sleep I told Sunnyboy, Tyson, and Syrup that they could have some of my junk food, and to just leave me some. While I slept on the couch Syrup and Tyson told Sunnyboy about the GB we ran on Kacey from start to finish. I went to sleep, drained from the long bus ride.

Around 1:30 in the afternoon, I was awakened by my urge to urinate. I went up to the top floor, which is the third floor, to use the bathroom. After I finished, I went into the icebox to get a cup of juice and a doughnut. "I couldn't believe those niggas ate all my junk food. I didn't get the chance to eat a crumb of anything." I became furious and slammed the icebox door. I rushed down to the basement and said to Tyson and Syrup, "Who ate all my stuff?" Sunnyboy was sitting there too, but I knew Sunny wouldn't eat all my stuff, so I directed my anger at Tyson and Syrup.

Tyson ignored me and continued talking on the phone while Syrup and Sunnyboy explained everything they ate. They also told me Tyson ate everything. Even when they told him to save me some, he continued eating until every crumb of my junk food and every drop of my juice was gone.

So, I asked him, "Tyson why in the hell did you eat all my stuff?" Tyson replied, "Man get out of my face." "Get out your face? Tyson the next time you disrespect me in anyway… I don't care what it is…I'm a knock you out, and if you think I'm playing try me." Tyson waited until I laid down on the couch and then he punched me in my face. I rose up from the couch like a sleeping giant. I stood to my feet and snapped on Tyson. I picked his 135-pound frame up in the air and body-slammed him to the ground. Now that I had him on the ground, I threw nonstop punches to his face. He covered his face with his hands, so I placed my hands around his neck like an eagle's claw, choking the life out of him until his face turned pale. While choking him I told him, "Nigga if you wasn't my cousin I would kill you."

Sunnyboy and Syrup were trying to get me off Tyson, but my anger wouldn't allow me to let go until Tyson gasped for air. When I stood up, I looked down at Tyson on the ground and kicked him in his ribs. Sunnyboy grabbed me and pulled me back. Tyson was lying on the floor holding his neck with tears racing down his face. Sunnyboy said, "Ya can't be fighting in here take it outside."

Tyson gathered himself and ran up stairs to the second floor where the kitchen was. I walked right behind him to the front door so we could go outside and finish fighting. But before I could unlock it, Tyson went into the kitchen. I heard a drawer open and silverware moving. My instincts kicked in, so I grabbed Sara's artificial tree pole out of the Christmas tree box to protect myself. The pole was no weapon to fight with in a small living room.

With Tyson coming towards me swinging the knife, I didn't have time to try to unlock the front door. The only way I could avoid being stabbed was to get to the bathroom on the third floor immediately. With that in mind I back peddled up the stairs with the pole gripped tightly in my hand to create separation between Tyson and me. I threw the pole at him to slow his speed so I could get into the bathroom and lock the door. When I released the pole, the knife was already in motion and had sliced my chest like a chainsaw. Panicking to reach the bathroom, I never felt the knife enter and exit my body twice. Now at the bathroom door, I collapsed onto the floor. Blood was shooting out of me like water from a fire hydrant, splashing everywhere. I placed my hand over the wound, but the blood wouldn't stop flowing.

As helpless as I was, Tyson was still coming towards me to finish me off. I couldn't fight him off, nor could I yell for help.

My cousin Big Man heard the ruckus from Sara's room. He opened the door and when he saw me bleeding, and Tyson with the knife in his hand getting ready to stab me again, Big Man grabbed the knife from Tyson; and with his 6'6 250-pound body frame, he kicked Tyson down the flight of stairs. Then he yelled out, "Call the ambulance now!" He repeated it until he heard Sunnyboy say he was on the phone speaking with an operator. I was nearly unconscious. Big Man picked up my fragile 140-pound body and took me outside, so it would be easier for the ambulance to pick me up.

As Big Man was carrying me out the door, onto the porch and down the small flight of stairs in front of the house, Sara was locking her car doors. When she turned in our direction she screamed and immediately rushed over to me. Without knowing I was stabbed she tried to make me stand up, but I couldn't. With little oxygen in my lungs, I collapsed again on the ground. Sara sat down on the curb and laid my head in her lap and cried loudly, "Lord please don't take his life."

Short on breath, I closed my eyes and heard Aunt Sara scream out again, "Lord please, please, please spare his life." I could hear Big Man, Sunnyboy and Syrup all saying, "Don't close your eyes, don't close your eyes Kojack." They repeated it several times. My eyes opened after I received a smack on my right cheekbone from Aunt Sara. I gazed into the sky, looking at the clouds above me, wondering to myself, "Will God receive me into heaven?"

In those moments, my entire life flashed before me. I saw that I had done nothing good, and I pleaded with God to spare me. My inner voice spoke words to God that I never said openly to Him. In my prayer I asked God, "Please give me the opportunity to make London proud of me. Lord I want the chance to turn everything in my life around just give me the chance."

Out of nowhere, a man I had never seen before, appeared ...standing over me. Instantly, he prayed and told Sunyboy, "Hurry up and get a towel." He did this to slow down the bleeding. With no shirt on, my blood was all over Sara's church dress and spilling onto the sidewalk. Once Sunnyboy brought out the towel, the man placed it over my stab wounds. He stood there until the ambulance arrived and continued praying over me until I was lifted into the ambulance. Once I was in the ambulance, my eyes closed slowly…this time I went under.

The EMT's pulled out the chest shockers that looked like two irons, to revive me. I was taken to Children's Hospital and the doctors were already waiting for me to arrive. They immediately took me into the operating room. Before I was placed under anesthesia, all kinds of tubes were placed in and on my body… tubes that were essential to my survival. Two of them were the most painful tubes that I can imagine could ever be put in a man's body. One tube went in my right nostril, and its purpose was to travel down to my stomach. The second tube took my breath and I held the doctor closest to me by his tie, choking him…the other doctors join in and they all held me down.

While a lady doctor placed a tube in my penis, I screamed and tears rolled down my eyes. I wondered if they were trying to kill me too. Once the anesthesia took over I was in la-la land. I don't know how long I was asleep, but I woke up for about one minute. Once the doctors noticed that I was awake, they placed the gas mask back over my mouth to send me back to la-la land. In that minute, I witnessed the surgery as the doctors were operating on me. I was split wide open from the top of my stomach down to my navel.

The next day, I was told I had 29 staples in me from the surgery. I couldn't talk; it was too painful for me to even think. The doctor explained to me why I was cut open from the top of my chest down to my navel. This was to make sure I didn't have internal bleeding. There were 22 staples in my chest and the other seven were placed where the knife had entered my body. The doctor also told me the knife was an inch away from my heart and if the knife would have punctured my heart, I would be dead. There were five doctors standing around my bed all looking at me; and one of them said, "Son, God has a purpose for your life because I don't know how you survived after losing such a large amount of blood." I didn't find out until I was home that I was also given a blood transfusion.

Hearing every word the doctor said made me appreciate life. Until this day, I wonder two things. One thing that I think about is, if Big Man wasn't visiting Sara (his mother) on that day, would I be alive? Two, I wonder if the man that prayed over me was an angel? It was something about the way he prayed. It seemed to me that he knew the right things to say to God.

I had to come face to face with a dilemma. My decision would ultimately change the way my family viewed me. When the ambulance arrived at Sara's house to transport me to the hospital, the police also arrived on the scene and Tyson was arrested and charged with attempted murder.

The next day, Tyson was arraigned in court and the question was asked, "Did Tyson really try to kill me?" The Judge wanted to know what had caused Tyson to stab his own cousin? Sara and Big Man told Eve that Tyson was trying to kill me; but Eve thought it was gossip and refused to believe it. Standing in Tyson's defense, Eve asked London if she could appear in court. But, before London appeared in court she wanted to hear my side of the story. I thought that someone had told London, but later I found out she was deceived.

London asked me what happened between Tyson and me. With the soreness in my chest and the pain in my heart I felt that I was betrayed; and I became afraid of disconnecting with my family. So, when London asked me the question, was Tyson trying to kill me? I shook my head from left to right signaling "No" to London. If I could have talked without feeling the soreness in my chest, the truth would have been told. Because I survived, London dropped the charges against Tyson and he was released from jail.

After two weeks in the hospital, I was back home resting and gaining my strength and weight back. I had lost 25 pounds off my 140-pound frame. Because of my weight loss, I felt and looked like a crack-head.

Now that I could talk, I wanted to tell London the truth, but I didn't know how to approach her. Knowing London's ways, I waited until she sparked an argument with me and then I let it out. But first I had to see what London knew about the stabbing. She told me, "Eve said I was in the bathroom and then I came out and that's when Tyson stabbed me because he was threatened by me." That was a rat-faced lie...she wanted it to look and sound like it was an accident, but it wasn't. I told London the truth of what happened. Then she approached Tyson at Eve's house and said, "I don't know if it was an accident or not, but if you ever in your life try to kill my son again, I'll kill you." Then Tyson apologized, only because Eve made him do it.

After a month, I returned to school; I was fatigued from walking up and down the stairs to class. My stamina was low and I couldn't stand up for long periods of time without feeling nauseous. Everyone wanted to know why and where I was stabbed. There was a rumor around school that Tyson had stabbed me over a bag of chips. I tried to explain the story over and over, but people wanted to believe it was over some chips. Two weeks later, when I was walking down the hall, I passed by the school's main office and saw Tyson. Unnoticed, I looked through the window to observe what was taking place. Eve was transferring Tyson to Miller, my school, to finish the year out.

I couldn't believe what I was seeing. This was like stabbing me in my back...Miller was my school. Now, it would be divided between Tyson and me. My Principal, teachers and classmates all asked me over and over, "Is that Tyson the one who stabbed you? Why would his grandmother transfer him to this school?" Tyson didn't go to school at all because niggas were threatening to take his life. The Principal of Elliott Junior High was tired of Tyson missing so many days from school, so they kicked him out and he landed in Miller with me because no other school would take him.

Things weren't the same between us and the animosity could be felt like the temperature on a hot day. I couldn't defend myself if he tried to kill me again. Even though I carried a knife with me, everyone could see that I was weak and fragile. A few of my buddies in school watched my back and made sure I knew Tyson's every move. Every day, he came to school late and left early. After two months, Tyson stopped coming to school. I later heard from a family member that he was bragging about stabbing me. Nothing hurt me deeper than to hear someone tell me that my own cousin was boasting about my struggle for life, when I was faced with death.

Chapter 6

Beef

After I was stabbed I knew "1991" was going to be a year to remember. The word "beef" on the streets means war, kill or be killed. Unless a beef is squashed, you have to watch your back at all times, no matter where you are, or who you're with. Some niggas will squash a beef just to get you to drop your guard, then put a bullet in your head or a knife in your back. No beef is ever completely squashed until you or the other person is dead.

Life is like a revolving door…one day you're coming, and the next day you're gone. Revenge is always in a person's mind whether you're a Christian, Muslim, or Atheist. A chance to get even with your enemy is a desire we all carry in us, one way, or another. Even if it's not spoken of, it crosses your the mind.

I thought the beef between Ned and me was over. He and his crew had graduated a year earlier, so I assumed they were above juvenile differences. Instead, they held on tight to their grudges; and even after they graduated, they would come back to Kelly Miller to unexpectedly visit a honey or start more beefs with me. They were praying on me to slip so that they could get at me, but little did they know, I was waiting for the same opportunity.

On graduation day, one of my classmates named Sugar invited me to her graduation party. Sugar and I were cool, I enjoyed her company and conversation. Sugar had a nice body and she was curvaceous with a phat butt. I never tried to get at her because she knew what I was about. Plus, she was aware of my behavior and knew I was up to no good. I respected her for her knowledge and the friendship we had. Sugar wasn't like most girls…she was smart and streetwise, and didn't play games.

After London took me out to eat at Phillips on the waterfront in South West, I washed up and prepared my clothes for the party. I had laid out my Sergio Tacchini sweatsuit with my Nike Air Force One tennis shoes. About 11 o'clock that night I was headed to the party…the temperature was about 80 degrees and breezy. I only went to see if I could pull a honey out to go home with me. But, when I arrived, there were only about five honeys and thirty niggas, including Ned and his crew. This was their opportunity to get even.

A few minutes after my arrival, my man Stan rolled into the party with his crew. Stan and I are cool, and I felt a little more comfortable because he was also an enemy of Ned's from school. After Stan strolled in, Ned and about twenty of his crew members went out into the backyard so they could plot their all out attack on us, especially me. I had decided that I was only going to stay for twenty minutes and then sneak out, unnoticed.

By the time I decided to get something to eat, Ned and his crew came back into the party. They surrounded the table where the food was placed. The smell of fried chicken made my stomach do flips. The food I ate at Phillips earlier had been digested and I was ready for my third meal of the day. Already enroute to the table, I couldn't turn back now. I pressed my way through Ned's flunkies. On my way to the table, I was viciously elbowed in the head, but I kept walking and grabbed a piece of chicken. I had only taken one bite, and was blown by the elbow I took. I knew I couldn't handle the bum rush, so I played it cool and calm, knowing I had to walk back through those niggas to inform Stan that we may have to throw down.

I braced myself and headed back across the room. The same nigga elbowed me again, this time in the face. I turned and faced him, "Nigga if you elbow me again I'ma whip your ass." Staring deep into his eyes, I saw fear. He needed his crew to back him up before he replied back "What Nigga, what?" I was immediately surrounded by his crew, so I replied back "Nigga you heard me!" Then I turned and walked away. A man should never turn his back on anyone, but I did.

Praying within myself, I knew it was time to go. As I tied my shoe-strings tightly, I told Stan what went down. When I stood up I saw Ned hand the nigga that elbowed me a gun. I tried to play it cool and not let them see me sweat. I got the hell out of there.

When I got to the door, I took off running in fear for my life never looking back. I was four blocks away and still running, when Stan drove up along side me. Not knowing it was him, I panicked until he made himself known. "Kojack it's me, Stan. The gun they had was a bee bee gun. I know because I have one myself, so what'cha going to do about that nigga Ned because he keep's coming at you?" "I'ma handle this nigga tonight." "Do you want me to roll with you?" "Naw, I got this one…this is personal."

Stan drove me to Sara's door. I went into the house, retrieved the loaded .380 pistol that I was holding for a friend, and headed back to the party on foot. When I got to the party it was over. Sugar's mother was informed about the gun that was pulled on me, so she decided to shut the party down.

I came up with plan B, directing my focus to hunt Ned down and leave him where I found him. As I walked onto Ned's street I saw the nigga who elbowed me. I walked up to him, "Nigga don't you ever in your life elbow me again or I'll kill you… nigga!" After I completed my sentence, I noticed his fear. I pushed his face and he replied, "Man, it wasn't even like that!" At that moment, my mind started racing and I reached for my gun, pulling it out of my waist-band. He immediately turned and started running saying, "what'cha got a gun?" "Nigga what difference does it make the next time you try to carry me I'm gonna kill you."

As I stood at the entrance of the street, I saw a crowd of niggas near the middle of street. Standing on the opposite side of the street I walked towards the crowd. My eyes were searching for Ned, but the street lights were dim and I couldn't identify anyone. Some older guy bumped into me, but before I could say a word to defend myself, everyone on the street came charging at me as if they were lions and I was their prey. They were saying, "Nigga! This our street! Who do you think you are?"

I wasn't about to let thirty niggas pound on me, so I pulled out my gun, aimed it into the crowd and open fired.... tat, tat, tat, tat, tat, tat, tat, tat, tat, tat. As my arm was stretched out squeezing the trigger, I witnessed every nigga that was rushing towards me like a mighty tidal wave ready to engulf me, all fall flat like a calm sea.

Some ran, some fell and the others screamed. When my clip emptied out the ten bullets, I ran. Less than three minutes after I fired on them, I could hear the police sirens. Now under tremendous stress, I ran in the opposite direction of the sirens. I was afraid to throw the gun because I knew it would probably be hard for me to find. So, I kept it on me, running full speed through the alleys until I got to the Kelly Miller School grounds. I turned my sweatsuit inside out so I wouldn't be identified as easily, just in case the police caught up with me. Breathing hard, like I ran a marathon, I collapsed with white foam in the corner of my mouth. I laid on the ground breathing in desperation, knowing that I had to slow the rate of my heart down before my body went into shock.

After I regrouped, I walked into Lincoln Heights like nothing happened. There was a block party going on that night...the entire neighborhood was outside. The music was booming loud at 1 o'clock in morning. Before I could stop to think about what happened, a beef kicked off. Right before my eyes, a gun was drawn and a guy's Nissan Pathfinder became the target of bullets. I witnessed his truck getting turned into Swiss cheese. Within seconds of the shots being fired, the police came racing to the scene as if they had already known it was going to happen. Everyone was hanging around to see what had just occurred. The crowd surrounded the Pathfinder in the presence of the police.

I overheard a guy say, "Man, didn't nobody get killed up here! Why is homicide on the scene instead of the police? Usually homicide doesn't come on the scene until after the police confirm a murder." I didn't consider the consequences of what I'd done until I got to my cousin Dee's house where I had spent the night on Call Place, ten blocks over from Lincoln Heights. My Aunt Sara's house was out of the question, plus Ned knew where she lived.

My conscience wouldn't allow me to go to sleep. Finally, I calmed down around six that morning and slept for a few hours. When I got up, I went home. I avoided television and all phone calls, hoping no one was injured from last night's escapade. The shooting played over and over in my mind. I sat in the room, wondering how I was going to handle this situation. I became afraid, and deep down I wanted to tell London that her baby had shot someone and that maybe the police would be looking for me. I had no intention of killing anyone, but the only way I could figure out if anyone had been harmed was to call Sugar. I waited until a week later.

"What's up Sugar!" "Hey Kojack, I been calling you at your aunt's house but they said you haven't been there. I just wanted to tell you that Ned and his crew is looking for you."

"For what?"

"I heard them say they're going to shoot up your aunt's house."

I played it off as if she was talking crazy or something. "Shoot up my aunt's house for what? And why are they looking for me?"

"Kojack you know what I'm talking about, they said you shot four niggas around here."

"That wasn't me and I don't know what you're talking about?"

"Well if it wasn't you, you got the beef and the blame."

"Sugar who got shot?"

"I know you probably don't know them by name... two people were shot in the leg and the other two where shot in the stomach. But they all are doing well, now that they're out of the hospital. Kojack, I know Ned never liked you, and I understand why you did what you had to do. I'm not saying it's good they got shot. But Ned is a wannabe...I told him one day he'll meet his match."

"Thanks for the heads up, Sugar...I have to go."

"Kojack, call me sometimes, don't be a stranger. Bye."

Chapter 7

Hustler

When I turned thirteen, I got tired of fighting…it had become routine. It was time for me to go to the next level on the street. I had to find a new hustle that would get my adrenaline rushing; but, I was stuck in my teenage years. Tyson, Martin, Chop, Omar, Jason, Wylie and I used to chill a lot. We had some good times, but being with them made me feel like a kid. Their presence reminded me of how we used to carry bags out of Safeway for money, go to the Redskins game and stand under the balcony on the front of the stadium where we begged white people for money. When the circus came to town, we'd sneak in there too. I had a dilemma. I was torn between two worlds…the streets and teenage life. I didn't know which one to choose, so I juggled them both. Perhaps that was a stupid move. All I knew was that I was definitely beyond anyone of them in the street life.

Older hustlers schooled me about stuff beyond fighting. This was my way to advance to the next level. I admired the advice and wisdom the hustlers had and taught me. I was fascinated with their lifestyle and their control over the streets.

Hustlers enticed me to sell drugs by giving me money and allowing me to trick the phatest prettiest crack-heads on the block. These women didn't even look like addicts most were school teachers, accountants and government employees. I was afraid and terrified of what London would do to me if she found out; so, I turned the game down. The hustlers knew how to persuade an 11, 12 and 13 year old. They knew the younger you were, the fewer questions you'd ask and the more money they'd make. I saw a lot of youngins get beat out of money. The youngins would sell a thousand dollars worth of drugs a day, which could amount to anywhere from 5,000 to 7,000 dollars a week and only have a pair of sneakers and one new outfit to show for their hard work and long hours on the block.

Old hustlers recruited youngins for only one reason, and that was to keep them from going to jail. They knew anyone under 17 would get a slap on the wrist especially if you were under 15 years old. But, nothing in life is free, there's a motive behind anything and everything. It took me a long time to realize that, but once I did, I was no longer ignorant or naïve to a hustlers hustle. The hustlers would let me hold their money, drugs and guns if I stood on the block with them, knowing the police wouldn't bother me because of my age. I never stole from them and that's how I earned their trust.

I became aware of why a lot of hustlers gave me money. They wanted to enslave and hold me in bondage as their property. Pimps own prostitutes and drugs own hustlers. If the white man could figure out how to tax drugs then it would be legal to sell out of a store. But until that time drugs will be sold on the street corners of America.

Bishop was in the game for a minute, and then he put his flunkies out there for him. Bishop and his crew controlled 15th street. Out of Bishop's crew, I became tight with Charcoal. He lived directly across from Eve. Chop and Charcoal are cousins, but they didn't express their love for each other like my cousins and I did. On the weekends, I left my crew and started hanging with Charcoal while he hustled. He had a bad temper and didn't play when it came down to his money. He was treacherous to crack-heads, knocking them out for fun. Another thing Charcoal did with passion was kill cats…I didn't like it but I watched him do it. Charcoal would take a brick, and bust a cat's brain out and laugh.

For some reason, Charcoal was always angry about something. One reason I got close to him was that I was curious about why he was angry all the time. "Charcoal, why are you always angry or ready to fight somebody?"

"Kojack I know you're not talking!"

"For real, Charcoal, it seems something is always bothering you." I was ignored but I later found out his mother was locked up for murder when he was a child, his father never was in his life and his grandmother was raising him. Charcoal taught me everything there was to know about the hustling game.

He would always tell me, "Kojack if you ever get in the game, hustle for yourself. Because niggas will kill you quick over a dollar."

I started observing the game from the do's and the don'ts. Like how to blend in with the crowd when the police came, always walk in opposite direction of them just in case they find someone's stash and place the blame on you for standing still. If you're selling dimes don't take less than eight dollars and on twenties it's eighteen. I was taught how to transform cocaine into crack by cooking it with water and baking soda on a hot stove. Every week I learned something new to place into my repertoire.

I became Charcoal's look out. My job was to inform him of the police or if anything looked suspicious like the stick up boyz. Because I did a good job, every week I was either rewarded with money and trips to the movies at Union Station or my choice of eating out at Houston's or some other expensive place where the hustlers hung out.

To keep my mind off Ned and his crew, I stayed on the opposite side of the bridge in Eve's neighborhood. Every now and then I would call and check on my aunt Sara to make sure nothing happened. It had been two months after the incident, so I knew they weren't going to run up in Sara's house. I already knew that Ned wasn't that type, all he did was talk.

One day I was standing at the bus stop on Benning Road waiting on the "96" bus. I snuck into Sara's house late at night with a female. I put her in a cab and I took my chances walking down to the bus stop in the morning. Waiting patiently, I noticed that my enemies had spotted me. They must have picked up my scent like a wolf does when hunting. Unarmed, I turned to face all four of them… they stood sixty feet away from me. I knew if I showed any signs of fear I was dead. With my hands behind my back I rocked my head back and forward with my bottom lip out. With my body language, I let them know I was packing. I was praying that my bluff worked. I knew if the bus didn't hurry up and come my only means of escape would be to run for my life. To further my bluff, before they got close enough, I placed my hands under my shirt as if I was holding onto a gun. Hesitant, undecided and doubtful of what to do next, I could see three of them ready to run; but one of them stood and just looked at me so he could get a good picture of me in his mind.

Within seconds, I was spotted by a friend driving on East Capitol Street where Bennning Road and East Capitol intersect; he asked me if I wanted a ride. I said, "Hell yeah!" Boy, boy, boy they had me and didn't even know it.

September was the start of my tenth grade year; over the summer I had turned fifteen. I went to Chamberlain and Eastern High Schools a half day each. At Chamberlain, I took up Business classes and at Eastern, I took my regular classes—English, math and history. Eastern was just like it's always been…honeys everywhere. I had been dreaming of this day for years, now I was walking down the hallways feeling like a King.

I had to maintain my composure. Whenever I went into a new environment I had to prove myself all over again. Every day at 3 o'clock when school let out, there would be a car show outside. Guys would drive up, down and around the block to show off their rides…cars like the Nissan, Pathfinder, Maximum, 300 Z's and the Acura Legend. The 300 Z's were the most popular car on the streets. Guys would speed down the street gliding like airplanes, while everyone looked on in amazement.

In school, the guys who got all the play from honeys were the guys who were hustlers and thugs. If you weren't one or both you got overlooked as a nobody, a wannabe, could be, but didn't have the heart to be. From school to the streets I was used to being the center of attention or at least the attention fell on my crew or my partner. From elementary to junior high, I was one of the best dressers. I never really had to compete until I got in Eastern. Guys in Eastern took dressing to the extreme. I couldn't keep up with them. Most of the guys had cars while I had to purchase tokens and a fare card to travel. Dressing was so extreme that many students dropped out because they couldn't afford the brand name clothes.

I had no interest in selling drugs until I started to see how women flocked to men that had money, cars and clothes. Selling drugs made a person's reputation even bigger than themselves. No longer was I fascinated by the lifestyle, I made it a reality. Since the start of school I had been plotting on how I could make my debut as a true hustler. With some help from Charcoal and Caesar, everything fell into place. One Friday afternoon I was fronted some crack, and by the end of the weekend, I had my own quarter of crack. With Charcoal's clientele already established, I had no problem selling my product quickly. I had $500 in my pocket, half of it went to Charcoal and I bought more crack with the rest.

From then on, I focused on the hustling. I remember when I was eleven years old, I placed a dollar bill on top of a newspaper and cut around it. Once I finished cutting the newspaper, I would place one dollar inside and another on the outside to make it look like I had a bankroll. I was no longer faking like I had money, because I did have it.

The D.C. Armory is four blocks away from 15th street. The Armory is one of the bases for the U.S. Army, it's also used as a recruiting center. Many soldiers purchase crack or exchange weapons for crack on our block...from AK-47's, 9mm, Mack 11s and Glock 40s. Selling drugs and carrying guns go hand and hand. In the drug game no one can be trusted, any violation can lead to death. So, I purchased a gun off the street which happened to be a .380, similar to the one I was holding for James, but newer. After I shot at Ned and his crew I informed James that I had to use his gun. He was mad that I used it, so I gave it back not wanting to cause a beef with an old school buddy. I really wish I'd held onto it a little longer but things worked out for me anyway...I got my own.

During the week I went to school and sold my drugs in the afternoon and on the weekends. Saturday was the most profitable day...I could easily clear $700 to a $1,000 before 3'oclock in afternoon.

Charcoal and I would make bets on who would be the first one to the strip. Whoever won the bet had to buy the other lunch from the Chinese store once it opened up at eleven o'clock. On this particular morning I had already made up my mind. "Charcoal is going to buy me some shrimp fried rice tomorrow." I love shrimp fried rice, that's about the only thing I would eat from a Chinese store. I woke up six in the morning, took care of my hygiene, grabbed my bag of rocks, placed my gun in my waistband, and was ready for work.

Just in case the police rolled up on me, I stashed my gun on the corner under the trash can where I could keep an eye on it. I kept my bag of rocks under my nuts only pulling out the plastic sandwich bag to serve a customer. One day I decided to observe my surroundings. I noticed two guys walking on the opposite side of the street in all black with their hands inside their sweathoods. My instincts told me to immediately "get up and walk."

I dropped my newspaper and walked into the middle of the street, and as I was crossing over they were crossing too. My reaction caught them off guard. Knowing there was distance between us, I walked into the convenience store and peeked through the glass door, watching their every move. They stood together conversing for about twenty minutes before they walked off. Once I saw the coast was clear, I went to retrieve my gun from under the trash can.

Before I could walk off, I noticed they had circled the block. With my gun in my waistband, I placed my hands inside my sweathood and grabbed hold of my gun; I loaded a bullet into the chamber. I waited patiently for them to get close enough so I could put a hole the size of a quarter in them. "Here they come, closer, closer, closer."

"What's up Kojack?" I recognized the voice but my eyes were locked and focused on the men in black. "Jack, I see you beat me out here, I owe you lunch nigga." It was Charcoal. I had told him about these two niggas headed our way. When they saw Charcoal and Charcoal noticed them, their body language and facial expressions changed instantly. Charcoal walked up to the niggas, cussing them out and threatening them. He made it clear if he caught them on or around 15th Street he was going to kill them. After Charcoal frightened them off he told me they were crackheads and explained why he only gave them a verbal warning. He was friends with one of the crackhead's daughters.

Just about every hustler I knew was dropping out of school to make money. I was afraid to drop out because I knew London would kill me. I only played hooky from school if I had something set up with a honey. I loved school because I could see the honeys. In my Geometry class, I couldn't sit still, nor keep my mouth closed.

My teacher asked me to come to the board to solve a problem. At the same time, I was in the middle of a jonin' session, in which it was my turn to fire back at classmates. The girl blurted out a direct comment about my mother. The entire class laughed. I felt I had to get her back, so I called her a heifer. My teacher mistakenly thought I was talking about her and I was suspended for a week.

London didn't come down hard on me because I explained what really happened. While suspended, I took the opportunity to stock-pile my money. The crack I was selling was so good that crackheads called it "butter." In our neighborhood, if you didn't have butter, you suffered major loss. The word got around the city quick that our neighborhood had the best crack in the business, flown in from L.A. From Maryland to Virginia, from the circus, carnival, government workers on Capitol Hill down to our Army, they all came to our block because of the butter.

I moved up in the game to where I had my own workers. I put Fray on because he needed some fresh gear and shoes. I set him up with a quarter to get on his feet.

Just like Charcoal showed me, I showed Fray the ins and outs of the game. To make sure Fray didn't serve an undercover cop, I stood outside with him across the street. Crackheads would approach me first, then I would send them to Fray. I was approached by one of my best customers asking for a loan until Friday...this was a Thursday night. When I gave a crackhead a loan, I doubled my price. I told him I didn't have anything on me...I was dry. With his crackhead senses, he detected that Fray was working for me and begged me to ask Fray for a dime rock.

While the crackhead held my attention, my eyes were on Fray but my ears were listening to the crackhead. With my focus unbalanced, I saw Fray place everything he had into a guy's hand. It never dawned on me to stop talking and come to my senses. As I looked, the guy turned around where I could see him and told me with a loud deep Barry White type of voice "Ah, you come here!" Before I could reply he unzipped his coat, drew his gun aimed and fired...Boom, Boom, Boom, Boom, Boom, Boom. I took off running. Knowing I was hit, I didn't want to fall. Turning the corner, I could hear more shots being fired as I ran. My fear automatically took over and I panicked. I made it to Eve's house, where I immediately checked myself. I wasn't sure where I had been shot, but as I was running my body shook and my nerves signaled to me that I was bleeding from somewhere. Out of breath, I pulled my right pants leg up and my sock was soaked in blood. When I saw the blood, I started banging on Eve's door...I knew I had to get to the hospital ASAP.

Eve called the ambulance and I was escorted to the emergency room.

The bullet went in and out of my leg ...I had been shot with a .22 long. There was no major damage done, but the doctor told me to stay off my leg for a month. I was given crutches; my leg was wrapped tightly in bandages and an ace band, and I was sent home with some pain pills and antibiotics. The guy who shot me was on the most wanted list (MWL) in my neighborhood. The rumor spread to watch out for a green Chevy Nova. He had robbed and even killed a couple of people. He shot one guy's nuts off, leaving him to survive with just one. Whoever got to him first would reap the reward of ghetto fame, even if they just wounded him. Everybody wanted to see him dead. With the police already on his trail, before I could map out a strategy, he was caught and charged with murder. Him being arrested didn't stop me from carrying my gun. Because I was caught completely off guard, I vowed to never allow that to happen again. But that night I felt safe and had no reason to carry my gun...so I left it the house.

In school I didn't like standing up or walking; and because of my baggy pants, I found myself adjusting my gun in my waistband a lot. One day, in my third period computer class, I got up to turn in my work. There was a line with about three people ahead of me. I waited patiently to see Ms. English until I was next in line behind Nicole. When all of sudden my gun fell down my pants leg, I instantly dropped my work, grabbed my right pants leg and awkwardly ran out the door holding onto my leg. Once in the hallway, I entered the bathroom, which was next door to my classroom. I dropped my pants to my ankles, grabbed hold of my gun, placed it back in my waistband, then took off running full speed to the exit door before the police came.

After convincing myself to go back to school the next day, I stashed my gun in a safe place, just in case I was arrested at school. In class everyone was laughing and talking about Martin Lawrence's T.V. show called Martin. I felt uncomfortable and was hoping someone would inform me about yesterday's event in Ms. English's class. But everyone went about their regular routine as usual, joking and playing. Third period rolled around and Ms. English called me to her desk. My heart dropped like a man jumping out of a parachute. I just knew she was going to ask me about the gun. Acting real cool I said, "What's up Ms. English?"

"Dawayne why did you leave your work on my floor yesterday and fly out of here like a bat from hell?"

"Ms. English I had to use the bathroom real bad and by the time I finished using it class was over."

"The next time that happens, you better inform me and here's your paper, keep up the good work."

I had an A on my quiz. I couldn't believe no one saw my gun fall out of my pants. Out of thirty people no one was looking...I guess they were focused on the quiz, instead of on me.

After a couple of weeks of laying off, my money was running low from shopping, gambling and the loss I took from Fray. Determined to reach my quota for the night, I was ready to go in the house and put my money up and return to work. I didn't like standing on the corner with more than three hundred in my pocket . But, before I could leave the block, Charcoal and a couple of niggas I knew who were on stick-up terms came on the scene. As much as I respected Charcoal I had to be on guard because I didn't know what these niggas were up to... the love of money is the root to all evil. Not that I wasn't taking my part, but these niggas took the love of money to the extreme. Whenever Charcoal got broke, he relied on robbing to bounce back. I wasn't into robbing or stealing...Charcoal tried to get me to go on a few capers with him but I told him that wasn't my hustle.

Charcoal walked up with his three-man posse...all of them were armed, and wearing their all black Champion sweatsuits with their hoods covering their heads. Charcoal walked over to me while I was sitting down.

My gun was next to me, stashed inside the bushes. He told me they were about to rob the liquor store and that they wanted to enter the store five minutes before it closed. While Charcoal informed me of what was getting ready to take place, his posse was peeking into the liquor store window, watching the cash register and monitoring every movement in the store.

I pulled my gun out of the bushes and took it off safety in front of Charcoal just to let him know if he or any of his boyz tried anything, I was ready. Then I took my bag of rocks out of my pocket and placed it under my scrotum. I didn't want to be a witness to a robbery that could turn into murder so I got up and left.

Just before I turned the corner, Bruce called my name, "Ah... Kojack wait up for me!"

Bruce and I were the only two hustling that Friday night before Charcoal and his crew came. Bruce knew I had my piece on me. My guess was that he wanted me to protect him from Charcoal, so I slowed up. As I leaned over the trash can waiting for Bruce to catch up, my backside was facing the street and my eyes were on Charcoal and his posse. As Bruce approached me I saw Charcoal and his crew run in the opposite direction. Unexpectedly, I was swarmed by police and a hovering helicopter with the spotlight beaming down on me.

Just before I noticed the police, I had a split second to throw my gun into the trash can; but I froze, everything happened so fast that I moved in slow motion.

The police jumped out of their cars with their guns drawn, "Put your hands in the air now." I knew if I made one false move I would be shot, so I obeyed the officer. Once I placed my hands in the air, I was thrown on top of the police car, hand cuffed and searched.

The lady officer searched me, patting my gun several times. Then she asked me a stupid question, "Is this a cigarette lighter?"

I said, "Yeah," knowing a bulge like my gun wasn't no where near the size of a cigarette lighter. She signaled to the other officer that I was carrying a gun. I was thrown into the back of the police car and transported to the police station. Bruce was questioned and they released him, nothing was found on him.

While I was in the back of the police car, I was trying to figure out how I was going to get rid of my crack. I knew I wouldn't stand a chance in court with a gun and crack. So, I leaned over as far as I could… the two officers were laughing at how I was going to jail for a long time… neither one paying any attention to me. Hand cuffed, I reached down into my draws and pulled out my bag of rocks and shoved it in between the crack of the seats. At the age of 15, I was charged with carrying an unregistered firearm, robbery and a stolen gun from (ATF) Alcohol Tobacco and Firearms. The robbery charges were dropped because I knew the owner of the liquor store and he wrote a letter to the judge on my behalf, telling him it wasn't me. There were over 300 guns stolen from the police department in 1991 and sold on the street for cash. It just so happened that I had bought a stolen police gun. My court appointed lawyer told me I would have to face some jail time. London and I agreed that I needed my own lawyer. I got six months probation.

When London came to bail me out she was informed I had crack-cocaine in my system. In shock, London didn't speak to me for an entire week. She never believed that my innocence was gone. I had been changing right under her nose. Because I made good grades in school, the thought of me carrying a gun and selling drugs never entered her mind. London didn't approve of anything the criminal life represented. Just the thought of me using crack blew her mind until I explained to her that I wasn't.

There are two ways that crack can enter into your system one is by using it and the other is by touching it. A razor blade and a dinner plate were the instruments I used to break down crack from a block into crumbs. By touching the crack with my bare hands the chemicals had entered my pores causing my urine to come up dirty. So, I was classified to be either a user or a seller by the court system and I had to take urine tests twice a week.

London was on my case, and she came up with a solution to all the problems she thought I had. I was transferred from Eastern to Anacostia High School. With the loss of my gun and my drugs I looked at the game differently. I reflected on the year of 1991, I didn't have the energy to climb the same mountain again. Now on six months probation, I was exhausted from the streets...I felt like I was on a roller coaster and the lights were out, not knowing whether I was going to end up dead or alive. Probation was the best thing that could've happened to me after all I had been through. This was the end of the ride for me, if I wanted to get off. So, I took off my belt, released my bar, got up from the roller coaster, and entered reality again as a spectator to the hustling game.

Chapter 8

Anacostia

Being on probation limited my ability to run the streets. I was only allowed to go to school and had to be in the house at 7 o'clock every night. My probation officer called me twice nightly, and some nights, he'd switch up his routine keeping me wondering and questioning when he was going to call. The thought always entered my mind to sneak out of the house, but I was afraid of not being in the house when he called. I wanted to do my six months so I could get off paper and curfew.

My first day at Anacostia High School, I saw a lot of guys I knew from 16th and W Street, Butler Gardens, Marlboro Plaza and Minnesota Avenue. I bumped into an old friend of mine, Black who still lives in the same apartment complex that my grandmother Beatrice lived in before she died. Black and I laughed about the time my chain popped on my BMX bike. I couldn't fix my chain and neither could any of my friends because it was tangled; so, I went into the house and told Beatrice. She came outside, telling my friends and me that she could fix anything. We all watched as she untangled the chain, placed it back on, and then proceeded to ride the bike.

As she started peddling, the chain popped again causing grandma to tumble down a flight of stairs. Humiliated, she threw the bike down, said a few cuss words, then went back into the house. I tried to help Beatrice after she fell, but even I had to laugh with Black and my other friends.

During the second week of school, I exchanged words with a guy who bumped into me and then had the nerve to look at me as if I was supposed to say, "I'm sorry," or act like nothing had happened. Naw, not me. Only punks did that. I turned, dropped my book bag and just like I thought, he was a punk. He didn't want to challenge me; I guess he did it because I was the new nigga in school. The next day, while I was standing at my locker talking to a classmate named Marcus Johnson, a guy walked up to me and said, "Nigga what'cha looking at?" Marcus and I looked at each other wondering who in the hell this nigga was talking to. He repeated himself, this time he had bass in his voice so he could draw a crowd. "Nigga what'cha looking at?" I instantly dropped my book bag and said, "Nigga what'cha trying to do?" When he saw I was no punk he yelled out loudly in hallway, "We got rec." Marcus and I were surrounded by fifteen scary looking niggas.

Now, I couldn't back down with a crowd eagerly encamped around us, so I started talking more trash to make myself look bigger and badder than these niggas. The more I talked, the angrier they became. They all turned and ran to their lockers. Knowing within myself they could only be running to get one thing, and that one thing could end my life. I immediately headed for the exit door leaving my book bag laying on the floor.

Lunchtime had just begun. Everybody was either outside or placing their books into their lockers. Once I got outside, I was walking real fast as if I was running. My instinct told me to turn around and look. As I turned, I saw the entire school running toward me with the niggas I was arguing with leading the charge. Already two blocks ahead of them I put my legs into overdrive and ran like a track star. In fear, I panicked, running through speeding traffic, with cars driving in both directions. Acting as if I was the invisible man, I took on cars speeding at 60mph, leaping across the cars, almost causing a three car accident as they nearly collided into each other. I continued running until I got to Steven's house where I collapsed at his door, gasping for air. My lungs felt like they were about to explode. Taking deep breaths couldn't slow down the pace I was breathing.

Once I got myself together I knocked on Steven's door but there was no answer. So I waited until he came home. Afraid to leave his apartment building, I stood in the window looking to see if I'd been followed. I knew no one could enter the building because it was secured. It had to be God, because I caught a resident of the building coming out as I arrived.

Three hours passed and finally Steven appeared carrying his gym bag. It never dawned on me that he could be at the gym playing basketball. When Steven saw me at his door, he knew something was wrong. I've known Steven since '83. I met him through Chicago who considered Steven family and we called each other cousins. Whenever I needed Steven's help, he was always there for me. Ever since the seventh grade, Steven promised me if I made the honor roll he would pay me $50 for every A and $25 for every B, anything less than an A or B didn't count. Steven kept his promise and I earned my money. He not only did this for me, but for every kid or teenager he knew in his neighborhood. He made sure we were taken care of, if we earned good grades on our report cards.

In every neighborhood in D.C. there's one guy who has everyone's respect. That one guy can either say a word to save your life…or have it taken. Steven was that guy in his neighborhood. Normally, I would handle my own business; but I didn't have a gun nor did I have anyone to back me up, except Steven. Because of the love Steven had for Chicago, he'd put his life on the line for me. So, I told him what went down at school that day and he, in return told me, "Before you go to school tomorrow come to my house." He took me home and that night I sat in the house and reflected on what could've taken place earlier in the day. I said my prayers and asked God to protect Steven and me tomorrow, then I went to sleep.

The next day, I was ready. I woke up listening to my N.W.A. CD "Nigga4life". I got on the bus and went to Steven's apartment, where he told me, "We'll wait until lunch time to roll up on the niggas." We sat in his house until lunchtime looking at "I Love Lucy and Wheel of Fortune". About 11:30 a.m. Steven started preparing himself, checking his weapons to make sure they were fully loaded and the safety was off. Steven placed both guns into his waistband and said, "It's time to go." I was thinking he would give me a gun to back him up, just in case, but he told me he'd handle it. We pulled up in Steven's car. School was just letting everyone out for lunch, but there was no one that resembled the niggas who tried to jump me. There were only three niggas I could remember off the top of my head.

As we sat there, Steven said, "I bet'cha those niggas are in game room." We pulled off. Steven checked his guns now that we were in front of the game room. My heart dropped when we walked into the game room. I didn't know what to expect. It was crowded. Everyone was either playing arcade games or standing around eating.

My eyes scanned the room, I recognized one of the niggas and pointed him out to Steven. With his eyes now on me, he never saw Steven approaching him. Steven stepped in his face and told the dude to step outside; he did as he was instructed. Once outside, I looked across the street and recognized the rest of his crew. Everybody that was in the game room wanted to come outside to see, but Steven commanded them all to go back inside. Without questioning Steven, they all obeyed.

Steven, with his notorious figure, ordered the rest of the niggas to come across the street; they approached slowly. Before Steven could get out a word they started speaking out, "Steven it wasn't me, I didn't have anything to do with it." Another guy said, "Steven I ran with everybody to see who was fighting." Once Steven spoke they all became quiet like trained dogs. Steven spoke, "This is my little cousin. Do anyone of ya want to fight him one on one?"

None of them said a word. Steven continued, "If anything happens to my cousin, you will suffer the consequences." They dropped their heads and walked away. Steven looked over at me said, "Wayne go ahead to school and if you have anymore problems knock on my door." I later found out the niggas that tried to jump me lived in Woodland project.

While things were cooling down between the Woodland niggas, another beef surfaced. I didn't know there was a rivalry going on in school with the school's two biggest crews going head to head. I got caught in the middle of it. Walking down the hallway, I could see an argument taking place between the Woodland crew and the Minnesota Avenue crew. Marcus and I stood as spectators, watching and listening.

Pea-Nut from Minnesota Avenue said, "I'ma start smacking every nigga out that's not from Minnesota Avenue."

As he spoke he looked at me with anger and suddenly rage came out of me. "Nigga who are you talking to?"

Nut replied, "You talking to me?" I replied, "Yeah, you nigga! I wouldn't fight you, I'd just smack you around like you were my son."

After hearing our voices roaring, teachers came rushing into the hallway sending everybody in the hall to class. After a few days, Nut was a no show in school. I started thinking…either he's locked up or he dropped out of school.

A week later our Principal called every teacher and student to an assembly in the school auditorium. When I opened the auditorium door to enter, there stood Nut and his crew. Nut called me a punk, I flicked off and charged straight at him. Before I could swing a punch, I was grabbed by some students in my class. I yelled out, "Step outside nigga!" Nut never budged and stood there as if I was a fool. I acted as if I was carrying a gun in my book bag just to increase his fear and to let him know I was the wrong nigga to mess with. With all the words that were exchanged between us I felt like he didn't take me seriously. So, to prove my point I invited him to come outside again, but he turned down my offer.

I left school immediately because one thing a man should never do (I mean "never" do) is act like he has a gun when he doesn't. The rule on the street is never pull out a gun unless you're going to use it. Because 95% of the time it will come back to haunt you. I didn't want to fake it, but my pride and my reaction took over. Nut had a reputation for carrying a gun, plus he had the respect of his crew and neighborhood as a nigga who would put you on your back.

Back to the drawing board…knock, knock, knock. First, I heard a gun slowly being cocked back. "Who is it?"

"It's me Steven, Wayne."

He opened the door, "Boy why aren't you in school, you know you can't hang around my house until after 3 o'clock. That's the golden rule."

Steven saw the seriousness on my face; I told him what went down between Nut and me. Steven asked me about the beef with Woodland. I told him everything had been cool, no problems. Steven and I jumped into his car and rode around Minnesota Avenue where Nut hangs out. With no gun on me, I let Steven step out the car first. Steven called Nut over to the car. After they talked, I step out of the car. Nut stood his ground like a soldier… we both talked and the beef was squashed. At 11:00 AM Steven made us go back to school for rest of the day. Because I didn't back down from Pea-Nut I earned the respect of Woodland, Minnesota Avenue and other crews in school and we all became friends.

With peace finally in place in school, I could fill my life embracing change. I started reading to keep myself occupied. Books like The Firm, Malcolm X and Martin Luther King, as well as Final Call newspaper and the Washington Post always nurtured my interest. Reading elevated my mind and allowed me to understand the role I played in society as a black man. I couldn't understand why a lot of black men were like me, lost. Why didn't we take control of our lives? I knew if Malcolm could go to jail and find himself, then I should be able to find myself while I was free.

In 1992 Spike Lee did an advertisement on T.V. promoting the Movie "X". Lee wanted every black student in America to skip school to see the premiere of "X". After watching the movie my outlook on life changed. I even thought of becoming a Muslim. I stopped eating both pork and beef, I was the only vegetarian in my household. I've always admired Malcolm for his boldness, wisdom and choice of words. Hearing him speak showed me that cussing and foul language weren't the only words a man could speak out of his mouth.

When I told London I wanted to become a Muslim, she reminded me of my Christian roots. She repeated over and over, "don't join anything you don't have knowledge of." London explained that being a Christian is more liberal than being a Muslim. I started tapping into my spirituality; and although I had prayed in the past, I started praying even more for direction. To make sure I covered my ground, I prayed to God and Allah, begging and hoping that I was praying to the true and only God. My prayers were answered with me using my own logic. I didn't join the Muslim organization because I followed my heart to remain as a Christian. However, I still purchased the Final Call newspaper from Muslims and still watched Farrakhan on T.V. on Sundays.

Reading had given me so much wisdom and knowledge that my family and friends started calling me Farrakhan. When Martin, Chop, Tyson, Jason, Omar and Wylie saw me. They started laughing then they would say, "Here comes Farrakhan." I thought, because they once looked up to me, I could influence them to go back to school and get their education. But I was teased because I decided to change, for the better. All of them dropped out of school to pursue what I had given up, hustling.

Wylie attended Miller, and before I graduated I had to make sure he was in good hands. I took time out to get to know the underclassmen before I graduated, so that Wylie wouldn't have to go through what I went through. Because of my rep with both males and females, Wylie became popular and untouchable. But, he became vulnerable to playing hooky with Martin and Omar. Jason, Tyson and Chop played hooky as well. I tried to talk to them several times, but they wouldn't listen…none of them would. They acted as if they were somewhat superior and more hip than I was because they played hooky. They thought most of the guys my age—sixteen, seventeen and eighteen—were just followers. They all wanted to fit in with the crowd, so they would sell and smoke drugs to be accepted into the street life.

Still on probation and taking my urine every week, I thought I'd make things look good for myself; so I started looking diligently for a job. Most students in school went half a day and worked the other half. I was trying to get in a (SIS) Stay in School position. A buddy of mine, Derrick Pope, was already working at EPA as an SIS. He informed Mr. Scott (My business teacher) that there was a vacancy available. In return Mr. Scott gave me the privilege to go on the interview, even though I acted a fool in class and flirted with all the honeys. Mr. Scott felt sorry for me, with my probation office visiting once a month and he wanted me to change my direction in life. I was still banging A's and B's on my report card, but whenever things got out of hand in class, Mr. Scott knew. In order for him to get control of the class, he had to get me a job. Every now and then I would put on a show in the classroom, captivating even the teachers. I was still jonin' and making the loud fart noise with my nose in class, which sent my classmates falling to the floor. Mr. Scott had had enough, it was time for me to go to work. One thing he respected about me was that I never talked back to him like the other students. I showed him respect because he was the only teacher in school who could get me a job. He took time out to prepare me for the interview by telling me what to wear—a suit and a tie—how to walk, talk, speak; make sure I had a fresh hair cut, and last but not least, get to the interview an hour early.

I took Mr. Scott's advice and a week later I had the job working from 1 PM to 5 PM Monday thru Friday twenty hours a week. The good thing about my new job was that it was subway accessible. Whenever I was out of school—meaning holidays, vacation or on summer break—I could work full-time. With my first paycheck, I looked out for Wylie and brought him two pairs of kicks, a pair of Nikes and some Addidas Sambas.

Chapter 9

Candy

Now off probation, I joined the Boys Club summer league basketball team. In the summer of '92 our record was 7-1, which qualified us to play for the city championship. We won by two points. I was known as a defensive specialist on the court. Some people called me "hack box or hacker" because of my aggressive play.

When I was younger, I couldn't wait until my skills developed to play on the court in my neighborhood with guys like Romeo Roach, Rock Roach, Sherman Douglas, Bill, Antwon Pringle, Kenny Diggs, Marty and Bird. These guys dominated the basketball court and they were all scorers. So, I decided that my neighborhood needed some defensive. I knew at an early age I wasn't an offensive player like these guys, but there was one gift I noticed that God gave me and blessed me with…long arms. I could pick a person's pocket, and by the time they noticed it, two points would be added to my team.

I had to prove to Romeo and everyone that I could play some defense just to get on the court. Being on Romeo's team, all I had to do was pass the ball to him on offense, then attack whoever was dribbling the ball on defense. With me playing aggressively, the ball was passed quickly. I averaged three to four steals a game, six to eight points off steals. I couldn't even look at a guy wrong on the court…they'd call ball.

Playing defense gave me a rush. I never slowed down; my stamina was above normal. I had now won the respect in my neighborhood as defensive specialist, but many of them told me over and over that I should've played football. Deep in my heart, I wanted to play football and start at the right corner back position. But with London always working, I never gave it a try. I wanted my mother's support because she was the only one who would root me on. As I got older I held it against myself for not playing football, even to this day I say, "I wish I would've played football."

Another reason I didn't try out for sports in high school was because Anacostia had the best football and basketball teams in the city. They didn't need me. Our basketball starting five my freshmen year was led by Mike Powel, Keith Thomas and Lavell Pinkey. Mike Powell was the man, but it would be Lavell Pinkey who would attend Texas Tex College to play football and later be drafted by the Rams. Lavell and I grew up together on 15th street. We took geometry together my freshman year. With Anacostia all star football and basketball teams, I did what I did best and that was to be cool and fresh for honeys.

Cool was my first name. They called me "Kool Kojack." I had my own style and most of all I was leader. I played and joked with the fellas in school but I was always around the honeys. Everything I did was done to impress the honeys. While I was on probation, I took time out to get my driver's license. I was ready to start dating. Catching the subway to the movies or a restaurant was now beneath me. Now that I had my driver's license, I was waiting for the opportunity to drive London's brand new '93 Champagne Camry. London had traded in her Rodney King Hon-die for the Toyota. The Camry had a CD player with a sunroof, the two things the Hon-die lacked. The Camry was clean and fresh with the new car smell. I knew if London just let me go around the corner or even drive to school I was going to get sweated like I was Al-B Sure in '87, better yet Bobby Brown in '89 from the ladies.

Just cruising around the city with my Chante Moore, Tribe Called Quest, Mary J. Blige, SWV, Boomerang soundtrack CDs with my R.E. Tapes…I couldn't figure out what I wanted to listen to. Driving London's car made me feel like it was mine. I was booking honeys left and right. I didn't have to say anything…they stopped me; some even forced me to pull over so we could exchange numbers. When you're driving a nice car, a man doesn't have to have a rap game; the car raps for you.

In my waistband I carried a 16-shooter page net pager that held all my numbers. I don't know why all the honeys wanted code #1 like code #1 means something; but if that was the code they wanted, I gave it to them. When I called them I still asked, "Did somebody page Kojack?" And then they would answer, "Yes this is so and so, what's up?" My Rolodex was on overload I had to do overtime trying to keep up with all the numbers that I had acquired. I really didn't know who I wanted to cut back because all of them were like that; so I enjoyed listing to the sounds of my pager going off back to back because it made me feel like a man.

Driving down Alabama Avenue, I saw my cousin Rusty talking to two women. I immediately made a u-turn and pulled up in front of them where I could see the women's faces. "What's up Rusty, you're a hard nigga to get in touch with."

"Yeah, what's up Wayne. Get out the car." Before I got out of the car, I could hear one of the women asking Rusty, "How old is he?" Rusty, in return said, "Ask him yourself." Once my feet hit the cement, I did a 180-degree turn around the car and stood in front of them waiting to be introduced.

I heard both of the women's names, but one made me curious to find why her mother would name her Candy.

There she stood beside me, a woman 28-years-old with a daughter. Candy was 5'5 and brown-skinned like Mary J. Blige. She had long hair, a body with curves, nice feet and breast size, 34-D. Her biggest assets were her "baby got back" butt and her personality. She was sweeter than the sound of her name and her smile made me blush a thousand times before getting out one word. She sparked a conversation with me, then asked for my hands. In my mind I was wondering, "why's she asking for my hands." Instead of me asking why, I knew she was going to answer the question for me.

"Boy you have clean finger nails, that's a plus in my column." Without me saying a lot she was already on me and digging everything about me; and I was feeling her vibes. She asked me, "How old are you?"

"I'm 17." I decided to tell the truth. What was I going to lose? Honestly, I already had enough on my plate; and if she wanted me to fit her in my schedule, I would have to see if she was all talk and no action. I don't like women who do a lot of talking…action speaks louder than words. We exchanged numbers and started talking over the phone.

Rusty gave me the 411 on Candy, telling me she liked young light-skinned attractive men like myself. I had tried many times to talk to older women in their 30's and 40's, not the ones that looked like the old lady in the shoe, but the beautiful sexy icons like Pam Grier, Jane Kennedy, Vanity, Apollonia, and Debbie Allen. I was turned down because of my age. I didn't care that I couldn't afford to take care of them…I just wanted them intimately. Ever since I lost my virginity to an older women at 13, I had a fetish for older women. No longer insecure or unsure of myself, I knew what I was working with and women's ages didn't scare me.

One day Candy invited me over to her house so we could talk. When I walked in the house I stood at the door until she asked me to sit down. Her mother was sitting directly across from me. I spoke "Hi, how are you doing? Nice to meet you. My name is Wayne."

Moms looked over at me like she was trying to guess my age. I was praying she didn't ask my age.

"How old are you?" she asked.

"17." At the time Candy was in the kitchen.

Moms yelled out, "CANDY CANDY THIS BOY IS TOO YOUNG FOR YOU, YOU'RE GOING TO JAIL, YOU PEDOPHILIA."

I looked over at her mother with the thought of speaking my mind. But I had nothing good to say so I kept it to myself. I stood up and left. Candy and her mother were arguing.

Before I reached the car, Candy came outside running towards me with a look of embarrassment on her face and said, "Don't worry about my mother, she's old. The next time I invite you over I'll make sure she's not home. Okay?"

"Cool." Then I went on my way. I don't know what happen after I left, but Candy seemed even more interested in me. She stepped up her calls from twice a day to four times a day.

The week before Memorial Day, London informed me that she was going to visit my grandfather in Williamsburg, Virginia for a week. I told London I didn't want to go…now that I was older I had the privilege of staying home. London took Benisha, Tilly and Wylie with her. Wiley couldn't question London because she knew he wouldn't obey me, so he had to go bye, bye with mommy and the kids. I was going to be home alone; but to make things even sweeter for me, London rode with my Aunt Channel in her Caravan. The keys to the Camry and some money were left on the table. Once I got home from school I ran through the house screaming, jumping on the beds and rolling all over the carpet like a dog with an itch on his back. With no rules to abide by, the first thing I did was clean the house so it would be clean and smell fresh. I knew I was going to live it up; and I hoped that I could get Candy over there Saturday night for a nice dinner, or maybe we would just chill and watch Russell Simmons' Def Comedy Jam.

I couldn't track Candy down, so I decide to go to the movies to see "Menace to Society." "Menace" was the talk in school; and even at work many people told me that they had seen it twice and recommended it as a "must see" movie. It sure was good...I paid to watch it three times myself.

Monday morning I woke up bright and early, with my clothes already laid out. I knew it was going to be a great week. I was going to show off the Camry when I got to school. Everyone thought I had a new car because the paper tags were still on. I tried to tell them it was London's but they didn't believe me... I guess because I was driving the car everyday...and their parents wouldn't allow them to drive their cars. They thought I was trying to be low key about the whip. After school, like most young men my age and older, I drove around with the music loud and the seat leaning back. This showed the honeys that you were cool.

I cruised the city with the sunroof open, like I was "the man". Still respected on the streets, my reputation grew even bigger because I knew so many women and I drove London's car. Most women thought London's car was mine and a lot of them assumed that London's Camry was an Acura Legend or a Lexus ES 300. I wasn't the perpetrating type... if a woman didn't ask I didn't volunteer. I used whatever I could to my advantage.

At the stoplight a car pulled up beside me...there were two honeys in the car. The passenger asked for my number, and as I yelled it out to her my pager went off. I retrieved my pager from my hip to see the number. By the time I looked up the light was green. The passenger said, "I'll call you!" I drove to the nearest phone booth, slid a quarter into the phone, and then asked, "Did someone page Kojack?"

"Yeah, this is Candy." Sounding seductive she said, "Are you coming over?" "Like the Jackson 5, I got to be there. I'm on my way." She started laughing, then hung up. I got back into the car, made a u-turn and flying like an eagle, I was at her door in fifteen minutes. When I knocked on her door I caught butterflies.

Candy opened the door, "Are you scared to come in? My mother isn't home; neither is my daughter." This was my second visit, I didn't know what to expect. With Candy flirting with me, I played shy just to get a feel for her strategy. Once I figured her out, I set the tone by flirting back. Then out of nowhere she said, "What kinda relationship do you want with me, be real and up front with me?"

Shocked that she asked the question I replied, "Don't beat around the bush get straight to the point because that's how I like it."

She replied, "Okay school boy."

"Who you calling boy? I'm all man, so don't test me by calling me boy like I'm your son, little girl."

I knew calling her a little girl was an insult. Little did she know I was getting turned on. As we went back an forth I said, "little girl" and she said, "little boy." The words rubbed together like two sticks and a flame was sparked between us. We didn't catch fire until we entered her bedroom. Slowly she took off her clothes without saying a word. As I watched her strip down to her Victoria's Secret underwear, I thought of R Kelly's song and said, "R. Kelly, shut up. Her body is calling me, not you."

Her skin had no marks or bruises. In a seductive way, she walked over to the CD player and turned on Chante Moore. I slowly undressed, then rolled on a Lifestyle condom.

After foreplay, Chante Moore's CD continued onto the second song, "It's Alright." As Chante sang, Candy sang along with her while looking deep into my eyes...

Relax your mind, we can be free together,

Take our time, even through the tears,

I'm staying right here, I'm waiting right here,

Oh, we're going through some hard times,

But it will be…alright

It's all right, it's alright…

By the time we finished, the CD was back on "It's Alright." I went through four condoms. I could've gone through five, but four was all I had.

Candy and I stared into each other's eyes, then we both started laughing. After she washed me off, I got dressed. Candy went into her pants pocket and gave me some money. "This is my last, but you can have it."

"Naw, Candy I'm okay. I got money."

"No here!" she demanded. So, I took the money without arguing. When I got into the car, I felt like a gigolo who just had sex for money. I went into my pocket to see what she had given me. There was a $20 dollar bill folded over a $50 dollar bill. I was amazed because this never happened to me before. Staring at the $70, I was puzzled about what kind of relationship we had.

Candy was oversexed; she wanted me every day. I couldn't believe a woman her age would have "white liver," a slang word for a woman who craves sex. Basically, she has to have it. Every time we had sex she gave me $50 to $100. I would beg her not to give me money, but she would find ways to stash it in my car, house, clothes, shoes or my underwear pocket. Candy did everything for me and she didn't allow me to do anything for her. She bought everything for me…from clothes to food. Whenever I was hungry, she would bring the food to my house, even at 3 o'clock in the morning if I asked her.

I wasn't used to this kind of treatment. Most of the women I had dated wanted me to take care of them, but here I was on the receiving end, being controlled by money and sex. To feel like a man again, I started dating other women…women who allowed me to be me…women who allowed me to pay the dinner bill, or at least treat them to the movies. The last thing in the world I wanted to do was break Candy's heart. In any relationship the one who shows the least attention to the other is the one who controls the relationship. I wouldn't return any of Candy's calls, nor would I answer my door when she came over unexpected. I ran from sex, love and Candy. I needed time to think. I wanted to tell her how I was feeling, but I hid my true feelings from her. I was thinking she only wanted me for sex and not as her man. With sex taken away the truth surfaced; and I knew all we had established together was sex. There was no love, just the lust for sex.

When Candy finally caught up with me, she cussed me out, calling me all kinds of foul names. I couldn't even get in a word; all I could do was listen to every insult. Before she hung up the phone, she spoke these words that I'll never forget, "One day, little boy, somebody is going to break your heart and when they do you'll see how it feels." As I laughed in her ear, I heard the phone slam.

I told myself, "Candy is tripping ain't no woman going to break my heart. I guard my heart like Fort Knox and you have to be slicker than a can of oil to get in."

Funky fresh dressed to impress ready to party
Money in your pocket, dying to move your body
To get inside you paid the whole ten dollars
Scotch taped with a razor blade taped to your collar
Leave the guns and the crack and the knives alone, MC Lyte's on the
Microphone, bum rushin and crushin, snatchin and taxin
I cram to understand why brothers don't maxin,
There's only one disco, they'll close one more
You ain't guarding the door, so what'cha got a gun for?
—MC Lyte from the album "Self Destruction"

Chapter 10

12-22-93

On the night of December 22, 1993, I was dressed fresh and ready to impress the honeys that were going to be in the club. But little did I know, this would be the night that changed my life.

"Thank you Jesus." I never thought I was going to live to see eighteen. On my eighteenth birthday I looked up into the sky and said, "Thank you" once again; then I got on my knees and kissed the ground. In my neighborhood, 18 is a lucky number for a black male to live and talk about it. I felt as if I survived the tidal wave of money, drugs, guns, going to jail, death and the street life.

In '91 a few moths after Tyson stabbed me, he was arrested for larceny and was given a year in Oak Hill juvenile jail. He wrote me a few times. In every letter he asked me to come'n see him. I didn't want to see this nigga and I didn't want to hear his name. He sent messages through Eve and London asking me to please come see him. After a while I started to think this must be important. So, I took the journey to find out. When I entered the visitor's hall I saw a lot of niggas who I grew up with that I didn't know were locked up. I noticed Chicago's buddy St. Louis was also in the visitor's hall. I later found out from Tyson that St. Louis was a counselor in Oak Hill.

When Tyson came out, I didn't know how to react. He didn't look like himself. I could tell he was under a lot of pressure and I knew why. St. Louis pulled me to the side and told me a lot of guys didn't like Tyson and they wanted to take his head off. I wasn't surprised, but knowing that St. Louis knew Tyson had stabbed me, he wanted me to give him the word so he could let the dogs loose on him. I stood up for Tyson and asked St. Louis to look out for him as a favor to me. He gave me that okay, then I took my seat beside Eve and Tyson. There really wasn't a lot for Tyson and me to talk about, until visiting hours were over, except for women we both knew and had slept with.

I wasn't a fool. I recognized why Tyson wanted me to visit him. He wanted niggas to know that he was my cousin, and with me visiting him, that automatically let niggas know to back off.

When Tyson came home in '92 he thought he was O-Dog from the movie "Menace to Society." He no longer cared about life and fell back into stealing cars and drugs. Coming from school one day, I stopped at Eve's house to meet London. Tyson and his Aunt Manda were arguing about the stolen car Tyson was driving. Two women were in the car with him. London stepped out on the porch and said to Tyson, "Don't get back into that car."

Tyson replied in front of me, "Shut the hell up!"

I looked at him like he was crazy and said, "Nigga you're not going to disrespect my mother like you disrespect Manda and Eve. Not in front of me nigga!" Then I got in his face.

He ran to the car and said, "Nigga I'll be back."

"Nigga, I'll be here waiting, you punk."

Ten minutes later Tyson jumped out of the car with a .38 revolver, which he pulled from his waistband. With nowhere to run London and Manda jumped in front of me trying to calm Tyson down so he wouldn't shoot. Seeing that he was hesitant I said, "If you shoot me, you better kill me because my father is going to kill you."

With Chicago now home from his six-year bid, Tyson came to his senses quickly. One of the neighbors called the police and within seconds the street was flooded with them. Once Tyson heard the sirens he jump in the car and flew like a jet before they arrived.

If I had told Chicago what happened between Tyson and me, Tyson would be dead. So, I kept it to myself only because I stood my ground. Deep inside of me I knew Tyson and I would never be close like we were years ago. I really didn't want to face the reality that I may have to kill this nigga. To protect myself and to keep the peace, I kept my distance, only because he was family. After Tyson stabbed me, he couldn't hide the fact that he was a coward hiding behind a gun. He carried a gun because of his low self-esteem, and he felt that everyone knew that he and I were not close.

From time to time London would ask me to take Eve to run some errands. I really didn't want to go over to Eve's house because I wanted to avoid seeing Tyson. But, London would be tired and sleepy, or I would be out driving and she'd page me and ask me to run Eve to the store. At least three times a week, Eve would call for a ride and two out of three times London would send me. One night, I had to drop some cash off to Eve for London. My cousins Caesar and Martin were playing tonk for money.

I gave Eve the cash, then I looked in on the card game and decided to join in. The hands that were being dealt to me were unreal…they thought I was cheating. I tonked on them seven straight times and they had to pay me. After I broke Caesar and Martin of all their money, Fat Head wanted to shoot some crap. I had my friend Lady with me. She sat in the car for two hours while I gambled.

Tyson came in the house with these two dudes, twin brothers, who we refer to as "Twins." Tyson asked me if I was going to the go-go at Celebrity Hall, a club located in North West on Georgia Avenue…it's the Saturday night hang out spot. I told Tyson twice I wasn't sure whether I was going or not. I was trying to stay focused on the dice as they rolled, but Tyson kept irritating me by asking me the same question over and over. So, I replied, "Why Tyson?"

"Because I want you to take Martin in your car." "Tyson, I don't know, I might take Lady out to the movie's after I finish gambling."

"Man, take Martin in your car because he's not riding in my car."

"Tyson you would rather take two niggas you don't know instead of your uncle? That's crazy!"

With those words I spoke, Tyson became angry and asked me again if I was going out. Then I became angry and told Tyson, "Don't ask me nothing else about going to the go-go."

Tyson replied, "Nigga who are you talking to?"

"You nigga! You see me gambling and you keep asking the same damn thing! No means no!" Tyson ran to his green Ford that was parked in the middle of street. He opened the door, grabbed a 9mm Glock from under the driver's seat, and walked up on the porch. He said, "Nigga say something now! I'll kill you right here!"

I stood there, nervously, as Fat Head said, "Nigga if you shoot him you' re going to have to shoot me too." Caesar, Martin and the Twins all told Tyson to put the gun down. Tyson pointed the gun at me and Fat Head stepped in front of me. I didn't want to show my fear because if I had panicked, I could've triggered Tyson's fear to shoot me. I stood as calmly as I could, allowing everyone around me to calm Tyson down. Once he calmed down, he got into his car and drove off. I grabbed my money off the ground, dropped Lady home, and then called Chicago and Steven to get a gun. Neither one answered my page; so I had no choice but to do this on my own. I went home and grabbed two steak knives out of the kitchen drawer.

Knowing where Tyson was headed (Celebrity Hall). I jumped into the car; and once I got to the club, I circled the block until I spotted Tyson's car. I did that so I would know where and how far away he was parked, so I could park closer to the door. This gave me the advantage I needed, so he couldn't get to his weapon before I got to mine.

I paid my money to enter the club, then I had to walk through the metal detector. I placed everything I had in my pockets on the table—keys, money, I.D., pager and my belt. As I walked through the detector, Tyson and I locked eyes. With my bottom lip out I didn't blink once. Tyson turned his head, then I was asked by the security guards to walk through the metal detector again. I was patted down like I was carrying a bomb. The metal detector went off three times and I was asked to leave the club. The security guards thought I was carrying a concealed weapon in my rectum. The pants that I had on had metal on the belt patch and that caused the metal detectors to go off.

I waited outside in the car for Tyson. It was now 12:30 AM. The club wouldn't let out for another two and a half hours. I would have to wait until 3 o'clock to get at this nigga for disrespecting me. I started thinking about how ungrateful this nigga is to London and me. London treated Tyson like a son and I treated him like a brother, up until he crossed me. I had never allowed anyone to disrespect me like that, and I was at the point where I was fed up with

Tyson. My mind wandered and my conscience made me think of the consequences. I sat in the car for two hours contemplating whether or not I should kill him. My conscience repeated over and over "go home."

I came to my senses while looking at the location where I was going to kill Tyson...there could be witnesses. So, I left the club plotting a different way to get him. Four in the morning I receive a page from Chicago and Steven, both telling me they were asleep and to call them in the morning. I didn't want to put any stress on them while they slept, so I held back the information and followed their instructions to call the next morning.

When I woke up I was ready to explode. All the anger and frustration I was feeling came out of me through tears. I was afraid of what I was thinking but there was no way my mind could avoid it. Knowing that I had shot five people in my past, I thought about how difficult it was to deal with the pain I left those people in. I explored every possibility that came to mind. It took months for me to build up my self-esteem, to face life, and to live with the shootings I had been a part of.

I dismissed my thoughts by praying to God for forgiveness. Only prayer cleared my mind to the point that it was no longer cloudy. At that moment, I was faced with killing a man, and not just any man...my own cousin. A few seconds later, London knocked on my bedroom door. When I didn't answer she walked in and saw my tears. She said, "Fat Head told me what happened last night. I got off the phone with Eve and told Tyson that if he comes anywhere near you, he'll be dead."

In my mind Tyson was already dead... I was figuring out when and where... I didn't want any witnesses. Once I killed Tyson, I wanted everyone to think otherwise. I didn't want them to think it was me. Two days later Tyson came over my house and apologized, but I still didn't trust him...and I knew he didn't trust me. We shook hands. I had a smirk on my face, thinking to myself, "I'ma get this nigga to relax and then I'ma crush him." After that, Tyson stayed his distance and I stayed mine.

In the summer of '93 I finally opened my heart to a woman named Alexis Burke. Alexis was 5'2", sexy, aggressive, and very humorous and had a one of a kind smile. She reminded me of the actress Nia Long. We had been talking over the phone every now and then since '92. Our relationship was open, honest, and we communicated well. I felt comfortable around her because I was able to be myself. We both worked on the weekdays and spent the weekends together, focusing on our last year in school. I knew I wanted to go to Hampton University and she was undecided.

Alexis brought a part of me out that I didn't know I had. Her deep tender affection unclogged my fear of loving a woman. After sex, she would lay on my chest and cry. She never told me why she was crying, but would ask me to hold her tight and rub her back. I felt funny inside and I could feel myself falling for her every time she shed a tear. Our bond was beyond intimacy, I had finally met a woman I could share my emotions with. I wanted to be near her; so, three weeks before school, I had London transfer me back to Eastern. I promised to keep up my grades and stay out of trouble.

When I told Alexis I was getting transferred, she was just as excited as I was. Eastern still had its reputation as a fashion show school. I wasn't worried about the fashions because I knew how to put on a show. Alexis loved the fact that we shared lockers and I carried her books to class. But, she didn't like the attention I got from other honeys. Even after the women found out Alexis and I were dating, a lot of them would leave love letters in my locker and blow kisses at me while we walked together down the halls.

I found myself explaining and had to convince Alexis that I loved her. I was blamed for things I didn't do and she allowed the rumors to come between us. I fought hard for our relationship to work, but it faded away slowly. We no longer talked over the phone, but we continued our sexual affair on occasion.

London worked at night and I had the responsibility of watching my four-year-old sister Bennisha and my infant cousin Tilly. London had taken the responsibility of raising Tilly because her mother was on drugs and couldn't afford to take care of her. There were times I couldn't hang out late at night or even go to the club with everyone else, because I was babysitting. Wylie ran the streets with Martin and Omar. London knew he wasn't as responsible as me so I was stuck with the duty of cleaning, caring, and cooking for myself and the kids. Wylie had a 10 o'clock curfew, and after London left for work at 11 o'clock, he would run out the door. Martin & Omar were waiting for him at the corner. There were nights I'd be ready to go out to the GO-GO and Wylie would wait until I got into the shower then he would leave the house. So, I couldn't hang out, unless it was the weekend.

There were nights I would be ready to explode because I couldn't hang out during the week. The only thing that brought me relief was that I could sneak women in while London was at work. I would have these women catching cabs, the subway or drive to see me. They would be gone by the time London got home in the morning.

Every Wednesday in school, the talk was about Eastside Night Club, where you had to be 19 years old to enter.

Every Wednesday Rare Essence, a popular go-go band, played at the Eastside located in the South West section of the city. Rare Essence played a mixture of the latest R&B, rap music and created music they made themselves. Most people thought that Go-Go bands in D.C. caused violence, but it was the people who caused the violence, not the band.

The Go-Go was D.C.'s notorious playground, where anything could happen, from car thefts to killings. The Go-Go was where hustlers, ghetto superstars, inner city rappers, celebrities from sports to known rappers like Dougie Fresh, Ludicrous, Biz Markie all have performed over the years with Rare Essence. Perpetrators, gamblers, prostitutes, thieves, addicts and the worst of criminals and crews all came together to party under one roof. I was anxious to go because that's where the women were. To go in the Go-Go you had to be fresh…if you didn't have a new outfit on, you were better off staying home. Only the flyest of flies walked the walkways of the Go-Go. I wasn't a rookie to the go-go scene, I had been going since I was nine and I'd been listening to the music all my life.

At any age, you could see Junk Yard Band, the youngest band in the city. To be able to see Rare Essence, you had to be nineteen or over. Only nine months shy of my nineteenth birthday, I figured out how to cut corners when it came to getting in the clubs. I had been sneaking to see R.E. since I was fourteen. There were only two ways of getting into the clubs if you were not the legal age. One, get a fake I.D. of someone you know and look like; or two, pay the security guards extra money to enter. I got myself a fake I.D. I had to make sure I remembered the address, social, height, weight and D.O.B.….I knew if I didn't the security guard would take my I.D from me.

London took leave from work one Wednesday night, so, I called my crew to see what was what. Everybody was ready and fresh. I was rocking my new Polo 2000 sweatshirt black pants and my low-top Tims. I snuck two knives in the club just in case anything broke out. I couldn't worry about my crew backing me up; I knew who would get down and who wouldn't. Out of fifteen of us, there were only two people I trusted if I got into a beef …Charcoal and J.P. I knew what to expect from the rest of my crew. I carried the knives because this was a new environment for me, I had never been in this club and I heard many stories about South West and 37th Place niggas running it. I had heard stories of niggas getting beat to death inside the club and the security couldn't save the person. So, I carried my own protection because if I was going down, then they were going down with me.

Once we entered the club, I had my crew surround me while I bent down in the crowd unnoticed to slip my concealed knives into my pocket. Standing to my feet, I walked the floor with my crew searching for a spot we could party in and patrol. The music was booming and the bass made me want to dance. Before I could ease myself into dancing, I observed everything and everybody, including the security. I had to make sure everything was okay before I let loose. J.P., Jody and Tyson got their names and our crew on display. Once I heard, "15th Street crew is here." I started bobbing my head and then I started dancing to the music. I looked through the crowd, watching every woman walking past and the ones dancing near me. Something about watching a woman dance turns me on. The movement and the signal it sends is "come'n get me." I wondered to myself if some women can move in bed the way they dance.

J.P. tapped me on the shoulder, signaling that they were about to walk over to the bar. While standing at the bar, I noticed Ned and five other niggas. We caught each other's eyes, we hadn't seen each other since I shot his boyz. My heart dropped, but my facial expression didn't change. Ned glanced over at me and kept on walking. I knew now that I could no longer dance to the music and that I had to watch my back.

I identified Ned to my crew. There were nothing but stares and Ned knew they had no chance against us in the club. So he and his crew left and we partied until it was time to go. After the lights came on, everybody ran to their cars and sped off. Because someone sprayed a car with bullet holes, I knew the next time I went to the Eastside, I had to be strapped…I couldn't go without a gun because Ned had seen me there.

On Wednesday December 22, 1993 every student in my school had to write one paragraph on American Education Week, which is honored every December in the D.C. public schools. Out of seven hundred students, my paragraph was selected and published in the school newspaper Cluster 3 Exchange read as follows:

American Education Week means a lot to me. It is a week to celebrate teaching and learning. Education holds the key to my future goals and accomplishments. Education has improved my thinking, listening, speaking, reading and writing skills. Beginning in the first grade, I have tried to use all that I have learned to be successful. I am proud of my accomplishments and I am grateful to the Lord Jesus Christ for helping me. As we celebrate "education" and American Education Week, I would like to thank my teachers who have helped me and other students reach our goals. I acknowledge the talents and abilities of teachers and I thank you for the time, effort and encouragement you have given me.
   —Dawayne Williams, Eastern High School '93

Later that night, my crew and I were planning to go to the Eastside to celebrate J.P.'s birthday. London was preparing Christmas dinner… she had taken off work for the holidays. I got dressed around 8 o'clock that night. I was fresh in my brand new Polo sweathood that I paid $240 for, a pair of faded blue jeans and a black pair of Deion Sanders' Nikes, and my Calvin Kline "Obsession" cologne. I was on my way to see Alexis before I met up with everybody on 15th Street at 11 o'clock. Before I got to the door, my cousin Heather called and asked London if she could use her car to do some last minute shopping. London asked me if I could take her and I agreed. I picked Heather up and we went to 7th Heaven clothing store for kids in Hechinger Mall. I knew she was going to be in there for an hour; so, I sat in the car listening to Toni Braxton's C.D., Seven Whole Days. The thought entered my mind that Tyson owned me some money.

Two months prior, Tyson had bought a Polo shirt from me, only giving me some of the money, and I let him owe me the rest. I let two months pass, thinking he would pay me on his own. But Tyson never said a word about the money when I saw him. I decided that I would use this time wisely while I waited for Heather. Seventh Heaven was five minutes away from where Tyson lived.

As I drove off, my conscience overpowered my thinking and my ability to listen to Self Destruction. I sang along with Mc Lyte. "You ain't guarding the door, so what'cha got a gun for? Do you rob the rich and give to poor." My inner thoughts repeated, "don't go."

I started questioning myself and could feel the vibes of my thoughts telling me something was about to happen. I convinced myself that nothing was going to happen to me. When I got to Eve's house, Tyson wasn't there and Martin's baby's mother asked me to take her home. I told Gena I was going to 15th Street first to see if I saw Tyson, then I would take her home. I drove to the Chinese carry-out on 15th and C Streets where Omar, Alvin, Jody and ten other people I knew were standing.

Alvin said, "What's up Kojack are you partying tonight for J.P.'s birthday?"

"Yeah you know I'm going, have you seen Tyson?"

Alvin said, "Yeah Tyson is in the carryout." Just as I spoke Tyson appeared in the entrance of the carryout door.

"What's up Tyson?"

"Nothing what's up with you cousin?" he said.

Then I replied, "Tyson do you have the rest of my money?"

"Nigga, what money?"

"The 30 dollars you owe me from the Polo shirt?"

"Nigga, I don't owe you nothing," he said as though he wasn't going to pay me.

"Tyson I'll give you your $60 back right now." I went in my pocket and pulled out my money. I had $500 on me that London gave me for Christmas gifts. "Look Tyson here's your $60 and I'll just go in your room to get my shirt and that will solve everything because you ain't going to take my money and my shirt." When I stopped at Eve's house I looked in Tyson's room. He had the shirt laid out on the bed. It seemed he was planning to wear the shirt to the club so I left it there.

I was sitting in the car talking to Tyson with the window rolled down. Tyson shouted back, "Nigga you better get out of my face cause I'm not giving you nothing."

Tyson was trying to test me as if I was a punk, so I spoke back. "Nigga you know you could never beat me with your hands."

Tyson repeated three times, "You better go head nigga before I kill you." Then Tyson reached in his pants like he was grabbing something.

As I reached to put the car in gear to drive off, he pulled out his gun. I froze and looked him in his eyes. "I know this nigga isn't about to shoot me," was all that was on my mind. But before I could finish my thought, I was interrupted by ten bullets sending me into shock. Pop, pop, pop, pop, pop, pop, pop, pop, pop, pop. The first two bullets swiftly greeted my back. Resting directly on my spinal cord, the other eight anonymous bullets demolished London's car. I couldn't move or even yell for help! All I could whisper to Tyson was "Nigga I'ma get chu!" I drove off slowly, my ears were ringing from the gun shots.

I could feel one of the bullet's traveling inside my flesh. I couldn't lean back in the seat like I normally would. Both bullets made me sit erect. Gena said, "I'm glad nobody got shot."

While Tyson and I were arguing Gena was looking in the opposite direction out the window. She had no clue who was shooting. Once she heard the shots fired, she placed her head in her lap. If she hadn't a bullet would've hit her in head. Both side windows were shot out, two bullet's greeted each head rest, there were two bullet holes found in the driver's door, another bullet hit the dashboard, which shattered the front windshield, and the last bullet shot out of the gun hitting the gas tank.

As I drove off slowly, I could feel myself blacking out. "Gena I've been shot."

Gena panicked, "Stop the car so I can drive you to the hospital."

I stopped the car. Gena jumped out and tried to move me out of the driver's seat, but she couldn't, my body was paralyzed; I couldn't feel anything. My feet and my hands reacted when I moved them, but the rest of my body didn't. I said, "Gena get back in the car." I couldn't move I knew I had to drive myself to the D.C. General, which was five blocks away. Once Gena jumped back into the car, I drove off slowly, running three lights. Normally, I wouldn't run a light without looking but this was a matter of life and death.

When I pulled into the emergency room exit, I came within an inch of crashing into the window. I hit the breaks; then Gena jumped out running full speed into the emergency room, "He's been shot! Please somebody get a doctor, he's been shot!" Three Nurses came rushing out to see who Gena was talking about. One Nurse tried to move me, but she couldn't. They sent for a stronger male doctor to lift me into the wheel chair. I tried to tell the doctor, "I couldn't sit back." But the Doctor still tried to push me into the wheel chair, rushing into the emergency room. I could no longer hold the dizzy spells back. I blacked out and fell out of the wheel chair, while the Doctor was rushing me into the emergency room. I fell face first onto the dirty hospital floor... and that's all I remembered. At home, London was in a deep sleep until the phone rang.

"London, this is Blue! Is Kojack alright?"

"Yeah, he took your wife Heather to the store."

"London did Kojack get shot?"

"Shot, shot, no!" Then Blue hung up. London went back to sleep for a few minutes then the phone hang again. This time it was D.C. General explaining that I had been shot twice in my back and she needed to get to the hospital immediately to sign papers for me to have surgery and a blood transfusion because I lost a lot of blood. London called Tyson's aunt Ebony who lived in the same apartment complex we lived in.

Ebony told London she was about to leave the house to go to D.C. General with her kids. London got upset because she needed a ride to D.C. General, too. London hung up the phone and called a cab, panicking and praying that she would get to the hospital in time to save my life. Ebony called back and gave London a ride.

When London got to the hospital, she saw her car shot up with broken glass everywhere. She rushed into the emergency room to find the doctor so she could sign the papers for me to have surgery. After signing the papers, the doctor told London she could see me in five minutes.

My entire family and a few friends were in the waiting room. London asked everybody if they knew who shot me. No one answered her, tears ran uncontrollably as she repeated, "Please somebody tell me who shot my son?" Before London arrived Eve had told everybody—family and friends that were present—she wanted to be the one that tells London.

My Aunt Sara screamed out, "That nigga ain't getting way with this one. He gotta go to jail this time." London became curious of who Sara was talking about.

Eve slowly walked up to London and whispered in her ear and said, "It was Tyson." London went off. The nurses and doctors had to calm her down.

My new Polo shirt had been cut in half; blood was all over my clothes and shoes. I had been stripped naked by women doctors.

Once again, it felt like déjà vu from when I was stabbed. I got the tube up my nose that goes into my stomach, and a tube in my penis to control my bladder and to make sure no blood was in my urine. I was sliced on the right side of my body, under my armpit and a tube was placed there to drain out unclogged blood. I also had two IVs and the heart monitor on me.

When I opened my eyes, there were two detectives standing on the right side of my bed while the doctors stabilized me. The detectives questioned me, "Who shot you? What kind of gun do you think it was? What street did you get shot on? Were there any witnesses?"

I wasn't telling them anything, "Man I don't know, I don't feel like talking, I'm shot." I thought they were going to put the handcuffs on me because I had my two knives on me but they didn't. They just kept asking off the wall questions. The doctor took all my belongings and placed them in a plastic bag. I kept my money and my pager just in case someone tried to steal it.

Five minutes later, London was standing directly over me. Hearing her voice made me feel I was going to make it. London rubbed my head and said, "God isn't ready for you boy." The tears ran down my face knowing that she was telling the truth. I gave London my money and pager; and I asked the doctor to give London my belongings.

When the detectives realized London was my mother, they questioned her to piece together information. London looked at me, "Go head and tell them." I turned my head signaling that I wasn't saying anything. London told them what they had been waiting to hear from me. They took the information London told them, but they couldn't do anything unless I told them Tyson shot me. I didn't say a word.

Before the detectives left the room, they gave me a card to contact them if I changed my mind about talking. Before the doctors took me off to surgery, London said, "You're going to be alright." As she spoke I felt a calmness come over me; and I prayed and asked God to protect me because having surgery was serious.

Chapter 11

Get Back

I was placed in the critical condition unit. I received a lot of visits from family, friends and co-workers. I tried to hold myself together and was able to, until Alexis came to see me. She cried the entire visit but once she left, the walls caved in on me. I started wondering if I would be the same person I was before? Would I be able to walk again? There wasn't much I could do... I had no strength to attempt to walk; all I could do was think. Half the time I was drugged up on pain pills. I couldn't get any sleep because every two hours a doctor came in to check my monitor and pressure. I was mostly irritated because I couldn't sleep. I hated the food. The only thing I ate was the fruit and vegetables, and I drank my apple juice. For nearly two weeks, I put up with the misery of pain and needles five times a day. The doctor told me I could go home once I started walking. I knew I had to force myself to walk, because I was home sick. One of the nurses came in my room everyday and helped me walk. I had to hold onto the rail on the side of the wall to balance myself. After a few days, I was walking on my own and talking to other patients in the hospital. I was in the hospital for Christmas and New Year's. Once the doctor saw my progress I was released.

I thought because I was home I would be able to get some sleep but the phone was ringing off the hook. Everybody asked me if I was okay and if I needed anything. My body was weak and frail; I had lost 30 pounds. My weight went down from 140 to110 pounds. To build up my immune system I continued to eat fruit and vegetables; and I took vitamins daily.

Chicago gave me a .32 handgun snug nose. He liked revolvers and I liked semi-automatic guns with clips. Beggers can't be choosers, so I took the gun and I carried it everywhere I went, especially school. The night Tyson shot me, Chicago was riding through 15th Street minutes later. One of Chicago's friends flagged him down and told him that I had been shot by Tyson. Tyson spotted Chicago's Lexus and ran through an alley. Once Chicago figured out that he wasn't going to catch Tyson, he came to visit me in the hospital. London and Chicago got in an argument because he wanted London's approval to kill Tyson, but London told him that the police were now involved and to leave it up to them. Knowing that Eve knew Chicago's reputation, he would be the number one suspect, besides me, if anything happened to Tyson.

My body had started to feel a little better, but I still couldn't stand for long periods of time... my head would become dizzy making me feel nauseous. I was out of school and work for a month. The weekend before I was about to go back to school and work, my brother Country (on my father's side) wanted me to go with him to a party at the Capitol Plaza Mall Bowling Alley where Rare Essence was playing. When we got there I saw Omar, Martin, Charcoal, J.P., Alvin, and Jody standing in line. Country and I busted in line with them, and I heard a few people mumbling about it; but this was my crew. They wouldn't let me go to the back even if I wanted to.

I recognized a familiar voice so I turned. It was Tyson. Everybody froze, it seemed as if he and I where the only ones standing there. I gave Tyson the stare down for about ten minutes. He never looked at me; his eyes were glued to the ground. I could see he was ashamed of himself; but I wasn't going to have any pity on him. I was thinking, "If this nigga looks at me once, I'ma kill him right here in front of everybody, even the P.G. police." The car was parked 30 feet away with my gun under the driver's seat. I said to myself, "Tyson look up." He didn't even give me a glance or a corner look.

Once we all got into the bowling alley, the word had gotten around that Tyson and I were beefing. Everybody showed me love and respect, especially the women. Nobody stood around Tyson, everybody isolated themselves from him. Wherever I walked or stood, my crew followed. Tyson got the message that none of us wanted to be around him. When the band started playing I lost track of Tyson. After a while I thought he left, so I loosened up a little and started dancing to the music. As I was dancing, I could feel someone coming from my blind side. Before I could brace myself to see who it was, the person was already up on me. It was Tyson crying, making a complete fool of himself. He ran from behind me and hugged me whimpering, "I'm sorry cousin, I'm sorry." His tears ran unstoppable, I felt a little sympathetic, but he had to die. Everyone looked astonished at the fact that Tyson was hugging me and crying. He couldn't hold himself together. I felt embarrassed because we became the center of attention. I wanted to act like I didn't care but I knew Tyson was falling right into my hands. I left the bowling alley before Tyson, so I could get my gun. The P.G. Police must have called for back up because 5-O was deep outside. About twenty squad cars came rushing with their lights flashing. I just knew I was going to jail, but once I left out of the club, a fight broke out and everybody started running towards his or her cars. I told Country, "Let's go." We took the Baltimore/Washington Parkway exit and went home.

The next day I got a call from Alvin. He told me that Tyson was in two accidents on the way home from the bowling alley last night. I knew that his conscience had to be killing him to have two accidents in one night. Two days later London sent me to the store to buy her some cigarettes. When I got back in the house, I went to the bathroom.

While in the bathroom London knocked on the door, "Lamont where's my cigarettes?"

"They're in my coat, check my top pocket." "Damn, damn, damn!" I yelled to myself, "My gun is in my coat." I was praying that London didn't find it.

After I came out the bathroom London said, "I want to talk to you right now. Where did you get this gun from? And why are you carrying a gun in the first place?"

I replied, "Ma, I'm not going to be caught off guard by Tyson anymore. He tried to kill me twice but he won't get the third."

Then she said, "Just press charges and leave it up to God."

I wasn't trying to hear that, all I wanted was my gun back. So, I asked, "Ma, can I have my gun back?"

"No, I'm keeping it."

"Ma, look I need my gun for protection you can't protect me, only I can protect myself. Tyson doesn't care about you or me and if he did he wouldn't have shot your car up with me in it."

London was pissed off now. She threw the gun up against the wall. I ducked hoping the gun didn't go off. London told me, "Get the hell out of my house right now."

I ran over to the wall and scooped up the gun before London noticed; and I ran out the front door with London chasing me. When I got outside, I thanked God that the gun didn't go off. London yelled out the window, "Don't come back in here either."

Later on that night London paged me and asked me to come home because she was worried about me. Before hanging up she said, "Don't bring that gun in my house." I stashed the gun outside before I entered the house. I waited until she was asleep and then I went and got my gun. Everywhere I turned someone was saying, "Press charges and leave it up to God." I didn't know how to leave it up to God. So I wrestled with myself because I never wanted to be considered a snitch. The situation I was in was difficult. Everybody, I mean everybody knew about Tyson shooting me. The pressure was getting to me to retaliate.

The next day, I was alone walking to school with my bookbag full of books. I had on my blue Eddie Bauer coat, wearing an EB is like wearing a pork chop in a lion's den. EB is the most popular coat to wear in the winter time. The coat costs $400 and it's not safe to be standing still if you own one. It's best to keep moving or you'll get robbed.

Actually, a person is better off not buying the coat to save them from being robbed or killed. Many people have died because of those coats. Every fall and winter the hunting starts and the prey are people with the EB coats. The cycle began in the 80s and it continues to this day. Most guys that were robbing people for EBs targeted schools, bus stops, subways and clubs for their victims. Having an EB made me commonly accepted by the honeys and I knew the risk I was taking but my rep of wearing expensive clothes made me who I was.

A block away from school, I was headed towards the school entrance door. I spotted a red Buick, with two guys inside. The passenger jumped out of the car with his gun in his waistband; he waited for the passing cars to drive by before he crossed the street. I reached under my coat pulled out my .32 and aimed it in his direction. The passenger yelled at his partner, the driver, "He's got a gun!" Before I could squeeze the trigger the passenger jumped back into the car and they sped off leaving tire marks on the ground.

I looked around to see if anyone notice me pulling my gun out, then I placed it back into my waistband and stood in line to go through the metal detector.

Our school security guards focused more on the backpacks than searching each student for weapons. The metal detector always beeped when anyone went through. The security guards would ignore the beeps because basically everyone had a piece of metal on them anyway. By the time I placed my books into my locker it was time for homeroom.

For some reason I could feel today was going to be a bad day. I couldn't concentrate. I was tired of people asking me the same questions repeatedly, "Did you get shot? Does it hurt when you get shot? Did your cousin shoot you? Would you rather be shot or stabbed?" When I told people that I been stabbed too, they wanted to know who, when, where and how it felt. Everyday in school, students…and even the teachers… questioned me. I was ready to explode, and I did. I got into a fight with a female classmate.

While I was walking to my seat a few classmates were horse playing and one of them was pushed into me. Not knowing my full strength, I pushed her back. I was still weak and fragile from the bullets in my back. She turned around and pushed me back, causing me to lose my balance. A few of my classmates stepped in between us, telling the young lady that I had been shot. After they told her, she politely apologized. I didn't feel I could make it through the school day so I asked Ms. Arrington if I could go to the school nurse's office. She granted me permission.

The school nurse and I were cool. I stopped in her office at least once a week to get some condoms. Occasionally, if she wasn't busy we'd talk for awhile. I felt comfortable talking to her.

She was about 40 years old, nice looking with a personality that drew me to her. I could see she cared and showed interest in me. If she wasn't married, I would've hit on her but I had too much respect for her to disrespect her in that way. I have to say she was sexy. I tried to get her to send me home, but instead of allowing me to leave, she wanted to know why, when, where I was shot and who shot me.

I figured she probably knew from the rumors, so I opened up and told her what was on my mind. "Ms. Destiny my cousin shot me in my back twice and I don't know what to do. My mother and a few of my family members told me to just press charges, but I don't want to snitch."

"Well, Mr. Williams what do you plan on doing after you graduate and what are your future goals?"

"I plan to go college once I graduate, own my own house, car, business, wife and have four kids, that's my plan."

"Well, in order for that dream of yours to come true you have to make that decision now. Everything you do now affects your future. If you kill your cousin you're going to jail, whether you like it or not. What does your cousin do for a living?"

"He sells drugs and he dropped out of school years ago."

"How old is he?"

I replied, "twenty."

"Dawayne do you want my advice?"

"Yes, I'm listening Ms. Destiny."

"There's two ways of doing things in life, your way or God's way. God is giving you an option …take it or leave it. Either you press charges on Tyson and save both of your lives, or you kill him or he kills you. Your life isn't in Tyson's hands, it's in God's. Me, you and your cousin… we're all God's children whether we're good or bad. But we must make the right choices in life. Your cousin needs help and you're the only one who can help him. His life is in your hands, you have the power to redeem your life and save Tyson from taking someone else's life, if not yours." Then she used her hands as a dem-onstration to allow me to see the reality and the seriousness of making the right choice. In her left hand she said, "jail or dead." In her right hand she said, "Press charges and pursue your dreams. Now which hand do you chose, Mr. Williams?"

"I chose the right hand Ms. Destiny." After we talked she gave me a big hug and told me to do the right thing. She sounded like she was advertising for Spike Lee, but I appreciated it. Ms. Destiny con-vinced me that I had to pursue my dreams in life.

A week before I talked to Ms. Destiny, Tyson called me, with his girlfriend on the phone. She asked for me, then Tyson spoke. I was surprised that he called. He told me he was staying with his Aunt Heather, and if I needed anything, just call him. With me knowing where he was staying, I utilized the detective's card I took from the hospital. Two weeks later Tyson was arrested and charged with attempted murder and assault with a deadly weapon. Tyson was hoping that I would drop the charges against him, so he pleaded not guilty. He wanted Eve to use her manipulation tactics. She did as she was persuaded to do.

Eve called me and said, "Tyson said it was an accident and if he wanted to kill you he would've. Tyson was high, and you know that boy misses his mother."

"Eve, if Tyson wasn't trying to kill me then why am I living with two bullets in my back? I could be paralyzed." I got tired of talking, so I hung up the phone on her. And I didn't answer when she called back.

With Tyson pleading not guilty, I had to go through jury selection, preliminary trial proceedings and the grand jury process. I missed a lot of days from work and school dealing with this case. Tyson was placed in the D.C. Jail until the case was resolved. Tyson tried every-thing he could to get me to drop the charges against him. His girlfriend offered me sex but I knew this was a trap.

Once the case was in process, Eve called again, "Kojack, the judge wants to give Tyson fifteen years. You know Tyson wasn't trying to kill you. Please tell the judge that Tyson wasn't trying to kill you so he won't have to do fifteen years. The judge could lessen his time if you write him a letter or tell him personally that Tyson wasn't trying to kill you."

Eve begged me, but my mind was made up and I had no regrets living with the decision I made. Tyson took the plea bargain and the judge offered him, five to fifteen years in jail with parole.

I was glad that Tyson took the plea-bargaining because I had already missed my class trip to the Bahamas and didn't want to miss my graduation day if the trial continued.

June 16, 1994 was our graduation day and Alexis and I said our final goodbyes. Even though I had tried to make our relationship work, it didn't. It was hard to let go. She had captured my soul and looking into her eyes upset me, knowing that we had to separate and move on with our lives. I received a few calls from Alexis over the summer; but our relationship faded away once she went off to college in Atlanta.

Chapter 12

Unique

For the oddest reason, every woman I tried to date had a man. To be honest, I loved talking to women in relationships because I didn't have to be committed… committed to dinner, movies, and spending time together. Women in relationships were more vulnerable and easier to have sex with than single women, particularly if they were not fully committed. I found out that some women were gullible with men they were attracted to and vice versa. With Alexis' and my agreement to see other people, I met a woman named Unique.

She was 5'7" with a brick house body and smooth, sexy legs that she used for ballet. Her hair was long, without a weave; she was light-skinned and had pretty feet. From the moment I laid my eyes on her, I was infatuated. I would walk past her in the hallway between classes and look at her in amazement. I was hypnotized by her perfume and my imagination explored her like I was watching the sun set. I observed every detail of her, she had to be my princess. I couldn't stop thinking about Unique, so, I built myself up to approach her. I was dismissed three times, but I was determined to conquer her.

So, I did nice things like carrying her books to class and buying her lunch or giving her lunch money. Over and over she told me she had a man, but I didn't care. Eventually we exchanged numbers, and once we started talking I found out we had more in common than I thought. Earth, Wind & Fire was our favorite R&B group, and we both loved listening to old school music from the '70s and '80s. Unique knew more about music from those eras, like the year the song came out and the names of every member in Earth, Wind & Fire. I had to put her to the test, but first I had to find my Earth, Wind & Fire CD.

"Okay, Miss Unique, since you think you're an Earth Wind & Fire fan, name the members of the group."

"That's easy... Philip Bailey, The White Brothers... Maurice & Verdine, and Al McKay."

"Okay you got that right, Unique, now what's your favorite song by Earth, Wind & Fire?"

"I like Reasons, Devotion and Shinning Star; and my other two favorites are All About Love and After the Love is Gone."

I replied, "All About Love and After The Love is Gone are my favorites too." Slowly we became close and our conversations over the phone were exciting and interesting to the point where we both would fall asleep on the phone, after talking for hours. But, we'd play it off like we heard what the other said, knowing we were really asleep.

I was impressed with Unique's integrity, intellect and confidence. Her inner beauty made her even more beautiful than her outer beauty. Unique's attentiveness made it obvious that she was the one for me. I never in my life felt tingly inside for a woman. When I saw her, I got butterflies; and if my friends mentioned her name, I melted like butter on hot toast.

Unique and her boyfriend were going through their ups and downs with their relationship. I gave her my best advice to show her that I wasn't the jealous type. I wasn't a player hater, neither did I hate the game. Whenever she disputed with her man, she wanted me to pick her up so we could talk. She was afraid of her man and what he would do; so, when I picked her up she would lean her seat all the way back. She did this just in case she was spotted by one of his friends. Sometimes we'd go to the mall. She would go her way and I would go mine. Before we separated, we would agree to meet at the car in an hour. Her man was a hustler. He fought to instill fear in her so that he could control her. I knew from our conversations that their relationship wasn't going to last long. I gave her a picture of me that I took at my prom. Her man found it. I got a call from Unique crying telling me he shot at her in front of her apartment building and the bullet just missed her head.

She also told me that he knew me, so I asked her his name and she told me. I knew who he was, but I played it off like I didn't know O-Boy.

One day I was riding though Simple City projects and I saw my man Marcus Johnson from Anacostia high school. As we were talking, a car pulled up. I saw a guy get out with a gun in his hand. I saw his face. It was Unique's man. I ran to my car and sped off. Later that night I saw Marcus again. This time we were in the club.

Marcus walked up to me, "Kojack man why did you run when you seen O-Boy?"

"Marcus man, I have to tell you the truth, I talk to O-Boy's lady."

Marcus laughed and said, "He wasn't after you, because if he was I would've known. That's my man. He pulled his gun on a nigga that owed him some money, Kojack. He pistol whipped the nigga and took his coke and money then spit on the nigga." Marcus assured me that he wasn't going to tell O-boy that I was talking to Unique. After Tyson went in, I didn't carry my gun often. It wasn't until I had that encounter with O-boy that I decided to tote my gun again

Unique was dangerous to be with, but I took the risk. After seven months of plotting and planning, Unique finally gave into my sexual advances.

I couldn't believe I made love to Unique, I was so excited that I went into the bathroom and looked in the mirror and said, "Yes, yes, yes, this can't be real." Usually I would give up on a woman if she didn't have sex with me within two months. The longer I had to wait the shorter my interest became and I would usually move onto the next woman. I did this to women who made me wait. But with Unique I couldn't get enough of her. Every time we had sex, it felt like the first time; and I wasn't going to risk losing her, so I broke my rule. A few months later O-boy was killed in a shoot out. Unique mourned for four months. I was right by her side and when she wanted to be alone, I gave her the space.

To occupy my time while she mourned, I focused on my college courses. When it came time for me to go to college, I had to make a big decision. I was accepted into Hampton University; but after Tyson shot me, London and Eve's relationship changed. They were barely speaking. Eve was the only family member London could depend on when she needed a babysitter. I knew London would be required to get up extra early to take the kids (Bennisha and Tilly) across town late at night to another family member's house. So, I decided to attend the University of the District of Columbia (UDC). I was able to attend school in the city, keep my job at EPA, and baby-sit at night while London worked.

Wylie was in jail at the time serving 180 days for fighting.

In May 1995, my doctor suggested that this would be a good time to remove both bullets from my back. They had moved to a safer place for the doctors to perform surgery. The doctors didn't want to take a chance at removing the bullets a year ago because one of them laid on my spinal cord. If they had moved it, there was a 75% chance I would've been paralyzed if there were complications. After surgery,

I was on bed rest with stitches in my back. To ease the pain I took Motrin 800s. London came into my room and checked on me every hour. She had been promising to buy me a new car for a graduation gift, but I had to pay off my credit card bills.

London said, "I just got my taxes in the mail we can go look for a car tomorrow if your feel better. But your bills better be paid off."

Wylie came rushing into my room after London left. "Brother, they're all gambling around the corner." Wylie had done his 180 days and was now free. He grabbed his money that he had stashed in my room and returned back to the crap game. I added up all my credit card bills while laying in bed. I needed $1,300 to pay off my credit cards. With $80 to my name I was willing to take my chances at winning or losing in the crap game. I got on my bike, sore back and all, and rode to the crap game. By the time I pulled up, Wylie was broke.

I spoke to everybody then I placed a bet. Once I got on the dice, it was over. I was known for quitting once I had won enough money; and because of that most guys wanted their chance to break me before I broke them and quit. There's a superstition about dice that guys believed when shooting crap…and that is…if a person makes all the numbers in a roll, the dice must be switched and that's what they did to me, switched the dice. Most of the guys I gambled with didn't know when to quit. It didn't matter whether they were winning or losing.

As people crowded around, I was in a zone, like Michael Jordan when he scored 55 points on the Washington Bullets….he was in a zone. Like when Deion Sanders returned a kick off, an interception and a pass for a touchdown against the Giants all in one game…he was in a zone. The odds were against me, 15 to 1. I had fifteen people all betting against me. Every time I made a number I slipped a hundred into my sock unnoticed. I tried to calculate in my mind how much money I had stashed in my sock. I knew that I had well over $1,300. This is something you never do—I prayed that I would miss, so I could roll out; but the dice were still in my favor.

Many of those who were betting against me where now on my team because they knew I was in a zone. I threw out thirteen numbers straight, and even when the dice were gated, I rebound and threw my number. Finally I crapped out. I stood up, brushed off my knees and tried to slip away unnoticed. But everybody said, "Where are you going Kojack?"

"I'm gone, thank you niggas for my new car." I laughed to myself all the way home, riding the bike at full speed. I won $1,700, plus I still had the $80 that I came in the game with. I paid my bills and saved the rest.

It took London and I a week of searching to find me a car. Car shopping is worse than shopping for clothes. We went through a lot of hassle, but we finally struck gold at the Tyson Corner Nissan dealership, where I drove off in my new 1994 Champagne Maximum. We left the car dealership at 2 o'clock in the afternoon; and I was able to make my grand entrance to pick up Unique at school at 3 o'clock.

When Unique saw the car she said, "Oh my God." She was surprised that I made a power move without telling her. I dropped Unique off at work then I cruised the city showing off my new ride.

After Unique graduated from school, we talked about our future together…things like her going to college with me…and possibly, us moving in together. I was pleased that we were on the same page and able to discuss our future.

Two months later Unique called me crying, "I got something I want to tell you."

Before I could reply my heart drop, "Unique what is it?"

"Dawayne are you going to be mad at me."

"No, what's up?"

"Are you sure Dawayne, because this can wait until I see you."

"Unique, what is it?"

In a soft sexy voice she said, "I'ma, I'm pregnant."

At the age of twenty, I was excited and thrilled about becoming a father, but Unique wasn't thrilled. She thought the baby would interfere with her dreams of becoming a nurse and a professional dancer. I tried to convince her not to have an abortion, but her mind was made up.

"Dawayne, can you give me the money for the abortion?"

"Hell no, you know I don't believe in abortion."

"Dawayne I'll pay for it myself. Will you go with me to Hillcrest Abortion Clinic?"

"Unique, it's not that I don't have the money. I want you to have the baby, believe in me, believe in us, we can make together. I can't stop you from going, but I can't go with you. It hurts me that you want to do this, like it's nothing."

She hung the phone up on me. Just the thought of seeing and knowing she was about to kill my unborn child made me look at her differently. Two days later she called me and told me that she had the abortion.

It hurt me that she had done it. Because of the pain I felt, I ducked her calls for three weeks. Finally I returned her calls after she left urgent messages at my job and with London to call her right away. When I called her to see what was so urgent all she wanted from me was to bring her some Wendy's. I took her the food and she apologized to me a million times. She suckered me in like a mouse to cheese. We were back on track.

To help establish my credit, London co-signed for me; and that helped me get my first credit card. Unique wanted a CD player from Circuit City but she needed a co-signer so, I co-signed for Unique to help her establish her credit. We both received our own credit cards with a limit of $3,500. The bill was sent to her address.

After two months of paying the bill, Unique filled out the change of address form and the bill was directed to me, the co-signer. She had charged a $1,000 worth of merchandise and I charged $500 at the time. Unique didn't inform me that she was sending the bill to my house. When London saw the mail with both of our names on it, she called me every fool under the sun.

Once London started fussing and cussing, I felt like the world was going to end. One of the most painful things in this world to me was listening to London after I screwed up. I wanted to plead my case but London was the judge in this courtroom. I had never been called so many dummies in my life. I felt like Fred Sanford was speaking to me, "You big dummy!" That's what London said to me over and over.

I couldn't take it anymore. Her words were like razor blades cutting me; so, I left out the house, got into my car and turned on the radio. It was set on 96.3 WHUR. I sat in the car listening to a song by a group called, The Main Ingredient. The song was Everybody Plays the Fool. My heart was broken; and after London dropped the bomb on me, I was thinking about dying. I had to get to the bottom of this, so I called Unique. She told me the reason she sent the bill to my house was that she couldn't afford to pay it. I understood that she was a little nervous that the balance was $1,550. This was her first credit card, so I tried to explain to her that the balance didn't have to be paid in full.

Unique told me, "I'm not paying anything until you pay your half of the bill."

We argued. I tried to convince her that we both needed to pay the bill off and that it would kill two birds with one stone if we both just paid what we charged on the account. Unique didn't pay another monthly bill and I was stuck with the bill until the full balance was paid. My pride was hurt and I distanced myself from her for two months.

One night I was in the club with my crew and I was surprised to see Unique there. She never went out to the club. She wasn't the club type. She was more of a homebody...go to work, come home, cook dinner, watch T.V. and then prepare for the next day. I didn't acknowledge her, and even when she spoke, I stepped off like she was invisible. Still hurting behind the fact that she used me, I played big in front of her friends and mine.

Later that night, I received a page from Unique; but I didn't call back until the next day. Deep down I missed her; but I wasn't going to show her any affection. Really, I didn't know how because I was still hurting from the abortion and the credit card issue. I kept Unique close to me just for sex. We didn't go out to the movies, dinner or shopping anymore; and I stopped giving her money for personal needs. It was just sex... and have a nice day.

Unique and I only communicated on a sexual level and we both realized that sex was the only thing we wanted from each other. Without telling each other that we wanted to see other people, we did it anyway, and this led to our break up. No relationship can last without trust, communication and spending quality time together. I knew this, but I didn't have the slightest idea if Unique knew it. I took a gamble with having unprotected sex outside our relationship and it cost me. I didn't know how to face Unique and tell her the truth about how I really felt about her. Really, I wanted to say, "I love you but you played me and now I'm going to get revenge by sleeping with other women. If I get caught, I get caught, but I'm too slick to get caught." That's what I thought. I blamed Unique because I cheated. She knew that I needed sex at least four to five times a week. A woman can tell a man no only a few times before he goes astray. Unique started throwing me shade, so, I went out and did what I wanted to do...not thinking I was going to get caught.

I received a call from Unique, "You dirty dog!"

"What'cha talking about, Unique?"

"Nigga you know what I'm talking about you gave me the Clap."

"The Clap! You didn't get that from me, so what nigga burned you? I knew you was sleeping around, now you trying to blame it on me."

"Dawayne, I know it was you because I haven't been sleeping with anyone but you."

"So you're trying to tell me that you haven't had any sex in two months? I know that's a lie."

Unique was beefing hard and we stopped talking over this for two more months. Honestly I tried to be faithful. I tried to protect myself, but my appetite for sex and rejection caused me to gamble. I couldn't tell Unique that I was the one that gave her the Clap because I didn't know who gave it to me. I narrowed the women down who I slept with in the past week. I counted 3 including Unique. I asked myself, "Who could be the suspect?" I had no clue. All I knew was that I had to take a trip to the STD clinic to stop my penis from dripping.

While I was in the clinic I saw the nigga Unique was suppose to be sleeping with behind my back. So you know what I thought, "He probably got the both of us, or maybe I got them, but somebody got me. Who knows?" Before I took the shot in the butt I had my blood taken for the HIV test too. I had never in my life been so paranoid. The test took two weeks to come back. I didn't get any sleep thinking about how my life would change if I had HIV or AIDS.

Two weeks later the doctor told me to come in the room and close the door. I was praying so fast that God had a stenographer angel in heaven dictating my prayers. The doctor looked me in my face and asked a few questions about my sexual history. I answered them to the best of my knowledge. He passed me ten condoms and told me "Son you're okay, but everything that looks good ain't good." He repeated, "Protect yourself because your dick can and will fall off if you use it on the wrong person."

After singing Anita Baker's song, I Apologize, I was able to convince Unique to come over my house so we could talk. She gave me the okay to come and get her. I picked her up and we went back to my house to talk things over. Unique seemed hostile and unapproachable.

The more I tried to talk, the more she insulted me, telling me she only came over my house at twelve at night to tell me that she has a new man. She didn't blink, not even once, when she said, "Dawayne, it's over we can't see each other again in life because I have a new man who loves me."

My heart dropped and I knew she was serious. The first thing that came to my mind, "Well, if this is it, can we have sex for the last time?"

Unique stood up and said, "Nigga please take me home." I tried breathing on her skin and rubbing her legs with a gentle kiss. Unique pushed me off and insisted that I take her home right away. In the car Unique started crying because I told her, "You're gonna miss me."

As the tears ran swiftly down her cheeks, Unique threw punches at me. WHAM, WHAM, WHAM. Unique struck me in between the eyes causing them to water up. While swerving from the blows to my face on the East Capitol Street Bridge, I lost control of my car, just inches before hitting the rail. I guided my car back under control, pulled to the side of the road and we started fighting.

London had taught me never to hit a woman and if I ever felt I had to, just walk away. I didn't punch Unique in her beautiful face like she was punching me. I had to defend myself so I grabbed her arms. I wasn't about to let her whip me like I was a punching bag. Before I pulled off, I warned Unique, "If you throw another punch at me, I will put you out of my car and you can get home the best way you can."

Three blocks away from Unique's house she threw a flurry of punches at me again. I got out of the car and took my keys out of the ignition, just in case she locked me out of my own car, which she tried to do anyway. I had to run around the car for awhile until I was able to unlock the door. I grabbed Unique and threw her out of my car and drove off. When I got in the house I called her to make sure she got in safely. Unique answered and told me never to call her again and then hung up. I let her cool off for a while.

Whenever I was in the mood I would call just to see how things were going with her. But she wouldn't answer any of my calls at home or at work. I got the message that it was time to move on and I blocked Unique completely out of my mind. I'm an expert when it comes to burying my emotion and thoughts. I told myself, "She'll be back." Every woman I've been with always came back to me.

Every time I went to the club, my car windows were busted out. This happened five times. One night, when I came out of the club as usual, my window was shattered and the front of my car was damaged. I never wanted to think Unique deliberately busted my windows out, but after repeated attempts I had to look at this closely.

Some guys go to clubs and target certain cars, especially the ones with tinted windows for guns and other items such as CDs, money, coats and purses. To make a clean break on a window, they would take a spark plug from a car and break it by throwing it to the ground. The force of throwing it would cause the spark plug to break into small white pieces like crumbs. Those crumbs from the inside of the spark plug would shatter a car window causing a clean break. To shatter a window the spark plug had to be thrown at the window with force; and like throwing a rock through a window it will shatter and brake.

I could tell the difference from a spark plug break and someone breaking the window themselves to enter my vehicle. So, I investigated my car; nothing was ever missing from it each time my windows were busted. My gun, CDs and my money inside my ashtray all were still in place. Eventually, to keep my car windows from being busted out, I switched up cars with London, or I rode with my buddies when I went out to the clubs.

After a year had passed, I realized that I had been wrong to let Unique go. The games I played backfired on me. I never meant for our relationship to end the way it did. I smacked myself upside the head every time I thought about letting her walk away and go into another man's arms. Even though I let go physically, my heart held on. All the thoughts and emotions I had buried were now resurfacing and coming back strong like waves coming upon a seashore. There's a saying that the weakest part of a man's body is his penis. That's a lie; the weakest part of man is his heart. As for most women in my life, I've left the brand name of my car tires on their heart by running over them.

I never thought my heart would be broken until now. My pride had hidden my true self from Unique and now I was exposed by my heart and love. Love was the very thing I ran from and I was now captured, feeling its wrath. The cement I had placed around my heart to protect me from love was now cracking, causing me pain…pain like I had never experience before. This is when I fully understood that love was real and nothing to be played with.

The hardest part of it all was that I knew I loved Unique and didn't tell her. Listening to slow intimate music overwhelmed my thinking and I could feel the words from the songs like my heartbeat. As I sat on my bed, the melodies from the music opened my mouth to sing along with Ce-Ce Peniston's, It was Inside That I Cried. What I really felt for Unique couldn't be held inside anymore, so it came outside of me like a volcanic eruption.

People say, "A grown man isn't supposed to cry." I never in my life had cried over a woman. I couldn't hold back the force of the over-flowing dam in my eyes, so I let go of the tears. They relieved my heart; but just when I thought I was recovering from Unique, I was hit by a Mack truck worsening my condition from critical to a coma. I saw one of Unique's girlfriends and she told me Unique had a baby boy. I was crushed and couldn't sleep or eat...my appetite was gone. Candy came to my mind and the truth is what she said came true, "One day somebody is going to break your heart Kojack."

Experiencing this heartbreak allowed me to see myself and under-stand what I needed to work on as a man. For the first time in my life, I didn't like myself. I felt ugly and self conscious; and my emo-tions became mixed on love and women. My self-esteem was smaller than an ant. What I thought I understood, I didn't. Love is real and you never know who you're going to love; but when you do know who you love, tell them because it can change everything. I had to lose love to gain it; and loving a person isn't worth the pain of losing them. I got exactly what I deserved from our relationship, and the truth of it all was that it made me a more mature man.

Deep in my heart I wished I would have given her the letters I wrote, but I felt silly for writing them. The men I knew didn't write letters to the women they loved. So, I balled up every letter I wrote and threw them in the trash. I appreciated everything I had experienced in our relationship. This was a real turning point for me and it took Unique to help me realize it.

Words cannot express how I look back on this time and realize Unique was the one for me. Honestly, I don't know whether Unique loved me or not, but I loved her and still think about her.

Chapter 13

Falling Apart

Love will make you do crazy things, but I would have never guessed that I, Dawayne Williams, would be sitting in my bedroom looking down the barrel of a loaded gun contemplating life or death over a women. I began to talk to myself and rationalized how easy it would be to inject myself with one good bullet to ease the pain of Unique's absence. I figured that we live to die, so why not speed up the process...at least I wouldn't have to think about Unique. Unique was the bulk of my misery and the other part was the streets.

On the streets everything was falling apart like a tree losing leaves in the fall. Since '91 a lot of my buddies were in jail, dead, selling drugs, robbing people, smoking crack and weed or both. It all started in 1992 with Bishop and his crew when they were arrested on conspiracy charges ranging from murder to drugs. Also in the same year, Chop was killed for robbing a man at gunpoint. The man returned and unloaded multiple shots to Chop's head. In 1994, Tyson, Martin, Jason, and Chicago were locked up for different beefs.

Kentucky Courts Projects is a block away from 15th Street. Kentucky Courts is a replica of the Carter apartments on the movie New Jack City. It was regulated and controlled; and it functioned just like New Jack City. The police didn't have any control and they were afraid to enter Kentucky Courts without backup. After a police officer was killed on December 30, 1993 search warrants were executed on the Kentucky Courts Crew for guns, drugs and bulletproof vests. (Source: *Washington Post*)

A select few on 15th Street were also arrested for conspiracy with the KCC, including all mentioned above. All of them were sentenced for five years to life for various crimes.

In the summer of '94, I was hanging with my crew: my cousins—Caesar and Omar, my brother Wylie and three friends—Alvin, Jody and Cuba. The hangout spot was still 15th Street. Now that everybody else was locked up, we had full control of the street. Every crew that has control of any street corner has to make their own mark. In whatever way it takes place; murder, drugs, robbery or gambling. Other crews must respect your territory, because if they don't, the lease you have will become theirs... and then where you gonna go? To be an extortionist on the streets, your reputation had to be more than violent. To reach this level as a vicious, no heart nigga with no remorse, Killer had to be your last name.

And if a nigga didn't want to pay up, then his family would have to suffer the consequences. A beef was quickly catching fire and I knew eventually someone was going to ask for my help.

Alvin and I were standing in front of Eastern High School, waiting for school to let out at 3 o'clock. With five minutes to go before the doors opened, we were approached by the Extortionist and his brother. I could see that Alvin was afraid, but I wasn't going to let them take advantage of him. My gun was tucked in the waistband of my jeans. I was secure with protection and I knew that they were just as secure as I was. The guy approached us as if he wanted to challenge us. I looked directly in his eyes to let him know I was up for the challenge. His eyes expressed seriousness, but his brother seemed timid. After scanning their eyes, I quickly checked to see if either of them had a bulge poking out of their waistbands. To my surprise they had no protection. It was then that I felt like the HNIC, Head Nigga In Charge.

I relaxed because I knew they were coming to talk, but I didn't sleep on them. There was silence, then out of nowhere, a conversation sparked and words were exchanged. The whole time, I was standing next to Alvin like his bodyguard, digesting everything that was being said. I listened attentively and made my presence known at the same time.

The conversation got heated and I stood in front of Alvin. "Money! Alvin ain't giving none of y'all niggas no money!"

The extortionist replied, "Nigga I'm not talking to you. You can speak only when I'm talking to you."

I fired back, "Nigga, if you talking to Alvin, then you're talking to me!"

Alvin was a marked man. He drove a BMW 735 green with tan leather interior and dressed better then Johnny Versace himself. There was a difference between Alvin and me. He was seen standing on the corner all day and night, whereas I wasn't seen unless I was coming from work or school. But word on the street was that Alvin was running 15th Street and all the money was circulating back to him. They wanted their cut or they were going to take his 735 until he paid the $10,000 they were asking for.

As the argument escalated, I reached for my gun. A police squad car pulled up directly across the street from us. Immediately I walked off and blended into the crowd of students to make my escape. A week later the extortionist got high off PCP and committed suicide by shooting himself in the head.

Also in the summer of '94 I lost two buddies I had known since I was seven—Charcoal and Cuba. Charcoal was killed for robbery and Cuba was killed in a drug deal gone bad. The guy Cuba was buying drugs from tried to rob him for his $6,000 and Cuba was shot three times in the upper body with a .357.

In 1995, I lost Steven, another close friend. He was killed at the Giant Grocery Store on Good Hope Road South East. He was shot seven times in the upper body and was pronounced dead on the scene. I didn't have the chance to go to his funeral because his family chose to have a private ceremony, family only. Steven was a good dude and was always there for me…I'll never forget him. R.I.P.

In the summer of '95, Jody was killed right in front of his house on 15th Street. There were rumors about him testifying about a murder he witnessed. Jody was the Billie D. Williams of our neighborhood. Standing next to Jody made me feel unattractive because he was handsome. He was known by the finest women in D.C., Maryland and Virginia. When he was living on 15th Street, Jody always had women driving by or stopping in carloads. Jody was a real classy guy. The day he was killed, 15th Street died.

Unfortunately, the shooters in every case I spoke of above, were never caught.

People who lived and died by the streets were often members of some click. We hated being referred to as gangs. We preferred being called crews, because that was what we were…a crew. Every crew in D.C. added crew to the end of their name. The news and the media hyped everyone up all across America saying that D.C. has gangs. Los Angles, Detroit and Chicago had gangs, but the Nation's Capital had crews. The Latinos in the area preferred being called a gang; but black males loved being called a crew. A crew consisted of three or more members and they used a project complex, street names and numbers, or a made up name to be identified. No one became known without a crew to back them up.

When Kentucky Courts crew was arrested, 15th Street inherited their customers. With the drug traffic and the increase of people standing on the corner daily, the police of Second District were ordered by the Chief of Police to set up roadblocks and patrol the area with motorcycles and cars. All drug transactions and soliciting was prohibited, and that caused 15th Street hustlers to move to another street corner. Seventeenth Street was already an established drug corner. Moving two blocks over wasn't an easy transition, but what made it easier was that everyone knew each other. We all went to the same schools and our parents grew up together. There was no jealousy or hating amongst us and there was enough money to be spread around so we all could go on shopping sprees together. Moving to 17th Street was like the merging of two companies. We were twenty-five strong young black men—ages ranging from fifteen to thirty-three years old.

At the time, we only had two guns on our block. One was my .32 and the other was a stolen police Glock 9mm that was purchased from a crack head. I had become obligated to my friends and I neglected Unique. There was a strong gravitational pull on me from my crew. Someone always needed to borrow my gun or needed me to squash a beef for them. My reputation made people rely on me. In many cases, I was insurance to my crew members. One reason is that I survived death so many times that guys felt I was a miracle, like a cat with nine lives. I was loved by few, hated by many, but respected by all.

This respect had come when I was younger, from fighting, selling drugs, shooting a few people and having a reputation with the women. I can't leave out the fact that my father was a street legend.

Because I kept up with the latest styles and fashions and drove a nice car, most people thought I sold drugs to be able to accomplish what I had at nineteen. But, I wasn't selling drugs and I was the only one out of my peers who didn't sell drugs. I only hung out with them. They were guys I had known all my life, and I felt safe and protected around them.

All my friends walked around with hundreds of dollars in their pockets and I was broke. Seeing them spend money made me covet money and their habits. So, to keep myself from living from paycheck to paycheck. I came up with an idea to sell T-shirts out of the trunk of my car. I had a connection with my cousin Rusty who owned Gracey's Urban Clothing Store on Martin Luther King Avenue, South East. I purchased one dozen T-shirts for $30 and sold my shirts for $15 each. From one dozen shirts I made $180, a $150 profit. With the profit money, I returned and purchased a wide range of flavor T-shirts that I thought my customers would like.

But I found myself second-guessing my investment. People complained about my prices so I dropped the price down to $10 and they still thought my prices were high. I was stuck with a trunk full of T-shirts that I couldn't sell.

My interest faded and I became angry with myself for going back on my word, for weakening to my society and the environment. It had been four years since I sold drugs, and I told myself I was only going to sell weed to regain my pride. The minute I purchased a quarter pound of weed, I felt like my spirit had left my body. My conscience and my integrity made me unstable and my sleep pattern changed instantly. There were nights I had to have sex to fall asleep. Sex helped me escape the confusion of feeling doomed by selling drugs.

I started off with a quarter pound of weed. Then I moved up to a pound of weed. I sold weed in small doses like nickel bags, dimes and twenties. To gain an edge on the competition in the city, I stuffed my nickel bags making them look like dimes to make sure all my customers came back to me. Word got around quickly, and within two days, it was all gone. I had to re-up every two days to keep my clientele coming back for more. Bagging up weed was time-consuming and the smell of it would open up a stuffed nose.

People smoked weed like they smoked cigarettes, on the hour, by the hour. There were many times I would be standing in the alley with twenty to thirty people lined up buying dimes and twenty bags from me. People pulled up by the carloads and their cars would block the intersection causing traffic to back up for miles on 17th Street.

Cars were holding up traffic everyday, raising suspicion; so the police started harassing us; we were subject to searches and arrests regularly. We didn't care about the harassment, as long as they didn't find our stash. When they came we'd move to the next corner and continue selling. The police would sit in their cars to make their presence felt, but after they left, we would move back to our regular spots on the corner and continue selling.

Weed made women desperate to get close to me. They threw themselves at me for a chance at some free weed. As much as I couldn't stand the smell of weed and cigarette smoke, I fell prey to smoking a joint every now and then...with women only. I let women know that fair exchange is not robbery. I didn't mind giving up a twenty bag as long as I was able to get something out of the deal. Most women didn't have any money, so they preferred to get high before we had sex.

As many times as I smoked weed, I never got high. I couldn't understand how women and my buddies would get high as the clouds in the sky...and I didn't even feel a buzz. Maybe I was smoking it wrong, or I didn't know how to inhale the weed properly.

I thought a lot of people didn't know where I lived, because I only brought family and a few friends to my house. But when you have the best weed money can buy, people will find you. I don't care where you are they will ride up and down the block until they find you. There were times when men and women threw rocks at my bedroom window because they wanted a bag. My sleep was interrupted numerous times because someone wanted a dime or twenty bag. Some people were bold enough to knock on my door at unexpected hours of the morning and nights. They had no morals or respect for me or my family. London became suspicious of the company I was keeping. I kept London out of my business. I didn't need her worrying about me. I approached a lot of people to tell them, "Don't come to my house and don't send anyone to my door for anything." My aggressiveness spoke louder than my words. But there were some I had to be violent with by pulling my gun out to show them I was serious. My house was my castle and I had to protect it before things got out of hand. So, I decided to give up selling weed. I put the word out that I was now selling crack.

The main reason I gave up selling weed was the money. There's no real money in selling weed. To make money off selling weed a person would have to sell large quantities. Selling weed is like pitching pennies, but crack is the total opposite. People selling crack can easily double their money; and once I started selling crack money was flowing, until I started squandering it and having fun.

Drugs are sold 24/7, 365 days in a year. I remember back in the 80s, drug dealers didn't sell drugs on Sunday… Sunday was holy… even to crackheads. But now, it's get money and more money. Hustlers don't care who they serve crack to… it can be your mother, father, family member, friend, or even a foe. A few of my comrades' parents were on drugs. They wouldn't serve their parents but no one else turned down their money. I've seen my homies fight back tears because their parents were on drugs and there was nothing they could do about it. At one time, Chicago was on drugs…it was when he escaped from jail. But, I never lost respect for him as my father. The thought of London on drugs would destroy me—more inwardly than outwardly.

London has never smoked or used any kind of drug in her life. The most crushing thing was to see one of my homey's moms tricking…there were a few of them tricking for drugs and money to buy drugs…that in itself was an emotional burden to carry.

Reading the Bible, I came across a scripture that opened my eyes and expanded my thinking. In the book of Ecclesiastes, Chapter 10, Verse 19 reads: "But money answers all things." Money allowed me to gain everything I wanted, but I still wasn't happy. I squandered money and spent it like I was playing Monopoly. My comrades and I traveled up and down the east coast from: Virginia Beach, Atlantic City, New York, Philly and Ocean City. Everything we wore was flashy and expensive. Versace, Coogie Sweaters, Iceburg, Moschino, and Solbiato were name brands we bought. We were the flyest niggas in the city.

Every two months C.B. threw a party. If you missed his party, it was like missing the bus and you had to wait on the next one for awhile. You better believe everybody around the city was hyping up the next party. Whenever the word went out for the next party, that date played over and over in your mind... even if you weren't going to the party.

C.B. and Chop's cousin Regal where tight back in the 80s. Chop admired and worshipped C.B. like he was Hulk Hogan. When I was thirteen, Chop and I imitated C.B.'s walk because it was cool and drew attention to us. To do this walk, I had to practice until I got it down, like Chop. I leaned my body forward with my arms swinging from side to side, with my bottom lip poked out to make me look like I was taking a mug shot. That walk created many fights so, in '88 I switched back to my regular walk.

At C.B.'s parties, which were always on Saturdays, carloads of women would pull up on our block to borrow money for the party from various hustlers who they called, Sugar Daddies. In essence, C.B.'s parties were the hustlers' balls. Even athletes attended and if you were seen at his party you were considered a Ghetto Superstar. C.B. had established himself as giving the best parties in the City.

One night, C.B. gave a party in the fall of '95 at the Sheraton Hotel in Arlington Virginia. My comrades and I had women mesmerized by our gear and our twenty bottles of Moet, which cost $80 dollars a bottle.

We took center stage and drew attention from everyone while we took multiple pictures at the camera stand. I had on an all white Versace sweatsuit, which cost me $700, with tan Tims. With my crew and other surrounding neighborhoods who joined in the fun, we were seventy strong. Rollo, the tallest of us all, popped open bottle after bottle of Moet. He would place his thumb over the mouth of the bottle, then shake it until it sprayed over everyone like a rain shower. At that moment we were no longer petty hustlers. As a crew, we had made our mark; and on this night, we made everybody curious and eager to know where we were from.

Most of my comrades didn't have a rap game like mine. They were scared to approach women and afraid of rejection. Their approach to women was pulling out money, which we called flashing. I wasn't the type of guy who would go out of my way to impress women with my riches. If my looks, rap or reputation couldn't get a woman, then she wasn't for me. I was considered laid back, cool and easy going by women and that's how I carried myself with respect.

Everybody who was somebody went to the club called the Black Hole to promote their names as individuals, or as a crew. I was standing with Alvin, Omar, Wylie and other members of my crew, soaking up the stares and glares from the crowd. Attention became natural to me because I had the greatest recognition out of my crew. I was the only one known by the Rare Essence band that played in the club every Saturday night. I would push my way through the crowd to get near the stage as the music played.

With my right arm in the air and my thumb raised, I would signal to White Boy or Donnell, the lead talkers of the band, that I was now in the club; and once they noticed me, they would repeat my name, followed by my crew. "My man Kojack and the 15th street crew are in here." That's what White Boy would say once he saw me.

My crew wanted me to change White Boy's saying 15th Street to 17th Street. The truth was I didn't want to change it…15th Street was like Africa to me, the motherland were we all came from. Plus, I didn't want anyone to know our real hang out spot, so I left 15th Street as it was, in honor of Jody who introduced me to Rare Essence and showed me how to get my name on display.

I wasn't aware at the time, but I was becoming a prime target for extortion. I noticed a car following me while I was cruising down Georgia Avenue at 4 AM on my way from the Black Hole. My eyes searched my mirrors to see if I could identify the driver, but the person had his high beams on so I couldn't see.

I did notice that he wasn't alone in the four-door gray Dodge Dynasty…there were four niggas tailing me. My gun was home stashed away in a safe spot. My right foot instantly pressed on the gas pedal. The acceleration made my car jump to full speed in a matter of seconds. Looking back through my mirror, I noticed a siren in the middle of the front window. I wondered, "Was this really the police or someone trying to rob me?" I knew if I pulled over then, I would be beaten for making the police chase me. At ninety miles per hour, I still couldn't shake them. Weaving through traffic and running red lights, I was afraid that I was going to crash, or that someone was going to crash into me. I panicked, trying to think of a way to lose them. I made a left turn onto East Capitol Street, and finally I was on a straight road that would lead me to the highway.

The police car was two blocks behind me. I slowed down at the 17th and East Capitol Street traffic light. "Light, please, please hurry up and change." With the light still red I squeezed through two cars that lagged behind the other cars. I sped through the intersection just inches between both cars and headed towards the South East Free-way, where I knew there was no traffic and my escape would be easier.

I knew it would be just a matter of time until squad cars would fill the streets, setting up road blocks and a helicopter would be hovering heavily above me with bright beaming lights telling me, "Stop the car before we shoot." I took my final look through my mirror and slightly lost control of my car, almost causing me to run into a lamp post. I guided myself back and never looked back. Now on the South East freeway I was in overdrive speeding at one hundred and twenty five miles per hour. I took the Kenilworth exit down to the 7-Eleven where I used the pay phone to call Mickey, a long time friend who I could depend on whenever I needed her; she allowed me to stay at her house until I sorted through the madness I was up against.

I snuck in the house through the back door to bag up some clothes and other personal things I needed. I was on the run, for what I didn't know; but I had to take precautions. One place the police weren't going to catch me was in my house. I still managed to go to work and attend school during that time.

While I was gambling in the alley on 17th Street, undercover police jumped out on me and my crew. All ten of us were told to place our hands above our heads and spread our legs wide. I was hand cuffed and thrown into the paddy wagon with all my comrades for gambling in public.

Sitting in the cellblock, I knew I wasn't going home for awhile. In my mind I thought I had a bench warrant. But, because I wasn't caught with the dice in my hands or the dice near me, I was able to keep my money and was ordered to pay a $50 bail fee, then I was released.

The next day, four hoodlums with ski masks raided our block with guns. The driver of the gray Dodge Dynasty stayed behind the wheel while the other three passengers jumped out with their guns pointed. They ordered everyone to empty their pockets of everything, even Chap Stick. One of my comrades was pistol whipped by one of the gunmen, and his green EB coat was taken. They got away with money, wallets, drugs, and my man Spider's coat. Spider was a young guy...he wasn't aware of what was going on and had just stopped on the block to talk for a minute.

The robbers thought Spider was me because of our resemblance, and the fact that I sported a green Eddie Bauer coat myself. When I was informed about the robbers and the fact that they drove a gray Dodge Dynasty, I went on a manhunt looking for those niggas. My comrades assumed who they thought it was and where they thought they could be...and that's where I went looking for them.

After a week of searching and riding out gallons of gas, I thought it would be best to let them come to me. I didn't have the slightest idea who they were; so, I continued hustling and observing every car that approached our block that looked suspicious. My gun was always nearby, loaded and ready...all I had to do was pull the trigger.

The rule on the streets is never mess with a man's money unless you're willing to die. Cee was the man on our block and whenever he talked, we all listened. Cee was older and wiser in the drug game. With twenty years already invested, and never caught on one charge, he had the respect of everyone...and we all trusted his decisions. Cee was the man to see if you wanted more supply. To make money in the crack game one must invest. The more you invest, the more money comes in. To move up to elite status there are levels of investing that bring in real dough. The larger the quantity you buy, the more money you make.

I gave Cee $875 to purchase some crack. Whatever amount one spends on crack he or she should double their money. So, in return with me spending $875 I would gross $1,750. But in the crack game everyone doesn't come with straight money.

For instance I sold dimes and twenties on the street. But crack heads would come with $8, and $9 on dime sales. And on twenty sales they would come with $17, $18 and $19. Crackheads never come with straight money so I had to subtract money off my profit.

Usually, when I gave Cee money, within two hours I would have my product. But now, it had been two days of waiting; and I was worried that something had happened to Cee. Not only me, but every foot solider in our neighborhood. Thirty people, including me, had given Cee money. We all waited anxiously, even the crackheads became worried and frustrated. We all looked like we were waiting for an airplane to drop some food.

After many phone calls, Cee finally called me back sounding pitiful and full of contempt. "Kojack, I lost the money gambling."

"Cee, I had the feeling you were gambling but don't worry about it I'm okay."

"Kojack, do you need some money to pay your car note? Because I'll borrow it from my girl."

"Cee my car note is paid, don't worry about me. Get yourself together, man. I'll bounce back one way or another."

Every hustler takes losses...some big...and some small. Cee lost $22,000 gambling and because of that our forest suffered the consequences of losing all our customers to the surrounding drug strip. I didn't trust purchasing crack from anyone else, so I retired from the drug game. In November 1995 I sold my last bag of crack, after Cee lost my money.

In the spring of '96 Cee's luck was back. Within two months, he won $62,000 gambling in Atlantic City. He went out and bought himself a fully equipped 1994 burgundy SC 400 Lexus coupe. I stood on the sideline hoping he would break me off with the money he owed me. But, like the Nation Wide Insurance commercial, my hands were open but nothing was in them. And Cee turned his back on everyone he owed money to.

Chapter 14

Hope

I convinced myself that I wasn't going to jail and I definitely wasn't going to be another statistic. I couldn't let hustling cripple me, then I wouldn't be any good at accomplishing my dreams. During this time I was still searching for myself. Fear of death made me stop and think about the life I had led and where I was headed.

Leaving 17th street was the start of my new life. I wanted to change my way of thinking, so I tried to come up with new ideas by utilizing my creativeness. Finishing college was a goal I wanted to accomplish. In January 1996, President Clinton issued a furlough to all government employees. Last hired first fired; this was the beginning of a down hill slide for me. Immediately after I was laid off, I applied for unemployment. Without a job I was unable to attend school and I had to sit out for the semester.

I took another risk at easy money and became a full time gambler. I was good at it. My gambling spot was at the Knights of Columbus in Forestville, Maryland.

Knights of Columbus was a small casino that had poker, blackjack and roulette. The casino didn't have crap tables like Vegas and Atlantic City. I learned roulette like the back of my hand. I easily won money, anywhere from $300 to $500 on days I went to the casino. I would always quit after winning $500. That was the most money I was comfortable with winning at the time. The truth is, I was underage, only twenty at the time, but that didn't stop me. The casino rules stated that I was prohibited from gambling, because I was under 21. But because I was a regular face in the casino, I was never asked for I.D. I pretended to be 21 and blended in with crowd.

While I was unemployed, I was living good off my winnings. I ran into a buddy of mine named L-Train in the casino. I knew L from back in the 80s from 15th Street. He broke up many crap games and bought flashy clothes, fur coats, diamond rings, bracelets, chains and expensive shoes. L-Train showed me that gambling was the new hustle. And there was no need for me to go back to hustling on the street if I used his gambling method to win. "Kojack this is how I flip my money. I take a $100 and turn it into $300 then I quit. If you do this every day, by the end of the week, you'll have anywhere from $1,400 to $2,100 in your pocket. Add it up Kojack, add it up."

Winning $200 a day was not easy, but I guarantee you that your job wasn't paying you "$200 a day."

What L-Train said to me made sense and I used his method and became a $1,500 a week winner. But there were times I had to take risks, like the time my cousin Fat Head was behind in his child support. The judge was going to lock him up if he didn't have $500 when he appeared in court on the next day. With only $150 in his hands, Fat Head trusted me with his life, knowing if I lost his money, he was going to jail. At the time, I was broke, but my bills where paid and I was waiting on a few loans that were owed to me.

I was at the roulette table with Fat Head. His sweat was the size of bullets and his heart was beating like a bass drum in a marching band. I lost $140 in five minutes. Now I was down to $10. I said, "Make me or break me." I took my last ten chips, which were worth a dollar apiece, and placed them on my lucky number seven. The wheel finally stopped, but the ball was still rolling. Everything seemed to be moving in slow motion. Fat Head was now on his knees with his eyes closed tightly, praying. The roulette stick man yelled out, "Seven!"

Fat Head jumped to his feet and waited until I was paid before he smiled and bear hugged me. His prayers were answered that day and we walked out of the casino with $1,600. Fat Head gave me $650 of the money, paid his child support, and kept the rest for himself.

I was so good at winning that I could predict what I wanted to win and I did it. Depending on the amount I wanted to achieve, I determined how long I was going to be in the casino. I never liked being in there any longer than two hours. One day I went into the casino with a $100 and within three minutes I won $1,700 playing on the $5 table. Usually it would take me an hour to reach a $1,000 but this was faster than I ever imagined. So, I decided to go for another grand just to show my greatness. I could handle winning, but losing crushed me in many ways. I lost $1,800 that day and that was the most I ever gave back to the casino without quitting. The green light on my gambling was yellow now and slowly dimming into red. But I wouldn't stop gambling, my determination to win caused me to lose everything.

With no money in my pocket, I had to create ways to support my gambling habit.

So, I charged a lot of things for my family and friends in return for cash. Sometimes I was given half of the money and was paid later. It really didn't matter at the time, as long as I had money to gamble. I had nine credit cards, and because of my recklessness, I eventually maxed out all nine cards totaling over $12,000. My credit limits ranged from $800 to $3,500 on various credit cards. I could only afford to pay the minimum balance, which increased my interest rates on each card. Then I had to pay for late and over the limit charges that increased, on top of my regular payments. The bill collectors didn't make things easier for me, they called non-stop, and I had to promise that I was going to send money I didn't have.

Things really got hectic for me after I sold my gun. I was in desperate need of money and the last thing on this earth I wanted to sell was my wardrobe. My pride wouldn't allow me to live up to selling my clothes cheaper than I paid for them. Standing in my room I calculated my entire wardrobe, shoes included. I estimated $22,000. I decided that I was going to sell the stuff I really didn't like. The majority of my clothes, coats, jackets and shoes were new, and mostly worn once. Everything I purchased came from drug and gambling money, money I never saved for a rainy day. I was able to get good value for my merchandise and I used the money to pay bills... and the rest I gambled with.

I went from Knights of Columbus to Donald Trump's Taj Mahal Casino in Atlantic City, which became my favorite casino. I couldn't break my losing streak and became frustrated with myself because I was drowning. I needed help. My pride wouldn't allow me to ask for help until I fell two months behind in my car note. London stepped in and helped me maintain my car note until I was able to get a job.

To release the stress I had on my shoulders, I went to the Eastside Club with Alvin on a Saturday night. While driving in my car, we stashed his gun where we could get our hands on it, in case we got into a beef. The Eastside had a high rate of cars being broken into. So, I left my doors unlocked so my window wouldn't be broken. I did this hoping that my car would be overlooked because my doors were unlocked. When we came out of the club, we got into the car. As we were pulling off, we were surrounded by Park Police in squad cars. There were ten cars and they ordered us to slowly get out the car with our hands over our heads. Leaving my car unlocked wasn't a smart move. While we were in the club the police were outside searching every car they could and they stumbled across the 9mm Glock we had stashed in the car. Because I was the oldest (twenty years old) and Alvin was only seventeen, I was charged with the gun possession.

The Police made fun of me, especially once they found out that the gun was stolen from a 5th District Police Officer. "You're never going to see the streets again Dinky." The officer called me Dinky instead of my name because I was wearing a DKNY sweat hood. Alvin confessed that the gun was his and I was released two days later. Because this was Alvin's first charge he was given probation.

A week later, Omar and I went to the Unifest. Union Temple Baptist Church is the sponsor of the Unifest, which is given every year in June. They have live concerts, food of all kinds, and games for kids and adults. I made a left onto 14th Street and Good Hope Road. Traffic was backed up and every intersection and street corner was filled with people walking to the festivities. I was stuck behind two thugs in a black Dodge minivan, and my air conditioner was on full blast because of the 90-degree heat wave. In front of me, I noticed that the passenger of the minivan stepped out holding a gun behind his back. I tried to escape before bullets were fired, but traffic was bumper to bumper. Unable to go anywhere, I watched the passenger and realized that he was arguing with the people in the car in front him. The two men in the car in front of them were undercover police officers.

One of the undercover police officers flashed his badge at the passenger as he approached the car. Then they jumped out of their car and chased him. The passenger immediately ran behind the minivan and quickly threw his gun under the van before the officers noticed that he had a gun. He then placed his hands onto the minivan to be searched...the officers never saw the gun.

With all the attention, the crowd surrounded the scene to witness the suspect's arrest. I wondered if anyone else saw the gun being thrown under the minivan besides Omar and me. I waited to see if the police would find the gun, or if a citizen would tell the police there was a gun under the minivan. No one spoke up and it was a race to retrieve the gun after the police pulled off with the suspects handcuffed. I drove over the gun and Omar retrieved it while I looked to see if anyone noticed us. With the gun now in our possession, I followed the police through traffic to make my escape. The traffic was still hectic, but the police made a pathway for us with their sirens. I turned onto the South East Freeway to make sure I wasn't being followed. While I drove, Omar checked the gun out. It was a Desert Eagle 9mm and it was fully loaded with Talon bullets, which were designed to tear huge holes into a human's flesh. Some people call these bullets cop killers because they were designed to go through a bulletproof vest. I held onto the gun for safety.

When the Chicago Bulls beat the Orlando Magics in the NBA conference Finals sweeping Orlando 4-0, I took the opportunity to go in my back yard and honor da' Bulls by shooting the Desert Eagle into the air. I had been waiting to fire the gun for weeks and it had been a long time since I felt the power of a gun. I cocked the gun back allowing the first bullet to enter into the chamber. Then I fired...boom, boom, boom, boom, boom, boom. Six shots were fired and within seconds, as I stood looking out my back door while locking it, police squad cars surrounded my entire block. They blocked off every exit so no one could escape through the alley. I was afraid that someone had seen me fire the gun and would soon give the police my address. So, I took the gun, placed it inside a cereal box, then put the cereal box into a Safeway bag and pretended that I was going to the store. While looking out my front door, I saw that I could easily get into my car and pull off like nothing happened...and that's what I did. I thanked God that no one saw me fire the gun.

Ever since February '96 up to that point of June '96, I had applied for several jobs, but no one called. With only two months before my unemployment ran out completely, I became impatient and depressed over how I was going to make it. Sitting in my room with the door locked, I turned on my radio and reflected on everything I had been through in my life, wondering how I had made it this far. I didn't want to live anymore and was tired of suffering from the pain and distress I felt in my heart for being a failure. I thought about everything from losing Unique, being broke, no job, dead tags, no insurance, credit card debt, gambling habit, sex addiction, and was frustrated that I was reduced to buying clothes and taking them back after I wore them. I retrieved my gun from under my dresser and looked at it in ways I had never looked at a gun before. I thought, how could such a small bullet kill a human being? Looking down the chamber of the gun I thought of easy ways to kill myself. I pointed the gun at my temple then placed it in my mouth. I thought this was silly of me, so I threw the gun down on the floor and smacked myself several times across the head and face for even thinking of killing myself…I couldn't believe I had come that close to killing myself.

Deep down in my heart, I wanted to change and I wanted better for my life; but I didn't have a clue about what I really needed to make that conversion. For the last four months I'd been going to bible study at a church across the street from my house.

If that particular church hadn't been convenient for me, I probably would've never gone there. On Tuesday nights at bible study I left feeling inspired and enlightened. The church was the only place I felt comfortable and fit in. Even though my lifestyle wasn't in order, I felt accepted and loved by people I never knew. They didn't care that I was young and that I sold drugs before, they were just glad that I accepted Jesus Christ into my life.

I joined a Christian church and was baptized for the second time. People said that once was enough, but with all the sins I committed, I thought that a second baptism wouldn't hurt. I had my first baptism when I was ten years old. When I began reading the Bible, I didn't read it because I wanted to become a preacher, prophet or teacher, nor did I study to persuade anyone that God and I are tight like that. I studied the Bible because I was drowning and I was in search of a need to keep living. I was tired of trying to make my life work and everything I had done, up to this point, had fallen apart. I was also tired of listening to men and women who told me their experience with God. I was now ready to find and know God for myself. I was tired of running. I didn't become a Baptist because London and Beatrice were Baptists. I became a Christian because I believed and was convinced that Jesus Christ would save my life.

Honestly, I didn't kill myself because I had heard my pastor say if anyone killed themselves, they wouldn't make it to Heaven; hell would be the final destination for anyone who committed suicide. I was convinced from that conversation that I wanted to go to Heaven instead of hell. My confidence and self-esteem grew from church and studying the Bible. My faith allowed me to think that anything was possible; and after the furlough was over, I got my old job back in August of 1996. I was given a raise and placed in a new office under new management. Along with getting my job back, I had to attend school. I was still under the title Stay in School/clerk typist. Now that I had a job, things were back on track for me, but I still struggled financially.

I continued to go to church, and with my eagerness to study the Bible, nine months later I was promoted to a deacon and my pastor allowed me to teach bible study on Tuesday nights. Every Sunday I taught the men's Sunday school class. As a Deacon, I had to visit the sick and shut-ins at the hospital once a month and I learned that sick people appreciate prayer a lot.

The thing I liked most about church was the music, so I joined the young adult choir. I thought because I could sing along with music while it played on the radio that I had a voice to sing, but the truth was I couldn't sing at all. I was placed with the men in the baritone section and my choir director told me that I sound more like a tone-bari. Everybody laughed at me, but God had another agenda for me. With no drums in church, my pastor wanted to add another dimension so he purchased a four-piece drum set. I prayed and asked God to teach me how to play. On days when there were no meetings, I would go over and practice on the drums. With the permission of the Chairmen of the Church, I made all kinds of noise in the sanctuary. Within two months I was playing alongside Brock, the guy I admired more than Michael Jordan. Brock led and directed the choir and we became tight. He was from the street and could relate to me better than anyone in church. Brock reminded me of Little Richard when he played the piano and organ. When he stomped his feet hard on the floor, I knew I had to kick the drums harder. It was because of Brock that I learned how to play the drums with passion and discipline.

With my titles and duties around church, I became quite popular. In my church congregation there were 200 members. Sixty of them were men and the rest were women and children.

When I first attended church, women only spoke; but they became more curious than usual to know the real me. I stayed to myself and was shocked to hear that the women in my church thought I was gay because I wasn't hounding them like the other men. There were many women I was interested in, but I was broke and couldn't take any of them out on a nice date. Women cost money and I didn't have any money to spend, so I thought it would be best to avoid dating until my money was right.

Because of my status as a Deacon, I counseled men and women that were either new or in need of spiritual guidance. With my street knowledge and the knowledge I acquired from reading the Bible, I was able to gain the trust of everyone I counseled. People would call me at work, home or on my cell phone for advice. I always gave my best advice and if I didn't know the answers, I would then send them to my pastor or anyone who I thought knew. What I saw happen to men in my church I thought would never happen to me.

I saw pastors, deacons and regular members get caught up in sexual affairs that caused them to lose their church membership. My intentions for counseling women were pure. Even though I was attracted to some of them, they never knew what I was thinking. When the thoughts of a woman came to my mind, I blocked it out. I was abstinent for nearly a year.

Coming from a highly addictive sexual background, I was able to accomplish this goal by staying busy and not allow myself to get bored. My only relief from all my problems was Church, but I was facing a problem that wouldn't go away...no matter how I tired to avoid it. Church was my safe haven and my escape from street life and women. But, this safe haven was only temporary. Usually I was the predator and women were my prey, but now it was the complete opposite.

Many older women played matchmaker in church by introducing me to their daughters and nieces. Some, I have to say, were not my type but I still talked with them over the phone. Many women tried to figure me out, but some gave up. They just couldn't accept that I was a real man with no motives. But, there was one in particular that I couldn't shake. I didn't look at her in a sexual way and never thought we would hook up. She knew the right time to call me and I would drop everything because she was always in need of my advice. I had to stay on her because she was always ready to give up. Seeing so much potential in her, I had to motivate her on a daily basis. Our conversations where friendly and informal...until she wanted to know more about me. The mistake I made was telling Abbey my weakness. Telling her my weakness gave her the upper hand, and now she knew how to play her cards against me.

There were many other women who disguised their motives just as well. I was now in an underworld of deception and sex. My thoughts grew and my desire to have sex became irresistible. I had a sexual relapse and my lust became stronger. One side of me wanted pleasure and the other side was timid and afraid to sin against God. Not knowing how to deal with my secret struggles disrupted the peace I had, and my relationship with God. Before my secrets were found out in the church, I evicted myself from its residence. I had seen women get caught up with married and single men in church, and when things didn't go their way, they went to the pastor and told him everything. The next thing they knew, their business got out and then it was…bye, bye… see you when I see you, son. Go join another church because sex isn't allowed in God's house unless you're married. Everything I thought was going to happen did happen.

One thing I will never do again in life is put all my faith and trust in a man or any human being. I don't care how anointed they are or if they claim to be anointed by God; no one should take the place of God in your life.

The Brock I knew didn't have a secret life, nor did he do anything wrong in my eyes. Whatever Brock wanted me to do, I did. No questions asked. I never thought Brock would turn against me. One day in choir practice Brock called me a demon in front of choir. He was upset with me because I made a mistake while playing the drums. I have to admit that Brock did like perfection and he knew that I made mistakes all the time. I practiced until I got it right and Brock knew that. But calling me a demon was disrespectful and that showed me that Brock had lost respect for me. He not only called me a demon once, but he called me one twice…in front of thirty-five choir members.

I responded to Brock. "Who are you calling a demon?" Brock looked over at me and said, "If the shoe fits, then wear it." Raising up from the drums I felt like whippen Brock George Jefferson's haircut off his head. I had to realize that I was in church, so I thought about my reaction and the words I really wanted to express. There were cuss words on the tip of my tongue, but I held them in for the sake of the choir…and I walked away.

My faith was shattered when Brock called me a demon and my conscience played heavily on my decision as to whether I should continue going to church. I knew that I was a vital part of the church with my title of deacon, drummer, and Sunday school teacher. But, I gave it all up for six months because I didn't want to be around Brock. Seeing Brock would've triggered my negative thoughts and there's no telling how I would've reacted towards him. I took a vacation to brainstorm and figure out how I could deal with the situation. During that six months, I was able to see what kind of person Brock really was. After all the conversations we had in the past about God, I thought he would've called and said, "Dawayne I'm sorry." But he didn't, so I thought I should be the better man and call him. So, I did, and we ironed out everything; I went back to church and picked up where I left off... even though things were different.

I didn't see it coming, but I knew one day my pastor would say, enough. Brock was headstrong and arrogant and there were several incidents when he disrespected the elite members of the church, telling them it would be his way or the highway. His behavior caused a church meeting in which he was voted out. My pastor gave him several chances to redeem himself, but, Brock seemed to get worse and his mouth caused him to lose his job and church membership. The most embarrassing thing I ever witnessed in my life was when Brock was told by the Church Trustee not to come back to the church again.

He ignored the warnings and his reason for coming to church was to speak with the pastor in person because he couldn't reach him over the phone. One particular Sunday morning, right before 11 o'clock service, Brock and the trustee had a big argument outside of the sanctuary. Their voices were loud and they could be heard throughout the church. Someone called the police and ten squad cars pulled up to my church as if it was a hostage situation. Brock was escorted out of the church and my pastor informed him not to return. Brock stood outside the church, crying like a baby.

Because Brock didn't have a car I felt sorry for him and offered to take him home. He cried incessantly. I felt his pain and realized that we would never have the relationship we had before. When I dropped him off, I knew this would be the last time I would see the man I admired for his God given gift. I wondered why I admired Brock and realized then that there's no bond like that of men. Breaking away from every male that had entered my life made me realize there was still an empty gap in my life. There was still a void in me that Church couldn't fill, because I was still running from my past.

Chapter 15

Rollo

After giving up selling crack, I disconnected myself from my comrades on the street corner. To them, I was a Judas because I decided to change my lifestyle. At the age of twenty-two, I noticed I had no true friends or buddies I could hang out with when I got bored. Growing up, I hung out with my cousins and my brothers Wylie and Country, but I never branched off from them to have a true friend outside of my family members. My choice to work, go to school and stay out of the way of bullets and the police caused me to be alone.

In 1998, Rollo came home from jail. We had a lot in common. We both loved sports—football and basketball, women, Popeye's chicken and expensive clothes. Even though there was a seven-year age gap between us, we got along well. Rollo insisted that I hang out with him. It had been nearly three years since I stepped into a club. I thought one trip to the club wouldn't hurt, but after seeing women I hadn't seen in years and embracing the love I felt in the club, I went to the club more and less to church. Eventually, I gave up church all together. Going to the club on Saturday nights drained me.

It showed when I played the drums on Sundays. I found myself oversleeping because I got in the house at four in morning and I had to be in church at 8 o'clock. I have to admit, with Brock not there, I didn't know how to function. The church got a new musician to replace Brock, but it wasn't the same.

No longer living paycheck to paycheck, I sold my car to Car Max and consolidated my credit card bills. All of my credit cards were paid off and I carried only one for emergencies. I vowed to never get back into credit card debt again. I fought hard and prayed hard for relief, and finally my credit union gave me my first break. Because I had $12,000 in credit cards, I was only given a $5,500 consolidation. I paid that loan off in year and a half. Then I got another consolidation for the rest of the credit cards and I paid that off in a year and a half. Within three years I was debt free and had no car note. I was now able to do things I wanted to do and treat myself to things I had deprived myself of for the past three years.

The first thing I did was stockpile my wardrobe with expensive clothes that took my two weeks earnings in a heartbeat. When I went out to the club, I had on $300 jeans, $200 shirts, $200 belts, $350 shoes, $200 glasses, and a $600 Movado watch. With $1,850 worth of clothes on a night, no one had to tell me I was fly...I knew it and that was all that mattered. I could see myself losing control with my spending habit again. Rollo and I took shopping to the extreme, buying things we really didn't need.

I told Rollo, "Man we spent all our money on clothes, but we have no cars...and we both live with our moms. Last month, Rollo, you spent $600 on a Versace belt that could've been your rent money, or maybe your car note money. Rollo, I don't know about you but I'm tired of walking around like I'm on top of the world and don't even have a car or apartment. We're scrubs man."

"No Kojack, we're fly scrubs."

"Rollo, I'm not playing look at where our money is going." Rollo agreed with me, even though I hurt his feelings. It was time for us to man up and become responsible. I came up with a plan to utilize and promote my popularity to the status of Ghetto Superstar and to acquire my own place and car. A Ghetto Superstar is a person in his or her neighborhood or city who everyone looks up to and respects.

On my twenty-fourth birthday I gave a big cookout at my cousin Ebony's house in her backyard. Rollo helped me pass out 150 flyers, which we gave mostly to women. Ever since I could remember, my birthday has always been a major event in my family because I'm the only summer baby. Everyone else's birthdays fell in the winter months or in the fall. So, throughout the years, my birthday party became like a family reunion, a time when we got to see one another without an unfortunate event happening.

Between London, Rollo and myself we spent over $4,000. I was expecting 250 people to come, so we bought food as though 750 people were coming…it was better to have more food than less. I was scared to walk into my own party. I had to take deep breaths several times. My heart was racing and I felt anxious.

Seeing cars up and down Alabama Avenue, as far as I could see made me think I was going to cry once I walked into the yard. To relax myself I counted down from ten to one. "Ten, nine, eight, seven, six, five, four, three." I paused on three for about five minutes, okay, "two." On one, I walked into the yard; someone notified London. Then, London signaled to the D.J. and he hollered into his mic, "the birthday boy is here!" He repeated it over and over. I was surprised to see everyone I knew, from family to friends, come out and support me on my birthday. There were over 400 people. I was grateful they all had a nice time. I received many compliments about how good the food was.

We had everything from crabs, chicken, t-bone steaks, fried fish, sausages, hot dogs, all kinds of salads—potato, pasta, seafood, tuna—fruit, and the list of food went on and on. Everyone praised the tub we had packed with ice and cold beer. It was made like a swimming pool with a landscaping design of white rocks around the outside.

I had my man D.J. B-Sharp behind the wheels of steel and he kept everybody dancing all night long. Looking over at the grill, I was amazed. I doubted that Rollo could pull it off, but he did. His Uncle the Head Chef, Mark, had a grill the size of a large dining room table. This was an added dimension that received praise. Mark had thirty whole chickens, twenty t-bone steaks, twenty hot dogs and a large flounder with crabmeat in its belly, all laying on the grill cooking together. Mark had on a real chef's outfit with matching hat; and he was sawing his knives together like a chef does when he's cooking. He put on a cooking show for the crowd by chopping, slicing, flipping and cutting food to be served to our guests.

Every year after, we added new dimensions like D.C.'s own comedians—Billy the Kid, Sam I Am and D.J. Storman Norman. Rollo and I had a bar built in Ebony's yard so that we could make a profit, and to keep our guests from making trips to the liquor store.

With the flattery and compliments of the cookouts. L-Train convinced me to give a cabaret. "Kojack, with your reputation, you can make money off your name. I got the plan and my cousin Co-Co knows everything about giving a cabaret. She gave 5 of them before. We can split the money three ways and walk away with $3,000 a piece."

L-Train master minded the whole layout of everything from flyers, drinks, raffle, and the D.J. He is very creative and good at persuading. He even came up with the idea for us to raise the money. Co-Co, L-Train and I each put up a $100 a piece. And we raised $3,700 to cover the expense for the cabaret by selling chicken and fish dinners out of L-Train's basement.

We had James Funk, a known and well respected legend in the city as our D.J. We gave away free food and drinks like Moet, Hennessey, Remy, Heineken, and Coronas. We also raffled off a tennis bracelet for $5 a ticket. Some young lady was the happy winner that night. From wall to wall people were standing around, styling and profiling. Before the party was over at 3 o'clock I gathered my crew from Kentucky Courts, Gangster Terrace, 15th Street and 17th Street and we all took multiple pictures at the camera stand. With only twenty minutes to go, a fight broke out. The two policemen I hired as my security guards grabbed a guy by his shirt with the intention of throwing him out. The guy snatched away from the policemen and swung in their direction, causing London to fall to the ground. Seeing this, my anger intensified and I pushed five people out of my way to get to the guy. I swung, hitting the guy with two punches to his chin that sent him to the ground. With so many people in the area I lost track of where the guy landed on the ground.

With the help of my crew now standing behind me, we searched to find who the nigga was. He must have been Flash Gordon because we couldn't find him. He must have hidden in the crowd and hit the exit door. We all ran outside to look for him. By this time, I could hear the D.J. say, "The party is over."

Standing outside looking around, without hesitating, I saw niggas opening their trunks and pulling out weapons of mass destruction. "Ah Kojack, where that nigga at? He had no business hitting Miss London. When I find him he's dead." That was what a few guys repeated to me while my eyes searched the parking lot.

Sooner than we thought, he surfaced, firing his gun. I ran back into M.J.'s Meeting Place, diving for cover. Lying on the floor, I heard bullets fired rapidly. Once the shooting stopped, the police came rushing to the scene. No one was arrested that night, but a friend of mine named Roy was shot in the leg. Several cars were turned into Swiss cheese and my night was ruined.

Two months after that ordeal, Rollo persuaded me to give a cabaret with him. "Kojack let's give a cabaret together just me and you." With Rollo pounding away at me I gave in. Truth is Co-Co tried to beat me out of some money, so, I decided to leave her and L-Train alone and do my own thing…not that L-Train was behind it, but I caught Co-Co in a lie. On the day of our cabaret, I crashed Co-Co's car. It was my fault; I wasn't paying attention and I ran into the back of a man's car. I was told by Co-Co that her deductible was $700; but when I spoke with her insurance agent, I was told her deductible was $500. And $500 was what I gave Co-Co. L-Train and I remained friends, but I couldn't understand why Co-Co would try to beat me out of $200.

Rollo and I split our profits fifty-fifty. I was hard on Rollo because I didn't want to lose any money; so I worked extra hard at promoting the next party. Six nights a week, Rollo and I were out passing out flyers. We went everywhere, from barber shops, hair salons, car washes to late night food spots, Crystal's Skating Rink and all the local night clubs in D.C. and Maryland. On an average day I would come home and rest after work and school until 12 o'clock at night. Then I would hit the club scene passing out flyers. Some were placed on cars and the rest were placed in people's hands as they exited the club. On an average night, my goal was to hit four clubs. There were nights I didn't get in the house until 4 o'clock in the morning. On the days I was too tired to get up, I took off from work. Being a promoter takes hard work and dedication. Many people I know have tried to walk in my footsteps, but failed because they didn't understand the logic to making money in the promotion business. They thought they could pass out a few flyers and that would be it…wrong.

People wanted to know how I was so successful at giving parties and cookouts. I always told them, "Pass out all of your flyers." When I first started out, I purchased 5,000 flyers; but after I gave my first cabaret, I started purchasing 10,000 flyers. The more customers you have, the more money you make. Second, don't worry about the people you know, worry about the people you don't know because the people you don't know are the ones you make your profit from. Third, it takes money to make money.

I didn't worry about making money on my first cabaret, even though I did make money. I had to establish my name and reliability for giving cabarets before I touched a little money. The key to giving a successful party is making sure your guests have no complaints. And even if they did have a complaint, I made sure I corrected the problem.

Working money cannot out spend drug money. I learned that after Rollo and I took back-to-back losses on two cabarets we gave a month apart, Rollo's money flowed in like milk and honey, while I had to wait bi-weekly for my paychecks. Bouncing back from those losses took me six months to recover, whereas Rollo was back on his feet in two weeks. Over all, I gave ten parties, four cookouts and six cabarets.

Honestly, I was very skeptical of women who I met in the clubs and at my parties. To be safe, I dealt with women I knew in my past. I did this to protect myself from hidden agendas that could go way beyond casual sex. I've seen guys meet women in the clubs and get robbed or killed the same night they meet them. I've never made my business public, but because of my increasing status and people labeling me as getting money, I became a target for robbery.

The vultures were now lurking around to rob me, and by watching my routine, I made it hard for them. I learned this routine from Chicago, Rusty and Steven. Don't let anyone cut into you, especially a new guy you don't know. Keep people around you who you can trust, people who can see things you can't see. Be very selective about women because women can be used as bait to set up killings and robberies. Last, but not least, when coming from anywhere on the late night, never go straight home from the club…always take the scenic route home to make sure you're not being followed by anyone. With these rules embedded in me, I was able to notice when things were about to happen. If you don't see it coming, you'll get blindsided.

In the summer of 2000 Martin came home after serving six years in jail. Martin, J.P., Rollo and I went to Club U to celebrate Martin's homecoming. We got drunk that night, drinking shots of Hennessey and downing four bottles of Moet. After the club let out, J.P. went his separate way and Martin and I were talking to three women we grew up with—Melly, Rasheda and Ronnet. Rollo was nowhere to be found, I lost track of him in the club. With Martin dominating the conversation, I stepped off to see if I could find Rollo so we could go home. Standing outside the club too long can mean trouble at three in the morning.

My instincts told me not to go to the car, so I continued my search for Rollo. While walking back towards the club, I noticed Martin had finished talking with the ladies. We both headed in the direction of where the car was parked, barely walking straight because we were intoxicated. I heard a voice call out Martin's name from behind us; and I looked at him to see if he recognized the voice. Martin ignored it so I paid it no attention. The voice got louder and bolder and I could tell the person was now closer than I expected. "Martin, what's up nigga?" Martin turned to see who called him. His eyes got big like light bulbs and his mouth dropped. Looking at Martin's reaction, I knew we were in trouble.

When I turned, ten niggas surrounded Martin and me. One of the niggas was doing all the talking while the others scoped out our gear. There was a beef between them and Martin that I didn't know about. The D.C. Police were on the nearest corner from us. In the middle of a quick conversation between Martin and the guy, he landed a punch across Martin's face knocking him backwards.

As Martin fell backwards, he ran and was chased by nine niggas. Standing alone with the guy who swung the punch at Martin, I threw a flurry of punches to his upper body—from his head to his lower body—to keep him off balance.

As I continued throwing punches, the guy curled up, placing his left hand into his waistband. I heard a click, and thinking he was about to shoot me, I pushed him with all my might to get separation from him so I could run. As I turned to run, the first step I took caused me to fall flat on my face. While I was on the ground, the guy swung his knife at me, just missing me before my face smacked the paved concrete cement of the sidewalk. He cocked his knife back in motion coming towards me again while I was on the ground. I jumped to my feet to run, but feeling awkward and dizzy from the alcohol, my eyes became blurry. Running towards the street, I didn't step down off the curb, and I fell on my face again. But this time when I fell, there were four niggas standing over me swinging their knives and barely missing me, as I curled up and rolled around on the ground. I quickly jump back on my feet and sprinted across 14th Street in the direction of W Street where the YMCA building is located.

With four niggas on my trail, my balance came back and I took off like a racehorse running in fear. Looking over my shoulder, I saw all four of the guys stop running once they noticed they weren't going to catch me. Now two blocks away from them, I was out of breath. I hid in some bushes, just in case they circled the block. I passed out and laid in the bushes for 20 minutes to give myself time to gather oxygen for my lungs.

While laying there, I heard the police and ambulance sirens going off. Martin immediately came to mind and I said a quick prayer asking God to protect him. I said, "Lord I'm hoping Martin got away like I did." I ran back towards the car where I last saw Martin. A guy who witnessed the dispute told me a woman driving by saw Martin lying on the ground suffering from stab wounds. She picked Martin up and drove him to the nearest hospital, which was Howard University. They robbed Martin of his money, cell phone and jewelry. I called Eve immediately, to inform her of Martin's condition.

I entered the hospital with multiple scrapes and scratches that burned my skin like hot grease. My cheekbone was swollen; my shoulder, hand and wrist all had burn and scrape marks, where my skin was pulled back, revealing white meat. After I found out Martin was in surgery, I checked myself in and rested there for the night. The next morning I found out Martin was okay; he had been stabbed five times in his upper body. He stayed in the hospital for a few weeks. With that close call of death, I chilled out and let my wounds heal.

After Martin came home from the hospital, I found out that we both nearly faced death over a he say, she say conversation between my cousin Kenny and a girl he tried to impress. As I reflected on that night, I wondered where in the hell was Rollo; if he didn't disappear, none of this would've happened. Rollo did appear at the hospital that night, but I became suspicion of his loyalty to our friendship. Every detail of that night haunted me and I backtracked everything that took place. On that particular night I was dressed in all black. With a black short sleeve, soft cotton Bernini shirt with black slacks and my black suede slip on Ferragamo's. That night, I had a hard time trying to figure out whether to wear my suede or my leather Ferragamo's. I thank God that I had on my suede pair because they had a better grip on the bottom. If I would've gone with the leather ones, I'd probably be dead because they're slippery. In any friendship, harsh and severe words will be said and every person doesn't know its worth until it's tested. People tried to pit Rollo and I against one another, but I would never allow that to happen. But now, I had to make a big decision... either I faced Rollo, or just cut the relationship off. I remember Rollo speaking with the guys who stabbed Martin that night at the club before we enter the club. Even though the beef had already existed before that night, I had to address Rollo to find out if he had told those niggas where I had parked my car that night.

Rollo was open and honest with me about that night, but I drew my own conclusion about the situation. Rollo's girlfriend was in the club that night and she also showed up at the hospital. He cleared his name and we continued to be friends.

I noticed that since Rollo and I started hanging together, my life style had changed. I picked up habits like smoking weed again, drinking and going to the same clubs every week. These were things I stopped doing for three years, before we started hanging together. I knew if I continued to abuse my body and mind, I would end up running from life and responsibility. I wanted nothing but the best for our friendship, so, I thought of ways we could help each other to become better men. I knew this would force me to face my own flaws; but I wanted Rollo to be able to face his own issues and fears as well. He seemed to be comfortable with his accomplishments in life, but I wasn't comfortable. I wanted more out of life than just having a car, an apartment and clothes. Instead of moving forward, I entertained his thoughts, ideas and creativeness. I lost focus and had to regain purpose in my life to get out of the dead end I had driven myself into.

I found myself drained from giving Rollo advice on women and life issues. I was a true friend to him and I trusted him with my heart; but Rollo didn't protect what I entrusted to him. I became cautious of what I wanted to reveal to him. I used to tell him about my sex life with women, until he put my business in the street. I found myself correcting Rollo on things I thought he already knew. We both were ignorant to a certain degree, but he continued to make mistakes that showed me he didn't have my best interest at heart.

When I moved into my apartment I needed Rollo's help to transport my leather sofa from Marlo's furniture store. Rollo had a Yukon Delinai that was big enough to carry my sofa. He gave me his word, but when it came time to pick up my sofa, Rollo bailed out on me telling me his engine light was on and he wasn't going to drive his truck until he put it in the shop. A week later my sofa came in and I paid a friend to deliver it to my apartment. That same night

Rollo called me asking if I would like to go to the club. I was feeling good that I now had the final piece to my living room set so I said, "Yeah." Two hours later Rollo pulled in front of my building with his Delinai shinning like he just came from the carwash. I heard the horn out front so I grabbed my coat, keys and wallet.

As I walked up to the truck, the music was loud and Rollo was dancing. I laughed at him, seeing he was in a party mood. I joined him as we both danced in our seats in the truck. The new Rare Essence song, You're Not Ready for This Right Here, was playing in his CD player. The jungle music was like fire in my bones, but I had to ask, "Rollo did you put your truck in the shop this week?"

"Naw, ain't nothing wrong with my truck."

Rollo continued dancing, while I stopped dancing and then I laid back in the seat. Looking over at his dashboard, I saw no engine light on. Thinking to myself, "Rollo is petty. If he didn't want to take me to get my sofa, why didn't he just say no?" I guess he forgot that he lied to me.

We got into a heated argument that nearly broke up our friendship. What I learned from Rollo was that expensive clothes, cars, and women don't make a man. Clothes are costumes and a man shouldn't be judged by the material things he possesses. What a man should be judged by are his character, love, and what comes out of his mouth. Real friends don't compete against each other, and they don't talk about each other behind their backs. Rollo exposed me to what a true friendship should be and what it takes to be a true friend.

When I was a child, I spoke as a child, I understood as a child: but when I became a man, I put away childish things. (I Corinthians 13:10) I could no longer approach anyone in the way I approached them as a child... I had to be real with them and myself because that's what friends do.

Chapter 16

Favoritism

The key for me was to stay in motion. I've tried to make the transition from one stage of my life to the next. Knowing I went backwards on top of the mistakes I've made, gave me trouble moving forward. One thing that has paralyzed me for years is favoritism. I've been victimized by my own family. Favoritism has been like a poisonous snake's venom that has crippled me emotionally–making me feel unwanted and not loved and I couldn't figure out why? It has not only affected me but also my brother, Country, and my cousin, Syrup, until this day.

Before I was born, I was rejected by Chicago's family. London made several attempts to notify Chicago's family of my existence. But to them, I didn't exist because Chicago was afraid to admit to his mother, who is my grandmother Theresa, that I was his son. Even after Chicago's family accepted me at the age of four, I was mistreated and rejected like I was a stepchild. I was discriminated against because Chicago's family held a grudge against London for years, for which I was caught helplessly in the middle.

Country was praised by grandma Theresa and my two aunts, who played right along with the game of playing Country and me against each other. Country is older than me by eight months. He received all the attention from Chicago's family. With all the love and affection given to Country, I became skeptical; and at a early age, I built an emotional wall to hide my true feelings. Country got it all, and he even had Chicago's whole name ending with Jr. London gave me a name she felt was suitable because of Chicago's abandonment and denial of me.

There was only one thing that Country lacked? Like I've said before, "Chicago spit me out." I'm his clone. If you've seen Chicago, you've seen me. I say this, in truth, to bring to light this ordeal. Country doesn't look like or even favor anyone in Chicago's family. I say this not to hurt him or anyone else, but I must speak the truth. Sorry, but I must go deeper. Family members and friends have asked me, "Is Country really your brother?"

I always replied, "Yes, he's my brother and always will be."

Inside Grandma Theresa's house, Country was treated with the utmost respect. When it came to eating he always got his plates first, whether it was breakfast, lunch or dinner, even dessert. I could beat Country to the table, but grandma Theresa would wait on Country first. My two aunts, Pam and Brook, bought Country gifts on holidays and birthdays, while Syrup and I stood around hoping they would acknowledge us with the same love, but they didn't...this continued for years.

Syrup and I got love on the streets. When I say love, we were acknowledged as our father's offspring. My Uncle Jr. has been incarcerated since the 70s. He was also a street legend on 15th Street for the work he put in. He's serving life in jail for murder.

There have been numerous times when Country, Syrup and I were all walking together, and we were approached by older hustlers who knew Chicago and my Uncle Junior. The older hustlers would recognize Syrup and me because of our resemblance to our father... but not Country. Syrup and I were given money, and Country wasn't. His feelings were hurt repeatedly because we encountered people all the time who recognized Syrup and me, and not Country.

As a child, I had no understanding of what favoritism was. London never showed favoritism towards Wylie and me. With Grandma Theresa and Eve living a block away from each other, I couldn't avoid seeing Grandma Theresa or going over to her house for a visit. Even though favoritism existed I'd rather stay over Grandma Theresa's house than stay over my aunt Eve's house to avoid the ironing cord whippens. Theresa believed in getting the switch off the tree out in front of her house. I didn't mind getting beat with the switch because it didn't leave whelps on my skin like the ironing cord had done. Theresa barely beat me, once in a blue moon, but that was only when I had done something major.

Syrup and Country were also a part of my crew when I was younger. Syrup was cool and laid back, he loved girls and was an honor roll student. When he graduated from the sixth grade he received a certificate from the President of the United States honoring his hard work and excellent grades. Country loved to draw and play basketball. At the age of twelve, Country stood six feet tall and now he's 6'3". Country stood out like a sore thumb because of his height. But it was me with the brave heart who fought his battles. Little brother made sure big brother didn't get walked over by anyone. Even in our late teens and early twenties, Country used my reputation to gain respect and protection.

But underneath, he hated me from the day he met me at the age of four. I remember how he looked at me like I wasn't supposed to be born. In his heart laid anger, pettiness, jealousy and competition. It was all stirred up by favoritism and my resemblance to Chicago.

Country acted as if he wanted to be me. At times, he didn't understand my struggle for love and he thought I was jealous of him. I was never jealous of him. All I wanted was my grandma Theresa's love and affection that she showed Country. I didn't want it just for myself, I wanted Theresa to love all her grandchildren the same. Syrup suffered with me and we became close because we understood each other as children. But as we got older Syrup stopped coming around because things never changed.

I expressed my love through money, support and being there for Country when he was in trouble. Even the good times we shared playing basketball, chasing women and joning on each other. When he needed a job I talked to my supervisor and he was hired at EPA. When he needed the money for school, I paid for him to go to college and gave him the money he needed for his books. But once he got on his feet and established himself, he wouldn't let me borrow $20.

Like always, he looked down on me and I noticed something about him. He only came around when he needed my help. But when I needed him he was nowhere to be found. He'd rather help out his friends than his brother. I refused to be used by him or anyone who couldn't accept me for who I was. It's not my fault that I am who I am. I didn't chose to be myself. If I can accept you, then be a real man and accept yourself, because I'm not your enemy and never was or will be.

When I got older, I started searching for the truth behind the favoritism. The question I had to ask myself was why I had to suffer in silence when the truth was staring me in the face. All suffering has a beginning and an ending. I had to override my fear to cure my years of pain. Before I made my approach, I prayed to God for direction. I knew this wasn't going to be easy but I had to do it. The hardest thing in life is to live a lie and die with regret, never knowing the truth. Over and over I told myself "no regrets, no regrets."

So, I made a special trip to Grandma Theresa's house, just to talk. When I got there she wanted me to take her to the post office and Murray Steak house. Then we ended up back at her house where we sat in the front room. As grandma thanked me for being so kind, the words I held in for over twenty years finally came pouring out.

"Grandma, when I was younger my feelings were hurt and I carry the scar on my heart, even until this day. I've cried because I wanted you to love me and accept me as your grandchild. I never cussed at you or gave you any problems that would've made you act the way you have towards me. I've always done what you told me to do and that still wasn't enough for me to win your love. All I want to know is why you showed favoritism towards me?"

Grandma sat in her chair, shocked that I had finally spoken up and asked the question she probably thought I would never ask. Her eyes were locked on the floor and they never looked up. Patiently I waited for my answer. The room was silent. She was so quiet I thought about leaving, but I told myself I wasn't leaving this house without the truth. So, I sat there watching grandma as she became emotional. I saw a tear leave her left eye and slowly run down her cheek.

Finally she broke the silence, "Lamont I'm sorry. I've shown favoritism amongst my grandchildren. Between Country, Syrup and you Lamont I've given Country more and I know that you know that. The reason I gave Country more is because Country's mother was young when she had him. And at the time Country was born Chicago was seventeen years old and Country's mother was thirteen or fourteen. Chicago told me that she lied about her age saying she was sixteen. But when we found out that she was pregnant, her age was revealed. I didn't want Chicago going to jail over this, so I told Country's mother I would take care of him."

Hearing the truth brought freedom to my heart; even still, knowing why she showed favoritism wasn't an excuse. But I accepted the truth for what it was worth. Hearing the truth may not have been what I wanted to hear, but it was what I needed to hear. Grandma Theresa hated the fact that London had forced Chicago to pay child support. It was held against London for years…even Country held a grudge against her and me because of child support. Chicago still owed back support, which he never paid. Knowing all that I knew, it still didn't add up, I did no harm to them. To me it doesn't make sense that favoritism was played against me.

"Masculinity is bestowed. A boy learns who he is and what he's got from a man, or the company of men. He cannot learn it any other place. He cannot learn it from other boys, and he cannot learn it from the world of women. The plan from the beginning of time was that his father would lay the foundation for a young boy's heart, and pass on to him that essential knowledge and confidence in his strength. Dad would be the first man in his life, and forever the most important man. Above all, he would answer the question, Do I have what it takes? Am I a man? For his son and give him his name. Throughout the history of man given to us in Scripture, it is the father who gives the blessing and thereby "name the son."
- John Elridge, Wild at Heart

Chapter 17

Chicago

When I was younger, I tried everything I could to win my father's approval. Country and Syrup received more attention from Chicago than I did; their relationship was already established before I came into the picture at four years old. With Chicago in and out of jail our relationship never got the chance to develop. Country and Syrup knew how to hold a conversation with Chicago, but I didn't. I was always quiet and observant of my father. I knew we looked alike, but I really wanted to see if we had the same ideas—character, personality, gifts, and talents. There were times when I would emulate him and he would just laugh at me.

Out of my thirty years on planet Earth, Chicago has been on the street for eight of them, during which time, I had seen him put more effort into the streets than into his children. I felt neglected, deprived and cheated of my father's love. As a child, I thought life was perfect and maybe one day London and Chicago would get back together. That never happened and I grew up hoping one day Chicago would save me from all my fears. Trying to be a man at an early age allowed me to attach myself to whatever was available. Suffering without my dad led me to the streets, women, drugs, alcohol and gambling.

London did her best at providing shelter, food, clothing, protection and good health for me. I give London the utmost respect. She's a strong black woman who has worked long hours over the years to make sure I was well taken care of. From the projects to owning her own home. From three children, (Wylie, Bennisha and me) to inheriting my little cousin Tilly and Wylie's daughter Kimeko. London has never forsaken me, not even in my wrongs. She did her best with teaching me how to be a good man. A good woman can raise a good son, but only a good man can teach his son how to become a good man.

Chicago wasn't able to teach me how to be responsible, dependable, reliable, honest, open minded, have courage, be brave, face fear head on, sex, friendship, how to be a good father, kids, never give up on dreams and money. London was only able to teach me what she knew and everything else came through life's experiences.

At a young age, without a father to protect me, I took the journey to face the streets. Chicago's friends, and even my family members were on the sideline of my life, rooting for me to turn out just like Chicago (in prison). When I was arrested with the .380 gun, grandma Theresa said, "Lamont is going to be just like his father." Those words ate at me like acid when I heard them. I never in my life wanted to be like my father. I wanted to be better and I wanted people to respect and accept me for who I was…not my money, clothes and cars… because those things will fade away. I wanted to establish my own identity in life; but I noticed that I had inherited my father's weaknesses and traits.

There was no way I could've avoided the pain, anger, frustration, lust, lying and street life. Because this was where God placed me, I had to make the best out my life. I can't blame Chicago for not being there for me, even though I wanted to many times.

I didn't ask to be born or to live in the condition I had been placed in. I realize, now, that I'm an adult and I have to make the right decisions that would benefit me in the long run. I have to admit that I'm responsible for deeds that have caused life threatening damage to people physical and mental. Because of my lack of knowledge and the absence of my father, I did what I saw others do to survive. All the men in my life played a major role in molding me into the man I am today, especially Chicago. From childhood to adulthood, I had to figure out what kind of man I wanted to be. With no other male role model in my life, Chicago was the only man I compared myself to. Trying to be better than Chicago wasn't an easy task and I nearly died trying to overcome the same burdens he carried as a man. We both experienced failure, difficulties and the obstacles. I refused to believe that God was going to allow me to suffer like Chicago. I wasn't going to allow my life to be taken by my environment. Understanding my life helped me understand Chicago's life.

I made up mind to approach Chicago because I needed to free my mind of all I held against him. So, in 1999 on Father's Day I was in church. My pastor asked all the fathers to stand up. As they stood up, I observed their children hugging and kissing them. Honestly, I was touched and had to fight back the tears. At that moment, I realized that I had never embraced my father. I never got a pat on the back, a kiss, or a hug like the ones I witnessed in church that day.

I wanted to break down crying when I saw fathers and sons bonding. So, I decided that instead of crying, I would just leave church and visit Chicago. The D.C. Jail where Chicago is in the CTF unit serving his time was just five blocks away from my house. From time to time I visited him when I was in the mood or when he asked me to come.

At the jail, I waited in the visitor's hall for twenty minutes. Chicago finally walked out, cool as ever. His hair was still full of waves and his clothes were neatly pressed like they had been to the cleaners. As Chicago walked towards me, he was greeted by every inmate who had a visitor. They spoke his name as if he was the warden. Once the inmates noticed me, they all said, "Look at Chicago's twin." And another inmate said, "Chicago man, is that your son or your brother?"

Before he sat down, I stood up and wrapped my arms around him tightly squeezing all the love out of him. As we sat down, Chicago looked down at my feet. I was sporting my fresh pair of 991 New Balance tennis shoes. After I left church I went home and switched up my gear to look cool, just in case I caught one of the inmates' women slipping. There were always beautiful women visiting their brothers, uncles, fathers or husbands.

The first thing that came out Chicago's mouth, "Man where did you get those shoes from? I never saw them before. Those joints are like that?" I knew he wanted them, so I gave them to him. This wasn't the first and it wasn't the last time I switched shoes with Chicago. He and I wear the same size shoes, nine and half. Every time I visited him, I snuck in money… from $20 to $100 so he could have food, canteen, clean underwear and cigarettes.

I never told Chicago this, but when I was sixteen he asked me to do a delivery for him. All along, I knew what was in the bag without looking into it. I was paid a $100 for the delivery, but I was pulled over by State Troopers for speeding. I was listening to Toni Braxton's Breathe Again. The music was loud and I was caught up in the words of Seven Whole Days. While singing along with Toni, I didn't notice that I was speeding and being followed by the police. As I was pulled over, I was scared to death; so, I cooperated with the State Troopers and was only given a ticket for my violation. But, if they would have searched the car, only God knows the penalty I would have had to pay. After that day I vowed to never speed again.

When I graduated from high school, I was given a certain amount of invitations—seven all together. I gave an invitation to everyone I knew who would come and support me on my big day. I held onto one for Chicago, praying that he would come. When my name was called to walk across the stage, the applause roared. I could hear London and a few family members I invited screaming my name. I could sense that Chicago was there after the graduation was over, so I waited and waited for him to come and greet me in the hall-way…but he never came. I tried to hold back the doubt in my mind. During my elementary and junior high graduations, Chicago was locked up. I thought that maybe this would be his last time to see me walk across a stage to experience a once in a lifetime achievement.

After the graduation was over, I jumped into London's car and rushed over to Chicago's hangout spot. When I pulled up, I braced myself for another heartbreak. Chicago was standing on the corner with his flunkies, laughing at how much money they all made for the day. I walked up to him, hoping he would at least say, "Congrat-ulations son, I'm proud of you." But he didn't say anything except, "Sorry I didn't make it, I woke up late." I was crushed like a demol-ished building. I couldn't stand there and look at him as my father. I never begged him to do anything. All I wanted him to do was show up at my graduation and that would've made up for all the lost time. I couldn't build up the courage to say, "Chicago you have hurt me from the moment you laid your sperm into my mother." I just walked away with the little pride I had left. I wanted to cry, but he wasn't worth my tears.

As we talked, the noise in the visitor's hall was drowned out by our deep conversation. We talked about things I never imagined. Chicago opened up and the words he spoke washed away my anger and gave me hope that we could begin healing. "Lamont, I had Country's mother, London, and Emmanual's mother all pregnant at the same time. I was afraid and didn't know what to expect as a father. With three kids on the way, I ran from responsibility. I kept hoping it would go away, but now I understand the pain I've caused. When I was younger my father wasn't in my household. We didn't have a relationship...he never taught me anything. I guess I did what I saw my father do to me and I regret doing it to you. I wish I could've been a better father." He admitted that it bothered him even until that day.

I had all the right in the world to hate my father. When I looked at it, I had no father but God, who took the place of my father in my life. With Chicago not knowing how to be a father, what good would he have been to me? I forgave Chicago because I now understood that my past wouldn't have been any different with him. I learned a valuable lesson from Chicago's mistakes and that was, "Take care of your children because you never know if they'll have to take care of you one day." The same mouth you feed may have to feed you.

Chapter 18

Thousand Deaths

Boy, I tell ya…when Dallas and the Redskins played against each other, everyone in D.C. lost their minds. The rivalry between these football teams was serious. Believe it or not, there are more Dallas fans in Washington D.C. than Redskin fans. There's no other team in hockey, basketball or football hated more than my beloved Cowboys in Washington. On the week Dallas and Redskins played you could see everyone wearing jerseys, flags, banners, bumper stickers, and bandannas to represent their team. On one particular game day, I had on my fresh Dallas jersey and was standing in front of my fifty inch Hitachi screen T.V., shouting and screaming at the top of my lungs at every play.

The phone rang, interrupting me as I shouted at the game. I answered the phone, "Hello?"

"Lamont." "What's up London, are you watching the game?"

"Yeah, I'm watching the game. I just called to inform you that Tyson is home."

"Oh yeah?"

"Yeah, he's home. I just found out from Eve."

I played it cool with London and continued watching the game after she hung up the phone. I knew Tyson was coming home one day, but I just didn't know when. Over the last ten years I had blocked Tyson out of mind, it was the only way I was able to move on with my life. I was caught off-guard with the news and all kinds of thoughts started to cross my mind. But the one that stuck to me like bubble gum on my shoe was, "I can't let this nigga get the third chance to try and kill me." Compared to ten years ago, I had too much to lose. I had a fiancée, a beautiful daughter and a duplex condo with three bedrooms, a bath and half and a lovely deck that I love cooking on. Now living in Largo, Maryland I felt secure and was glad to be living outside the city.

My mind was trapped and every other thought was either Tyson or my immediate family. The thought of jail entered my mind and the thought of being killed was entertained as well. Only one thing made me reason carefully, and that was my daughter growing up without a father…so, I started spending more time with my daughter, Promise.

I wanted her to at least remember and have memories of me just in case. I stared into Promise's eyes, searching for an answer, hoping my three- year-old could give me a reason not to go down the road I had repeatedly thought of traveling.

My fiancée saw a change in me, and I tried to explain to Oliva about my past with Tyson. But she couldn't relate and neither could she comprehend what I had experienced in my life. We argued numerous times because she found out that I had a Mack-11 semi-automatic gun with an extended clip that held fifty bullets. A few months before Tyson came home, Martin had asked me to hold onto it for him. After Tyson came home, I wondered if Martin gave the gun to me for protection, or if he really needed me to hold it. The 9mm Ruger I had was tossed in a high speed police chase that Omar was in…he had barely made it across the Maryland, D.C. line where he was arrested. So, with the Mack-11, I was strapped again. The safety was off and I was ready to release it if a beef kicked off.

During Tyson's ten years of imprisonment, I was blamed for everything that happened to him. He was stabbed twice in two separate incidents where he nearly died. When I heard about the first incident, I was told he was stabbed from head to toe. There's a large scar on his face that makes him look like Two Face the cartoon character on Batman. Whenever Tyson got into a fight, Eve would call and tell London it was my fault. She would say I tried to have Tyson killed or jumped by niggas that I didn't even know. The truth was, if I wanted Tyson killed, he would've been killed. He got into his own beefs in jail, not me. A lot of guys who knew me personally didn't like Tyson after they found out that he betrayed me twice. These were guys who were locked up with him.

When Tyson shot me, my own family members and close friends wanted to kill him. I told them all, "Let me handle my own problems." I was afraid someone would go to jail because I gave them the word to take care of my dirty work. Plus, I didn't want the regret hanging over my head if I became an accessory to murder. The only person who wanted Tyson more than me was Chicago. Chicago had the opportunity to kill Tyson when Tyson was transferred to Lorton Correctional Facilities in Virginia. With Chicago's reputation, Tyson made it known that Chicago was his Uncle, for protection. Chicago respected my wishes by letting Tyson be. Once the Warden found out about our beef, Tyson was shipped to Ohio and Chicago was shipped to Arizona.

I had family members calling me everyday telling me, "Tyson is home, watch your back because that nigga ain't changed in ten years, he's still up to no good." Day after day I received phone calls and updates on what Tyson said about me and what he was doing. I continued with my everyday routine, working and spending time with my family and church.

My mind wouldn't stop thinking of ways I could kill Tyson....even in my sleep I would dream of killing him. One night I dreamt that I walked up to Tyson and blew his head off, then I unloaded bullets into his body so the coroner wouldn't be able to identify him. Waking up from a dream like that made me feel like taking a subway ride so I could think. Downtown Washington, D.C. has many tourist sights and places I could go to clear my head, so I decided to visit a few museums and walk around. After a few hours, I got bored and I entered the Archives Subway Station on 7th Street North West, where I stood on the platform waiting for the train to arrive.

After twenty minutes, the train finally arrived, pulling up directly in front of me so I could walk directly through the chiming doors. Before the doors opened, I looked into the windows of the train where I noticed a guy smiling, as if he knew me. I couldn't recognize him, so I went into my memory bank to see if I could recall his face but I drew a blank. I didn't feel he was an enemy, so I entered the train doors as they opened.

As I turned in his direction, which was to my right, I had a full view of his face…this was a face I hadn't seen in years. From the window I couldn't identify him because of the scar on his face. He spoke, "What'z up cousin?"

Then he stuck his hand out for me to shake, so I shook his hand and replied, "What'z up Tyson? I heard you was home?"

"Yeah, I'm in the half way house." During the entire conversation, Tyson wouldn't turn where I could see the scar on the left side of his face. He leaned his head on the window as if he was asleep. Shortly after the conversation ended, Tyson got off and I continued riding the train to my metro stop.

I couldn't let my guards down like I've done in the past. The problem with me was that I underestimated Tyson. Every time something happened between us, I never saw it coming; but this time I was fully prepared to expect anything. Now that we had seen each other, I started preparing myself for war. So, to avoid peer pressure from family members and friends, I distanced myself from them. I was tired of hearing the same thing repeated everyday, "Tyson this, Tyson that." I stopped answering my phone, and if Oliva answered the phone, I told her to tell whoever called me, except for London, Rollo, Roger and J.P., that I wasn't home. I was cracking like a hatching egg from the pressure; and I needed isolation to think and plan.

I would no longer react first, then think about what I should've done after the fact. I became a man who planned by gathering information, calculating, and determining what the outcome could or might be. A lot of reasoning went into my thoughts before I reacted.

On nights after Oliva and Promise were well off to sleep, I would go downstairs, grab my gun and ride the streets, hoping I would see Tyson. My alibi would be, "I was home asleep with my family." I knew where Tyson hung out and where he laid his head. I had everything well planned, except my escape. Getting away was something that would have to happen naturally. There were many weekend nights I went looking for Tyson but never saw him. I knew Tyson was in a halfway house in North West, but I wasn't able to pinpoint which one. Every week he was given a weekend pass to go home and return on Sunday night.

One day, when I was going home from work, I rode down 17th Street and noticed Tyson standing on the corner. My facial expression was a thug-looking mug shot. His face expressed shock…he looked surprised as I drove by. Tyson was slipping and I knew if I had my gun with me I could cut Tyson off at the alley and crush him like a roach. I didn't ride to work with my gun on me, nor did I carry it unless I was going on a mission. From the eye contact that transpired, Tyson figured that I was out to kill him.

From that day, things really got hectic and the tension took a strain on my entire family. Wylie, Omar and Martin had been tight since we were younger. Because Wylie is my brother, and Omar and I are close, Tyson thought it would be in his best interest to separate Wylie and Omar from Martin. Tyson had no one he could trust or turn to but Martin, his uncle. His plan worked, Eve told London she didn't want Wylie and Omar coming around her house anymore. The reason was she had heard from an unknown source that Wylie and Omar were going to kill Tyson for me. I don't know where that rumor came from, and I honestly didn't care.

One day I borrowed London's car to take care of some business. I dropped her off at work, then I went back to her house to use the phone. When I heard a knock at the door, my first reaction was to look out the window. I saw Manda, Tyson's aunt, out front in her car. As I went to open the door to see what Manda wanted, she drove off leaving my two little cousins, Eddie and Halle, standing at the door. Occasionally, London would watch Eddie and Halle for Manda; but Manda didn't know London wasn't home and that I was using London's car.

I tried to stop Manda before she drove off. I yelled, "MANDA, MANDA, MANDA." Manda slowed down as if she heard me, then sped off.

I ran to London's car as fast as I could, telling Eddie and Halle to get in the car. I sped around the corner, hoping one of the red lights had stopped Manda so I could tell her London wasn't home. As I turned the corner I could see Manda still driving fast as if she was trying to get away before I caught up to her. Just what I was hoping came true, Manda was caught at the light. I pulled in front of Manda, cutting her off.

"Manda, I know you heard me call your name before you pulled off. London isn't home, and next time, please make sure the kids get in the house before you pull off."

By this time Eddie and Halle had exited London's car and now they were entering Manda's. Manda caught an attitude and cussed me out, calling me everything under the sun. Then, she had the nerve to threaten me, "Nigga, that's why Tyson stabbed you and shot you, you punk."

"Yeah, I bet you he won't do it again, bet you that!"

"Nigga, I'm gonna get Tyson to shoot you again."

I flipped out and completely lost control, "Go get Tyson and when I kill him, I'll kill you too!" As we argued, traffic came to a halt, and the police pulled up behind us telling us to move along before he gave us both tickets. Before I drove off, I told Manda, "I'll be waiting at London's house! Go get Tyson!" Then I drove off.

When I entered London's house, my rage was uncontrollable. I felt like throwing the first thing I saw. I paced the floor, looking out the windows and the front door. Tyson never showed up...neither did Manda; but I wondered what I was thinking because I didn't have my gun.

The next day, I went to church. After leaving my old church, I had joined Jericho City of Praise. I was out for four years; but in spite of all I'd been going through, my love for Christ continued to grow. I was glad to be in an environment that gave me a fresh start. I learned a lot from the mistakes I had made in the past and I didn't allow my old habits to travel with me to this church. My pastor Betty Peoples' message unclogged my mind like Drano unclogs pipes. I was able to reason and analyze what I needed to do in that situation from the message I was receiving. My Pastor repeated, "Face your fears." I thought about who or what I feared in life?

It was definitely not Tyson...the only person I fear is God. Honestly, though, I do have to admit that the only person I feared was Eve. For years, and especially when I was a child, Eve instilled fear in me. She was the only person who came to mind. I lived in bondage and struggled as a man with things I wrestled with. Being afraid to open my mouth had caused me great pain over the years. "A coward dies a thousand deaths, but a brave man dies once." I had died repeatedly, but I could still never overcome my fear of Eve.

The truth is, I blamed myself for being too timid to tell Eve how I felt years ago. But the way I was trained by Eve and London was to never say no to Eve. I tried to obey this rule until it interfered with my college classes. On nights I had class or homework, Eve would need a ride to the store. By the time I got home from school, I would be exhausted. At least three times a week London would either tell me that Eve needed to go to the store, or Eve would call. Living under London's roof at the time, I obeyed her. Even though I was mad at times…especially when I picked up Eve and one of her children was at her house with their car parked out front. I'd become angry that they wouldn't take the responsibility of helping their mother. I had sympathy for Eve because she had diabetes.

Honestly, I love Eve and I've always shown love and respect towards her; but, I didn't appreciate the way she rejected me when I greeted her. She rejected me by turning her head when I hugged and kissed her cheek. After she did that a few times, I stopped kissing her on her cheek and I kept my hugs to myself. I didn't want to be around Eve because I felt she didn't like me because of what happened in the past between Tyson and me.

Taking Eve to the store three nights a week took a toll on me. With work and school, I fell behind on my homework. I realized what I needed to do, so I told Eve that on nights when I had homework, I needed rest and I couldn't take her to the store. London got on my back for telling her no, so one thing led to another and I decided to drop out of college. Really, I told myself I was only going to sit out for a semester; but one semester turned into another and resulted in my not going back at all.

Still listening to the sound of my Pastor's voice, I became bolder and equipped with the words to express my inner thoughts that had been longing to come out. I realized I had the strength in other areas, like using my wisdom, which was more important than my physical strength.

I could finally speak my mind without getting an ironing cord whippen. Leaving Church, I headed for Eve's House. When I got there she was coming out, headed to Church herself. I asked her for a minute of her time, which she didn't mind giving. I spoke these words to her, "Eve I respect you for standing up for Tyson, but you were wrong for trying to persuade, manipulate and intimidate me. From the time Tyson stabbed me, and especially when he shot me, I didn't appreciate all the rumors I had heard over the years about things said behind my back. Every time I tried to move on with my life, you brought Tyson's name up as if you wanted to keep something going between us."

The look on Eve's face was full of guilt, brought on by the way I spoke, which made me feel like I was chastising her. She apologized for everything that had taken place over the years. After I finished speaking, she spoke, "Tyson missed the relationship he had with you and London. Out of everyone in the family, he was closest to you and your mother. It hurts him and he cried the other day because he realizes he betrayed the only people who ever loved him, besides me and his mother, Faith. No one in the family considers Tyson family anymore, because of what he's done to you."

I replied, "Eve it's not in my heart to kill or do anything to Tyson, all I want to do is move on with my life."

The conversation ended and we parted. I needed advice on how to handle the situation. No man can just walk up to their enemy and say let's talk or iron out differences… it's not that easy. Listening to Eve allowed me to know what Tyson was thinking.

My mind was still bombarded with thoughts of revenge and I needed to talk with someone I could trust before I took action; so, I called one of my older cousins Rusty. He came over to my house and we both took a ride in his truck to talk. On occasion, we've had deep conversations and I knew I could trust him in this situation.

After I told Rusty what I was thinking and planning to do to Tyson, he replied, "Wayne if you kill Tyson you're going to jail. The street rule is if you was or were going to kill him, you should've done it ten years ago. Look at what you've accomplished—a house, soon to be wife, a daughter and a nice car. That's a lot of responsibility to be leaving behind if things don't work out the way you plan."

"Rusty you're right. I didn't look at it that way."

"Now, here's what you should do and I mean this from the bottom of my heart. You and Tyson should have a sit down. Wayne, you have to be the better man. Use your mind, explore what I said and let me know what you think. Okay?"

I thought about it for a week and it made sense to have a sit down with Tyson.

But before I could get around to talking with him, I received a phone call from my youngest cousin Kenny, telling me that Tyson shot Martin's car windows out of his Mercedes SL 500 last night. The beef was over some money that Tyson was expecting from Martin. When Martin didn't come through for Tyson, Tyson shot his car up. Kenny told me Tyson wanted me to call him. After I wrote down the number, I wanted to throw it away; but, after thinking about it for minute I decide to call Tyson.

We talked, and Tyson wanted to call a truce. I assured Tyson that I forgave him and I wanted to have a sit down with him and the rest of my cousins, which included: Martin, Caesar, Country, Wylie, Omar, and Kenny, because they needed to be present so we could put an end to the rumors and squash the beefs amongst us. A week later, I was cruising down 17th Street where I spotted Tyson, Martin and Wylie standing on the corner. I pulled over, parked my car, and walked up to Tyson, Martin, and Wylie... we all hugged and begun talking.

Within a few minutes of our conversation Caesar, Country, Omar and Kenny either walked up or parked their cars to join in on the sit down. Once I saw everyone in place, I knew this was the perfect time for us all to say what we had been waiting to say to each other for years. Not only was there the beef between Tyson and me, and Martin and Tyson's beef, but there were grudges, resentment, jealousy, anger, competition, lies, plots, betrayal and sexual improprieties, in which we all have been guilty of over the years.

Looking back into our teenage years, I believe we all lost control of ourselves once we reached puberty. We didn't have that talk with our mothers about sex. None of our fathers were there to tell us not to sleep with each other's women; nor was there a man to tell us how to carry ourselves as men. We all acted foolishly and along the way, we had lost trust and respect for each other. We had allowed women to play us against each other and that caused confusion amongst us.

The truth behind Tyson's shooting me was that I slept with Caesar's ex-girl friend in 1993.... at that time I was eighteen years old. Before December 22, 1993, the day Tyson shot me, we exchanged words on two separate occasions. He claimed he saw London's car parked outside of Caesar's ex-girlfriend's house, which was a lie... yes, I went over her house once, but I wasn't dumb enough to park in front of her house. I had parked blocks away from her house so no one would notice or identify the car. Tyson found out that I slept with Caesar's ex-woman because Caesar and Tyson's women are buddies. Not to justify my wrong-doing, but she was older, wiser, more mature and slicker at her approach towards me. I never saw it coming, and if I knew then what I know now, I would've never given in to her. She told Tyson's woman and Tyson's woman told him and one thing lead to another... and I ended up with two bullets in my back because Tyson held a grudge against me that I wasn't aware of. I wondered for years what made Tyson shoot me? I asked myself, "Why did he do it?" I wracked my brain trying to figure that out for years.

Three years after Tyson was in jail serving his time for shooting me, I received a letter from him. It read, "Kojack I've been in my feelings because you slept with Tracey."

When I read those words everything came together. The one piece I needed had finally surfaced and now I was able to paint the picture of what made Tyson shoot me. Tyson liked Tracey and when he found out that I had slept with her, he took matters into his own hands. Tracey had told me before, now that I could remember, that Tyson was trying to get at her. I had ignored it and thought nothing of it. Until I receive that letter, that's when my memory came back to me. I wrote Tyson back asking him if Tracey was the reason he had shot me. He didn't deny it, but he did say I shouldn't have gone against the grain. I can respect that now, but then I had no clue as to how sleeping with another man's woman would affect me, especially my relationships.

I had to face the reality and the realization that my skeletons were a form of betrayal to my family. We all have betrayed one another by sleeping with an ex girlfriend or someone we cared about deeply. We only slept with each other's women, because deep down we'd been scarred by our fathers. We didn't have those father to son talks we all needed to have. We needed to know the boundaries a man could and could not cross. So, we grew up with no boundaries, and not knowing the consequences that we would face if we crossed the wrong man for his money, manhood, woman, or family. Those are the four things I learned to respect as I got older. It took me a long time to understand what I had done and how deeply I had scarred my family for my actions. I can't speak for the rest of my family members who are just as guilty; but I do speak because I realized my faults as a man. I didn't know any better.

To avoid the pain would only cause more separation, discrimination and prejudice amongst us… and my entire family. So, I stood there in front of a circle of blood, everyone being the veins and myself the heart. I spoke with authority and made sure every word was clear. As I spoke, I could see the seriousness on their faces. Martin, Tyson, Caesar, Wylie, Omar, Country, Kenny and my youngest cousin Ninja. I turned my focus to Tyson and spoke, "Tyson, I forgive you, now you have to forgive yourself. I've moved on with my life, I can no longer live in the past. If I wanted to kill you I could have many times. We're young black men who have survived death only because of God's grace. We've witnessed many of our friends get killed over petty stuff that could've been avoided by walking away, or just apologizing. I don't know how you look at life, but I know that I'm here for a reason. Tyson, I understand that your mother died when you were young and your father didn't take the responsibility of being the man in your life, neither did mine. But that doesn't give you permission to go around taking your anger out on your family. Believe it or not, I had to pray for direction when you shot me and on the day I heard that you came home from jail. If it was intended for me to kill you, nigga you would be dead."

After I spoke, we all took turns talking and apologizing to one another for past and present faults. We ended the meeting with a prayer, led by me, and by hugging each other. The next day, which was a Sunday morning, I drove to Harmony Cemetery to visit Faith and Beatrice. I have other family members buried in that cemetery, but my focus was on Faith and Beatrice. The cemetery isn't my favorite place to visit. Watching London break down made me shy away from going to the cemetery over the years. But today was a special day, a day of relief for me, and I was prepared to shed a tear, or two. Standing over their graves I couldn't hold back the tears. I knew if they knew what had taken place between Tyson and me over the years, they would have turned over in their graves.

Chapter 19

Olivia

A dream or a vision is like a riddle, and sometimes hard to figure out. Dreams are the life of the mind. All good things are born out of dreams. I only write down dreams that I know are given to me by God. I've had many dreams over the years, but only a few have shown me my future. On the night of April 17, 1998 I recorded a dream in my spiritual diary, not knowing the significance of it in my life. Dreams are like locks…if you don't have the key to enter, then you won't get in. I'm not talking about a lock like a door lock. I'm talking about a safe, the vault to your soul and the combination you fight every day to figure out. Here's my dream…

I was in a fatal car accident. As I got out of the car, I was approached by the owner of the car that I struck. He was fussing at me and I told him, "I'll pay for your car to get fixed." I continued on my journey by walking until I saw a mountain with a ladder. The ladder reached up to the top of the mountain. The mountain seemed easy to climb, so I decided to climb to the top of it. Climbing to the top wasn't as easy as I thought.

Now in the middle of the mountain, I looked down from the ladder. Seeing how far I had climbed scared me and it caused me to become dizzy and I lost my breath. I began to think I was going to fall from the ladder to the ground. The ladder was rocking from side to side. I was surrounded by clouds and angels appeared on my left side and my right side.

The angels on my left side said, "He's going to fall," and they laughed at me, causing me to become even more unbalanced than I was. Their laughter drowned out my concentration to focus on climbing. But the angel on my right side was closest to me and he spoke into my ear saying, "He's God's child, he knows what to do when he's about to fall...pray." I opened up my mouth and prayed to God.

God answer my prayer and I became determined to reach the top of the mountain. Standing on top of the mountain, in front of me, was a house. I entered the house, walking towards the bedroom where I noticed a woman standing next to a bed. She was talking with another person. I wasn't able to tell whether it was a man or woman. I approached the woman standing next to the bed. When she recognized me, she looked surprised that I had climbed the mountain and made it into the house. She instantly took off running, leaving me puzzled about why she ran. I ran behind her but was unable to catch her before she got to the door.

Once I got to the door, I saw her running around the corner. I closed the door and sat in front of the window looking out, wondering to myself, "Why did she run from me, why?"

At my bank there was a young lady who always flirted with me. She would say she didn't chase me, but she did. Her name was Olivia. On this particular day, Olivia called me over to her window and asked me if I had a girlfriend. I replied, "no." We exchanged numbers, but nothing happened over the next two months. We only talked twice over the phone and decided to leave it alone. For some odd reason Olivia's girlfriend and co-worker at the credit union asked Olivia for permission to talk to me. I had to make a choice... do I go after Olivia, or do I settle for Apple?

Even though she was fine and light-skinned, with a petite shape, Apple lacked something on my checklist...she lacked communication skills. One thing I have to have is a woman who can speak her mind. Apple seemed to be shy and stuck-up, like she knew she was all that and a bag of chips.

Olivia had more to offer ...she was streetwise, professional and had a sense of humor. I was able to be myself around her. I liked the fact that we flirted with each other, which gave me the notion that we had something in common. But, what I liked most was that she was hip to all the designer clothes I sported. Some of my gear was hidden from the naked eye, but Olivia had an eye for things like that and I admired that about her. One day I was sporting a pair of blue denim Gucci jeans that looked like regular farmer jeans with a tan colored neckline that matched with the stitching. Olivia knew right off the top of her head, "Those Gucci ain't they?"

I said, "Yeah! How you know, Miss Movado?" I called her Miss Movado, referring to her watch.

In the past, I sometimes had to make the choice between a woman I liked or was dating, and her girlfriend who liked me too; it was hard for me to decide which one I really wanted? Usually, I would wrack my brain, but in some cases, I went along with the flow. But now that I'm mature, honest and a man about everything I do, I placed the choice into Olivia's hands by telling her the truth. "Olivia, if I talk to Apple and she starts telling you about me, then I'll come between you and her. Because you liked me first and we did talk for a minute, there would be no trust between you and her. Plus, if I talked to her and things worked out, she would never trust you around me." I gave Olivia a lot to think about.

A week later, Olivia and I went out on our first date. I thought I would impress her by taking her to one of my favorite restaurants, Copeland's, located on King Street in Virginia. The mood, the setting, the candles and the atmosphere were just right...everything flowed. Looking into Olivia's eyes—I knew this was only the first date—but my heart confirmed, "She's the one."

After Unique and I broke up three years ago I was afraid to spark another relationship. First, I was still in the daze of the song by Frankie Beverly and Maze, I Can Get Over You. I was still hoping and praying Unique would come back and unbreak my heart. But she didn't, she moved on and got married. Second, I was scared that my heart may get broken again. Third, no women I had dated after Unique were really worth my time.

I did try to have a relationship with a woman who I had been crazy about for years, but then I found out she had a man in jail she was visiting, which I didn't mind because we were only friends. One day, I stopped by her house. As I was knocking on the door, she pulled up with some dude in his car. I walked down the steps to get a closer look into the car to see if it was her. She wouldn't get out of the car and the dude repeatedly asked her "Who am I?" I walked over to my car and drove off. I should've known she had a man because she wouldn't stay over my house past 8 o'clock at night.

When I met Olivia, I was still somewhat wounded and vulnerable. The song by Carl Thomas was the hottest song on the radio at the time we started dating. I Wish I Never Met Her At All. That song was a clue to me that I didn't pay attention to, because I fell in love.

Because our first date went so well, I looked forward to the next one. As Olivia and I got closer, I started finding out things about her that I didn't like. I didn't like that Olivia had a male roommate. He was a cool dude that loved lifting weights. Whenever Olivia invited me over to their apartment, I observed everything about him. I checked him out to see if anything seemed fishy about him or Olivia.

I was going to cut Olivia off if I picked up anything that resembled intimacy. But I never felt that vibe and I wasn't convinced either way...I was more fifty-fifty about their relationship. To ease my mind, I asked Olivia about him and she said, "Dawayne don't worry about Simeon, he's gay." I never felt, nor did I sense that he was gay from the times I was around him. From my understanding Simeon went both ways, sleeping with women and men. I was surprised when Olivia told me he was having a baby. After meeting his child's mother I dropped my guard, I no longer looked at him as a threat.

Olivia made it clear before I found out Simeon's status as bi-sexual; at least that's what she wanted me to believe. "If you can't accept Simeon, then we can't be together." I took this as a joke, but she wasn't playing. While we were on the subject, I had to tell Olivia about my friend Demi. The first thing that came out of Olivia's mouth was, "Have you had sex with her?"

I was honest, "Yes, but that was four years ago. We've known each other for seven years and only had sex once." This was funny because Olivia had a girlfriend who knew Demi. If I didn't tell Olivia the truth about Demi and me, she would have found out from her girlfriend.

Demi and I were set up on a blind date by Syrup in '93, that's how we met. I had been in many relationships where we started off as friends, knowing each other's secrets and weaknesses; and it always led to sex. It didn't matter whether I was in a serious relationship or not; what mattered was that I had already established a bond with a woman whom I felt obligated to…a sense of duty to continue our relationship as friends. I kept Demi updated on my present rela-tionship and she updated me on her relationship and life. In most of the relationships that I established with women who considered themselves my friend, best friend or my so-called play-sister, if I had sex with them the relationship changed. With all of the rela-tionships I had on that level, none of them lasted long. Some people you have chemistry with, and some you don't, except Demi and me; we agreed to stay friends and not throw our friendship away over sex. We had too much history together and we helped each other grow by counseling each other through the storms of life. She was there for me and I was there for her.

I made it clear to Olivia that Demi and I were just friends, nothing more, nothing less…only friends. To make Olivia comfortable about our relationship, I introduced them to each other. I could tell Olivia was intimidated by Demi's age and the fact that she thought we might still have our fling going on. Demi is six years older than me.

Our relationship advanced and we were around each other seven days a week. No longer was football my outlet, I found myself trying to explain the game to Olivia. Occasionally Apple would come along to the sports bar and watch the game with us. There were times Apple made me wonder about her. She was nice looking and guys lined up to get her number, but she showed them no attention. Honestly, I wondered if she was gay because everything Olivia did, she did. Whatever Olivia liked, she liked. Wherever Olivia went, she wanted to go. If Olivia had her hair done a certain way, Apple got her's done the same. There were times when Olivia had to change her clothes because they where dressed alike.

The best way to get to a man is through his stomach. Olivia can cook her shoes off her feet. Her mother taught her how to cook well. At the time, I was limited as to what I could cook, until Olivia taught me everything she knew. Now that I can cook, you can't keep me away from the stove. Every Saturday night was seafood night. We'd eat crab legs, French fries, fried rockfish and shrimp until we fell out with a stuffed stomach.

Olivia decided to move out of the apartment with Simeon and move into her own apartment. With us together all the time, we discussed living together. I wasn't ready to move in with a woman yet because I hadn't experienced the bachelor life. But, I thought, either I move now or wait a few more months to move out on my own. So, I moved out of London's house into Olivia's two-bedroom apartment. I made sure the icebox, freezer and cabinets all stayed full. I had a food stamp connect and every month I bought $300 worth of stamps…I was given the EPT card with a pin to shop for groceries.

With everything going well, I turned my focus to my job. For seven years, from 1993 to 2000, my title had been Clerk Typist. During those years I had been promoted from a GS-1 to a GS-5. I was told by my supervisor that in order for me to move up the pay scale, I would have to do two things; graduate from school and I would be guaranteed a permanent position in the Federal Government and I take on more projects and assignments. Those were my options to land a permanent position. Without those two things, I would not be able to be promoted to a GS-6 or 7; I was stagnant and stuck in a ditch.

Only a sophomore in college and earning nine credits a semester, my patience became thin. It was going to take me three or more years to finish college at the pace I was going. I took on the challenge of securing myself a permanent job with benefits. In my SIS position, there were no benefits, only annual and sick leave, which I accumulated every pay-period. My title changed once I took on more work. I had become a Document Control Officer, Clerk Typist, Data Entry, Computer Specialist and I operated, ordered, stocked and delivered computer supplies, when they were needed, to the staff in my building. I also played secretary on days my services were needed. On Tuesdays and Thursdays, I operated the computer store for my division, which included 130 people. Determined to succeed, I started applying for jobs at other government agencies.

I was offered an interview at GPO (Government Printing Office) for a higher grade that would've promoted me to a GS-7. I was well qualified for the position, with benefits. After the interview I knew I had the job. Within a week they had checked all my references. My supervisor had informed me that she was called by the GPO human resource office and she thought I had a good shot at getting the job.

Everything seemed to be going in my favor until I found out that my supervisor didn't renew my contract as a Stay in School.

As a SIS my contract had to be renewed every six months, June 30th and December 30th. My supervisor decided not to renew my contract because she thought I had the job at GPO. I couldn't understand why she would ask me if I would've liked for her to renew my contract, when she had already made up her mind not to. I didn't find out that she didn't renew my contract until June 30, the same day my paper had to be signed and delivered to the personnel office. I was released from EPA and I didn't get the job as expected with GPO. My supervisor called me back and asked me if I wanted to come back to work. I told her I wanted more money and a permanent position before considering working for EPA again. I did this to pressure her into hiring me full-time with benefits. Two days later I was told, "Dawayne, I just can't do it."

After I lost my job with EPA I began temping with Randstar Temp Agency. I grew frustrated at the money I was making. I worked on jobs that paid me seven and eight dollars an hour. The walls really closed in on me once Olivia told me she was pregnant. Only a year into our relationship; I was surprised. From my understanding, this wasn't supposed to happen, not at this time and not this fast. I stayed on top of Olivia when it came to her birth control pills. I wasn't ready to have a child...I didn't even have a decent job to provide for the child.

Olivia told me she stopped taking her birth control pills because she forgot to take them and now she was pregnant. We had never discussed our future together. I barely even knew Olivia, but this was the beginning of sorrow for me. One thing I did know was that this was my chance to prove and overcome and be a better father to my child than Chicago was to me. During Olivia's pregnancy, we bonded like we were on an island all alone. Every weekend I would buy three DVD's for us to watch; our DVD collection built quickly and we both got fat from eating too much.

With only a few pieces of furniture in our apartment, I decided that we needed to have everything organized by the time the baby was born. So, we bought furniture, toys, and Olivia was able to buy a car. We accomplished our goals in time for our baby to be welcomed home.

Our child was expected to be born in July, the same month of Olivia's and my birthday. Olivia's is on the 7th and mine is on the 11th. In her eight month of pregnancy, Olivia developed toxemia, a condition in which the blood contains poisonous substances (bacteria in the blood). The doctor told me to get Olivia to the emergency room ASAP or my child could die...I did as he told me.

June 2001 my daughter was born premature at three pounds and two ounces. I had experienced the greatest thing a woman can give a man. Words can't express how I appreciated life more after seeing and holding my creation in my hands. With Promise in the picture I became motivated and determined because I had a purpose and a responsibility to now live up to—fatherhood.

Growing up around my brothers, cousins and sister, I had the chance to experience sharing. If one of us didn't share, we were labeled as selfish. Looking at Olivia, I started to notice that she was used to having her way. When she didn't get her way, she refused to give me mine. I saw this as a way of trying to control me. To me, self-esteem played a big role; but her parents and I contributed to Olivia's greed as well.

I tried to explain to Olivia, "Promise comes first, that's our responsibility. Are you ignorant of that?" Before Promise was born, I had bought Olivia everything she asked for. She had all the latest designer clothes and purses from Coogi, Prada, Ferragarmo, Channel, Gucci and Louis Vuitton. But now, we had a new bill on our plate that I took very seriously. I paid the daycare, and I did my best to make sure my daughter didn't want for anything.

Olivia would get upset with me and start arguments, which would lead to her not speaking to me for days…all because I wouldn't buy her a new purse. On the nights before I had to work, Olivia wanted to argue over things that really could've waited until the next day. This was very disturbing. I tried hard to ignore her. I would grab my pillow and a sheet and sleep on the couch. Olivia wasn't satisfied until she kicked me out the house. She even threatened to call the police. I never felt so embarrassed, self conscious and humiliated in my entire life.

Over the course of two months, Olivia kicked me out four times, causing me to pack my belongings into trash bags. Every time I was kicked out, it would be late at night twelve, one and 2 o'clock in the morning. Olivia knew I didn't have a car, so I had to call London to pick me up. London would be furious that I interrupted her sleep. On the last trip to get me London said, "If you go back that's on you because I'm not coming to get you. Don't call my house and wake me up for this petty girl friend of yours who likes to play games. If she was a woman, she would let you leave in the morning. I'm pretty sure she knew I had to work in morning." I had no choice but to move back in with London.

The truth was that Olivia was heated with me because I caught her in a lie. One thing I hated with a passion was for a person to lie to my face. I had to address this lie she told, or I wouldn't be a man. God knows I tried to block it out of mind. I overlooked it and even ignored it to a degree. From the day Olivia and I moved in together, I picked up on her sneaky ways. She would go places with Simeon and wouldn't tell me. She either knew or I told her everywhere I went.

On the night Martin was stabbed, I was going to ride with Olivia and Apple to the club. But Olivia didn't want me to ride with them. That caused me to borrow London's car that night; so, when I got to the club I saw Simeon standing with Olivia and Apple. Simeon rode to the club with them and I was told I couldn't ride. Later on, after I got my thoughts together, I told Olivia I didn't trust their friendship, based on the way she did things.

Simeon only came to our apartment when I wasn't home. Instead of Olivia telling me the truth, she lied to me with a straight face. I didn't want to come between their friendship; but it became obvious that they had more than a friendship.

Olivia was more obligated and committed to Simeon's friendship than our relationship. I explained to Olivia why I felt the way I did and I came up with a solution to the problem. I told her, "I don't want Simeon in my house unless I'm home. If you can't respect that, then we don't need to be together." She felt that I didn't trust her. Everything was about Demi, Demi, Demi. I had to tell her, "Olivia, Demi has a man and I respect their relationship by not going over to her house when her man isn't home. I would never jeopardize or cause confusion in Demi's house or her relationship by playing the games you play. One thing you can say is that Demi never came over our house."

After I put my foot down, Olivia took me for granted. One day I came home unannounced. When I walked up to my door I could hear another man's voice. I knocked because I left my keys in the house on that day. Olivia came to the door and opened it after I told her it was me. I stood in the front door and observed Simeon sitting on my couch watching TV. My daughter was crying, and Olivia had on a small dress that barely came to her thighs. The dress she had on showed me that she had no respect for me. I wondered how she would feel if I walked around in tight underwear in front of her so-called girlfriends.

I wanted to break every bone in Olivia's body and she knew it. I walked over to the T.V. and cut it off. Then, I told her to put on some clothes. Simeon got up to leave and I commanded him to sit back down, telling him, "We gonna get to the bottom of this right now! Don't leave! Sit down!" I picked up Promise, rocking her from side to side and calming her down by placing her pacifier in her mouth. She eventually fell asleep in my arms. Once Olivia returned to the living room, I addressed everything concerning their relationship.

Apparently, Olivia never told Simeon that I didn't want him in our house without me being present. Simeon said he had spoken with Olivia about him visiting and she said it was okay. He made it clear that he never slept with Olivia and that he doesn't want to be the cause of our break up. After that confrontation, Olivia held a grudge against me, which led to us having serious arguments, in which I got the short end of the stick by getting kicked out.

Chapter 20

Peace of Mind

The best thing that came out of Rollo's and my relationship was that I met a good friend named Roger. Rollo used to date Roger's sister Karisa. Roger and I gave two cabarets together and from there we became really good friends. Roger always said, "Kojack you're the brother I never had." Considering Roger only had a sister, I became the brother he had always wanted. Roger introduced me to a lot things I had no knowledge of ... even though he's a few years younger than I am. I was fascinated by his age and wisdom, and the fact that he had accomplished more than me at a younger age. Roger has twice as much as I have and we get along because our love and respect for one another go way beyond what other people think or say.

Roger is a flat foot hustler, a jack of all trades. His father taught him how to work with his hands. He can hunt rabbits, fish, paint, landscape, work on cars, do plumbing, electricity...if you name it, he can do it. Roger taught me how to work with my hands and how to think outside the box. I looked at Roger differently. From the day I met him I knew we were going to be friends for a long time. He knew what I didn't know and he seemed to have everything I dreamed of having. Roger has a nice house, a wife, three boys, four nice cars and he's a good father. I finally met a person who I admired for who he was and who allowed me to have the faith that I, too, could someday accomplish my dreams.

During the time Olivia and I were going through our problems, I was in the midst of planning Roger's birthday party. The party was going to determine whether Olivia and I were going to buy a house. We needed more space and I was tired of the apartment complex we lived in because of the increase of crime. Things went just as planned, so Roger and I decided that we had to give another party. The next party we planned was in six weeks. We went right to work planning and plotting and designing how, when and where we wanted to give the party. We needed more space, a club that could hold more people than the place we rented last time. So, we decided to rent a club called Studio 63 located in Capitol Heights, Maryland.

On the night of the party, the vultures appeared, trying to corner Roger and me. I was able to put a face, and even a name, with the niggas who had been planning to rob me for three years now. Roger, with his street knowledge outsmarted them. There were three...two following Roger around the party and one clocking my every move.

I was standing outside the club when everything went down. I had no idea that night that death was knocking at my door again. Standing guard with me were a few foot soldiers, guys I knew watching my back; we stood watching the women in line. I was approached, innocently, by a skinny black nigga in a sweat hood. I knew the guy by name, but I didn't know he was planning to rob not only me...but the front door as well....where Roger's wife and mother were taking money. The guy had become jealous of Roger and me because we were considered by the people and the club owners in the area to be the best party-givers in the city. We had a saying that we placed at the bottom of our flyers, "We're giving you the best parties in town, like Jay-Z said, you don't know, 'We beat them charges like Rocky.'"

At the same time I was approached, I heard Pumpin Archie, our D.J., shout over the microphone, "P.G. Police, go to the front door immediately. P.G. police you're needed at the front door." Standing outside in front of the door I wondered what in the hell was going on. There was nothing wrong at the front door because I was standing there watching and clocking all the money at the entrance of the club. Vick stood in front of me to distract me from what was taking place inside.

His eyes were gloomy looking and bulging, like he wanted me to read them. He said, "Kojack what's up? Do you need a gun?" At the same time he was speaking, he was reaching into his pants.

Automatically I reached into mine, "Naw Vick. I'm strapped and my man and them are too." When he saw he was out numbered, Vick stepped back. Then I entered the club to see what was wrong. Nothing looked suspicious to me, so I searched for Roger. But before I could reach Roger, his wife told me Roger had messaged her on the Nextel telling her to tell me we needed to leave the club now. With no hesitation, I grabbed the money off the table and we belted out of the party at 2 o'clock. We could've taken in another thousand dollars, only because the party wasn't over until 3 o'clock. When we left, the door was unattended.

Once I got into the car, Roger called me on my cell and informed me that two niggas tried to corner him inside the club with guns. I don't know how they got the gun into the party. Either they paid the security we hired to let them in, or they knew the security well enough not to get searched. Roger was able to escape and inform the D.J., who was able to alert the police over the loud speakers, which gave us time to escape before things turned sour. The next day we found out that a woman was robbed at gunpoint of the $300 cash raffle we gave away. We sold the tickets for a dollar apiece…I didn't have to ask who robbed her.

After that party, I decided it would be my last one. I accomplished my goal…what more could I ask for…I went out on top. Adding up the risk I took to make fast money wasn't worth the reward. My life and other people's lives were placed in jeopardy and I wasn't going to accept death that way; nor was I going to accept anyone else's life being taken randomly for the sake of mine.

The best thing for me was to keep on moving, no stopping. Olivia didn't think about the bills when she made the decision to kick me out. The games were over and I wasn't coming back this time before the bills were due. She was now officially on her own. She didn't last in the apartment one month without me. Still holding a grudge, Olivia wouldn't allow me to see my daughter. She even took Promise from the babysitter and placed her with another sitter where I couldn't contact or visit her. We argued back and forth over this because I paid the sitter, but I couldn't have visitation rights.

Once Olivia got tired of the crying, feeding and changing diapers, she gave my daughter to me on weekends. After Olivia got comfortable with the weekends, ten months later, she finally allowed me to meet the sitter.

Olivia had told the woman all kinds of bad things about me that weren't true. Judgment was already passed on me by a woman who didn't even know me. I was eagerly waiting to meet her. I wanted to see how her living environment was and I wondered if I would have to call the health department in case her house didn't look fit to keep my child. I wondered if she was mean, spiteful or abusive to my child. I built my foundation with her by communicating. We became friends and she noticed the real me, the real Dawayne Williams…the father side of me that Olivia didn't want her to see or know. She could see the love I had for my daughter and the love my daughter showed toward me.

We became well acquainted with each other. She told me the real scoop, and she let me in on a secret that she had held for a year. "Dawayne, how much did Olivia say I charge her to watch Promise?"

"$340 a month."

"Olivia been lying to you for a year now. I only charge her $200 a month to watch Promise. She pockets the rest."

I couldn't believe what I had heard, I refused to believe Olivia would do that to me. I paid the sitter, health care, bought pampers, wipes, milk and clothes; and on top of that, I was keeping my daughter weekly.

A week gave me more time with my daughter so we could bond, plus I didn't want Olivia over-burdened; so I decided it was in the best interest of us both. Promise would spend one week with me and the other with Olivia. This also gave me the opportunity to have a free weekend.

When the sitter told me Olivia was beating me out of my money, I wanted to beat the hell out of her for stealing from me. I knew if I placed a hand on her, I would lose it and go to jail. When I asked Olivia if this was true, she seemed shocked but didn't deny it. So, I went to D.C. Superior Court to the family division and filed for joint custody of my daughter. When our case got before the judge, I was told I had filed in the wrong jurisdiction. The reason was that my daughter was born in the state of Maryland and had the same address as Olivia. I thought because I lived in D.C. that I could file in D.C. but that wasn't the case. The judge instructed me to file in the state of Maryland where my daughter's current address was. I had to pay $80 just to hear the judge tell me to file in another state; and I found out that in Maryland I would have to pay another $100 to file the paper work. I decided to give Olivia a break and pay the sitter the correct amount of $200 a month. After that day in court, Olivia calmed down and I continued to move forward.

Four months after I moved back home with my mother, I saved up enough money to move into my own one bedroom apartment with beautiful hardwood floors and a balcony. I got to experience being responsible. I was in control of everything and it felt good. I felt even better that all my affairs were in order. I was enjoying freedom and peace of mind. Coming home to my own place after a hard day of work allowed me to think better.

I had no worries in the world, none…until Olivia showed up at my door unannounced late at night. At the time I had company. I didn't answer the door, Olivia had no reason to show up. We weren't having sex and we barely communicated. She banged and banged hard and loud until I couldn't take it anymore. I threatened to call the police if she didn't leave. After a while she left crying. I didn't allow Olivia to stop me from dating. I told her if she showed up at my door again she would be arrested.

I furnished my place and bought myself a Hoopdee to get around…a 1987 Delta 88, tan with tan interior. It lasted me for a year and half until it broke down and I left it on the beltway. I have to say that was my best car ever. Then I went out and bought another Maxima.

Being a bachelor wasn't what I thought it would be. Starting a new relationship with a woman wasn't as easy as it used to be. Getting to know someone can take a long time and sometimes the process made me go back to what I was familiar with, old girlfriends. Back into the dating game, I was invited by an old lady friend of mine named Pepa to attend the premiere of the Rosa Parks Story.

The premiere was held at the Ronald Regan building on Pennsylvania Avenue. There was free food with beer and wine. I was well dressed for the occasion. All around me were congressmen, lawyers, politicians, judges, doctors and all the local news channels: 4, 5, 7, 8, and 9. They were all there, capturing the moment. Some had video cameras and some took pictures. The event was classy, I felt as if I was in the white house ballroom. The premiere was invitation only, with one guest per invitation. I didn't know what to expect, seeing so many important people. All were gathered together to view history once again. In school, history had been my favorite subject. But somehow over the years, I lost track of how important history was and always will be.

Rosa Parks had created the spark and gave light to the civil rights movement…I wondered how effective a boycott would be in this day and age. If we stood for something, then we wouldn't fall for everything and anything that's taking place.

While this thought rolled through my mind, everyone stood and greeted Rosa as she entered the building, escorted by reporters and news cameras. I was able to meet not only Rosa Parks, but Star Jones and Ms. Waiting to Exhale, Angela Bassett, who was the star and actress portraying Rosas Parks in the film. She's shorter than I expected, but gorgeous and sexy just like in the movies. After watching the premiere I have to say, "That was a night to remember."

In December 2002, London's name was selected out of a random drawing for a turkey to be delivered to her house by Michael Jordan and the Washington Wizards basketball team. The drawing London's name was selected from was sponsored by the Friendship House, located on Capitol Hill three blocks from the Capitol. London was one out of five people chosen. When she told me Michael Jordan was coming to her house, I was excited. Fireworks went off in my mind; I couldn't hold it in. I called all my friends and told them that Michael Jordan was coming to my Mama's house.

On the day they were coming, we waited and waited. The house was full of fans, friends and family members. As the minutes went by, we all grew anxious and wondered, "Are they really coming?"

Two hours after the expected time, the wait was over. Policemen on motorcycles blocked off the street in every direction. A tour bus followed by an Office Depot truck, white Land Rover, Ford Expedition, and a Channel Seven news truck all arrived together. Everyone on London's porch had pictures, jerseys and video cameras waiting to get autographs by Michael Jordan and the Wizards basketball team. Acting crazy, like I sometimes do, I got everyone pumped up by saying a line from the movie Ali, "The champ is here, the champ is here."

One by one, we watched Charles Oakley, Juan Dixon, Kwame Brown, Jared Jeffries, Jadhidi White, Jerry Stackhouse, Bryon Russell and the owner of the Wizards Abe Pollin, followed by the Channel Seven news crew, as they exited the tour bus. Seconds later, we all entered the house. A few of the basketball players had their wives and children with them. It was unbelievable to have millionaires visiting my mom's house with gifts. Michael Jordan was a no-show but the Wizard's other stars made my day and everyone else's. No one complained, but we all were looking for Jordan. Cameras were flashing faster than a speeding bullet. The Wizards gave London toys, gifts, food, watches, games, basketballs with the Wizard's logo, gift cards and a computer with a DVD player with speakers. Later that night, Channel Seven showed London on the 11 o'clock news.

I had never in my life seen London so happy; she deserved it. A year later, I would realize the role of the computer that the Wizards gave to London and how it would factor into my dream.

Chapter 21
Denial

Despite all the problems Olivia and I had, I wanted us to be a family. Honestly, it was hard for me to move on with another relationship. I held onto my childhood promise to marry the woman who bore my child. My fear of being a father like Chicago deflated me. I thought about Promise's future, and the question I asked myself was, "How could I be a good father without seeing my daughter every day?"

I wanted to see Promise every day and getting her every other week wasn't enough. I wanted the privilege of putting Promise in the bed at night, and before walking away, greet her beautiful cheekbone with a kiss. I wanted to be there when she awakened from a bad dream and take her into my arms and rock her back to sleep, telling her, "You're Daddy's girl, I'm not going to let anything or anyone hurt you." These thoughts attacked my mind, and I decided to give Olivia the second chance she wanted. For months Olivia had been telling London she wanted to marry me and that she had changed her ways.

At the time, I had plans to move into a house. My loan was already approved and all I had to do was find the house I wanted. I discussed it with Olivia because we had started seeing each other again. I was persuaded by Olivia to entertain her option to buy a house, she had been renting a duplex condo, three bedroom, with a bath and half, and a nice deck. Olivia wanted badly to purchase the condo and I couldn't blame her. She was renting from a married couple who wanted to sell the condo for what they owed on it, $95,000. Olivia and I would inherit the $25,000 equity. The equity in the condo convinced me that this wouldn't be a bad investment. I was thinking of buying the condo myself, but since we were going to get married, I thought it would be best for Olivia to pay off her bills; then we would buy the condo together. But I didn't know how far Olivia would go to accomplish her dreams.

Marriage is a big step, bigger than most people think. I had all the right intentions of marrying Olivia. I cut off all contacts with every woman I knew or whose phone numbers I had. I was ready to settle down. So, on Olivia's birthday, I proposed to her. During the prior few months, we had several serious talks about marriage. I had to make sure she was ready to take this step before I proposed. When we called and told London, she gave us her blessing but told us both, "Go to counseling if you really want your marriage to work."

I moved out of my apartment into the condo with Olivia and Promise. We thought it would be best this way to save money for the wedding we had planned for a year later.

Olivia couldn't decide whether she wanted to go to the Justice of the Peace or have a church ceremony. I wanted a big wedding, so we decided to do both. On February 26, 2004, we were married at the Justice of the Peace. Olivia's mother and London were present with Promise, smiling. The church ceremony was set for July 31, 2004. After we were married, things got real hectic...things fell apart, like dominos falling. Even till this day, I can still feel the effects of the pounding I took. They say, "No pain no gain." How we react to adversity says a lot about our character.

During that time, I began my journey to write my autobiography. When I first started to write, I did a lot of brainstorming and soul searching to pull everything together. Going back into my past was difficult and painful in ways I can't explain. I didn't know how writing would take its affect on me and my family. At times, I would be, happy full of joy and other times I would be confused, hurt and crying. All of these emotions came with writing.

I left my job at Home Depot and started working for Pepsi as a merchandiser. I worked forty-five to seventy hours a week. The pay was good, but the work broke me down mentally and physically. My job consisted of me lifting fifty to one hundred pounds. On two occasions, I injured my back, causing me to miss work. On my first injury, I was off work for two months. My second injury came a year later, but it wasn't as serious as the first. My doctor placed me on light duty, but my boss had the pressure on my supervisor to get me back to full duty ASAP. I was on light duty for a month. I didn't know my supervisor was out to get me fired. I was written up for things that were petty. I couldn't believe the Union allowed him to get away with it. I continued to do my job to the best of my ability.

On the day I went off light duty, my supervisor had the nerve to ask me to pick up an extra store on top of the six stores I already had. I told him, "No, that's how I hurt my back the last time. I was helping you out, then you wrote me up." He insisted that I pick up the store or else. I told him, "Make me!" Then I slammed the phone in his ear. After twenty minutes passed, he called back and told me to meet him at the plant at 3 o'clock. With the feeling I was going to get fired, I didn't do any more work for the day. I covered myself by calling my supervisor back, but he didn't answer his phone. So, I left a message telling him my back hurt and he needed to get someone to cover my route. After I left the message, I sat in my car for the rest of the day listening to Donnie McClurklin and Fred Hammond to lift my spirits.

Before I knew it, 3 o'clock had rolled around. I was ordered by my supervisor to have a seat at his desk. A guy from Pepsi Union came in the office and took a seat next to me. Before the meeting took place the Union guy questioned me about what was wrong. My supervisor started lying, saying I was insubordinate when he really was mad that I hung up the phone in his ear. I explained my case, but my supervisor was fed up and handed me a suspension paper after the Union guy told him, "You can't make an injured man work." He didn't care that my back was still hurting, all he cared about was his commission that Pepsi was going to pay him at the end of the year. From out of nowhere, I snapped. All the frustration, anger and rage had built up so quickly that I became furious and threw the two hardest punches ever, striking my supervisor in his face and knocking him to the ground. He laid on the ground covered up like a baby. He wasn't talking bad now.

Once I noticed what I'd done I threw everything on his desk on top of him and turned his desk over on top him. By that time everyone who heard the ruckus in the plant came running to save his life. I looked down at him and said, "Why keep writing me up if you're going to fire me anyway, just fire me then. Don't keep picking at me." Then I walked away, surrounded by twenty Pepsi employees who all moved out of my way as I exited the building before the police arrived.

Pepsi filed assault charges against me, but the charges were dropped after I figured out my supervisor's motive to get me fired. Believe it or not, all the write-ups were over a woman who worked at the Safeway store I serviced. My supervisor was intimidated by me because she liked me. He was engaged to another women who he had gotten pregnant. And he was cheating with the woman at Safeway and worried about me at the same time. I wasn't thinking about the woman at Safeway. We were just friends on the job. I never had an affair with her, I honored my vows to my wife. I told the Union about the affair and his motive to fire me because of his jealousy. An investigation was done, he was disciplined and I was fired because I hit him. The charges were dropped against me.

Before things had gotten to that point, I tried to explain to my supervisor that I was dealing with a lot of emotion over writing my book. A week before the incident took place I had squashed the beef with Tyson. I remember when I was in junior high school and Ms. Barnes told me, "Dawayne stop messing with people because you don't know what they're dealing with at home. One day somebody is going to snap on you." But I never thought it would be the other way around. I had too much pressure on me and my pipes burst.

Immediately, I started my search for a new job. My search was put on hold when Olivia became sick three weeks after I was fired. Over the period of two months from May to the end of June, I took care of my wife. She wasn't able to do anything for herself. I had to feed her, bathe her and clothe her. She mostly slept and I took that time to teach Promise how to walk, talk and use the potty. My wife had a ruptured disc that kept her in excessive pain. She was unable to work. I couldn't take seeing my wife suffer like that, all I could do was pray and ask God to heal Olivia. After going to the emergency room five times and seeing a specialist, Olivia was healed and healthy enough to resume working. My unemployment paid the bills, with the help of our taxes and our parents.

While working hard on my book I got the craving for some Lay's original Stax potato chips. I have to have some Stax while writing, they helped me think better. While I was typing, I asked Olivia to go to the store and purchase some Stax for me. But she was in a rush, so I had to go to the store myself. I drove into an intersection on Marlboro Pike. I turned my head in both directions checking the oncoming traffic and waited at the stop sign for traffic to clear in both directions so I could make a leftturn.

As I pulled out into the intersection, a car from out of nowhere raced towards me at 70mph on a 25mph street. I tried to back up, hoping the guy wouldn't hit my car. Seeing I couldn't do anything, I screamed. I could hear our cars collide. My air bag imploded in my face immediately. The impact from the other car caused my car to do a 360-degree turn, nearly wrapping around a telephone pole. I laid helpless and unconscious for five minutes. When I looked up, the guy who hit my car was standing at my window panicking, asking me, "Are you all right?" I couldn't talk, nor could I remember what had happened. All I know is that I had a serious headache. I was taken to the hospital by ambulance and later released with pain medicine.

My car was totaled, with front-end damage. I didn't have any car insurance because my unemployment was only enough to pay all my bills. The guy's insurance company said it was my fault and they tried to sue me.

A week later in July, it was count down to the wedding. Olivia's cousin from South Carolina wanted to keep Promise for a week. In the back of my mind, I wondered about a lot of things. One in particular haunted me with the birth of my daughter. Months after Olivia and I met, she revealed to me that she had been abused twice as a child. She never told me by whom, but she did say it was by a close family member, and she still sees this person periodically. I was bothered by this because I didn't know who this person was and she gave me no clues. I couldn't understand why she told me and not her parents about the ordeal that's still haunting her until this day. Hearing this made me over-protective of my daughter. Olivia begged me to let Promise go to South Carolina but I didn't want her to go, she was too young, only three years old. Olivia convinced me that I needed the time to think and regroup myself so I could find a job. She told me, "It'll only be for a week." That week turned into a month I'll never forget. Even though I talked with my daughter over the phone, I was crushed inwardly for many reasons.

I was broke, with no job, only three weeks away from my wedding ceremony, my car was totaled and now my daughter was three states away and I couldn't get to her. I wanted my daughter home, whereas Olivia didn't care. Now that she was healthy, Olivia became my worst enemy. She talked down to me because I didn't have a job. She wouldn't let me borrow her car. Even after Promise came home from S.C., I wanted to take her to the museum downtown and to the movies. Olivia told me, "You're not using my car. Catch the bus to the subway." It was becoming noticeable that Olivia and I didn't see eye to eye. We argued because she lied to me. I told her, "You don't send a child away for a month with people she doesn't know... family or no family." All along, Olivia was scheming behind my back. She was so caught up with hanging out with her girl friends that she forgot they were single and she was married.

I found it deeply disturbing that Olivia would allow Mischievous, her girlfriend, to be one of her bridesmaids in our wedding. Olivia's best friend had dropped out of the wedding at the last minute; so, Olivia replaced her with Mischievous. From the first day I met Mischievous, I knew she was trouble. She was aggressive and eager to meet me. Personally, I didn't like the fact that she knew so much about me and I knew nothing about her but her name. I had to come clean with Olivia.

I didn't know how to tell her that Mischievous had come on to me twice. I tried telling Olivia by dropping her hints. When I saw she didn't catch on, I came clean not only about Mischievous, but also Apple. Olivia cut Apple off at the snap of a finger, but held onto Mischievous' relationship. This confused me and forced me to ask Olivia, "Why are you still hanging with Mischievous when you know she tried to have sex with me?"

Olivia replied, "I know she's not your type."

Whatever that was supposed to mean I was about to find out.

On July 31, 2004 we were married at Olivia's mother's church. During the ceremony while our mothers were lighting the candles, London lit her candle and Olivia's mother's lighter went out. From what I was told, London asked Olivia's mother if she wanted to borrow her lighter. Olivia's mother rudely snatched the lighter away from London and lit her candle in front of everyone. There were over 220 people that witnessed this act. London had to force herself to act respectful and she blew it off for my sake.

Olivia and I were supposed to go to counseling before we got married, but somehow it was avoided. Even after the wedding ceremony, I tried to convince Olivia that we needed to go to counseling, but she refused, thinking she knew what it took to be a faithful wife. She had no clue. I guess she thought the advice she got from her single girlfriends would solve everything.

One day J.P. and I were sitting out on my deck grilling some t-bone steaks, bluefish, hot dogs and BBQ chicken. My neighbor smelled the smoke and decided to take this time to congratulate me and warn me of his twenty years of marriage. While he talked, J.P. and I listened to his wisdom. Mr. Cray knew what he was talking about as he spoke with great concern. Honestly, I felt like God was speaking to me through Mr. Cray. He said, "Son, don't cheat on your wife. If you cheat once and get away with it, you'll keep doing it. I know from experience that cheating will only cause you to lie to your wife, your child and yourself. I nearly lost my family and my house because of my mistake. Don't do what you see other men do. Keep doing what you're doing and take marriage one day at a time. Put God first and you'll make it."

My marriage was on life support and we became strangers.

Olivia was focused on building her career and being obligated to her girlfriends. If she had the same tenacity at home, our marriage wouldn't have suffered. We tried to make things seem perfect when our parents visited. But I lost trust in Olivia. I had little faith that we could make it. If only she'd listen to me, her husband, and not her girlfriends. I held nothing against any of her girlfriends, but I could tell the advice she was getting wasn't advice. It was jealousy towards me. None of Olivia's four girlfriends had, or could keep a man, including Mischievous. Honestly, I don't think they knew how. Every time I saw them, they had a new man. Either Olivia had low self-esteem or she just wanted to be single again. I was now faced with a puzzle to piece together. When placing a puzzle together, you have to have one thing and one thing only, patience. Olivia spent more time at her girlfriends' houses than she did in our home. I found it difficult to communicate with Olivia, and her attitude towards me and Promise seemed confusing and distant.

Even with sex, I noticed a complete change. When I wanted to hold, hug, and snuggle with her, she didn't. Affection had left my marriage months ago. Before we married we had sex daily, but afterwards, she didn't want to engage in sex at all. When I tried to have sex in the shower with her, she locked the door, at night Promise divided us by sleeping between us. So, I made Promise sleep in her own room, but Olivia came up with another excuse, "I'm on." I would wait and wait until finally I stopped asking.

The Internet became my pleasure island. I had given up watching pornography. I hated watching it because I wanted the real thing. That's why I got married. When I was younger, I couldn't get enough, but now I had seen my share. There were times I would purchase a $30 video and watch it once then break it...I broke up many pornography DVDs and video tapes after watching them once. Olivia would get upset with me because I watched pornography, as if I had committed a crime. The real crime was her not having sex with me. She treated sex like it was fare exchange. Buy me a purse and we could work out a deal, that's how she looked at it. Sex is really overrated and the wrong reason to marry. The foundation our relationship was built on collapsed after we stopped having sex. Somewhere in our relationship, she didn't develop true feelings and emotions for me; it was all about her.

I was beginning to believe something was going on. On Saturday nights, Olivia started coming home later and later. For some reason, she thought I was ignorant of the time she was coming in at night. I thought nothing of it because she told me she was out with the girls.

When a man gets caught cheating, he'll give in; but when a woman cheats, a man must have all his facts lined up because he can't catch a woman based on what he thinks or suspects. He can only catch her based on facts and evidence. While Olivia slept, I searched through her purse looking for evidence. But I found nothing; she even cleared her cell phone of numbers. I felt foolish doing that, and I decided to let Olivia hang herself, so I stopped searching. It's been said, "When you go looking for trouble you'll find it."

Promise was at London's house for the weekend. It was a Saturday evening. Olivia and I had just finished eating breakfast together. I had no plans for the day except to clean the house and work on my book. After the house was clean, Mischievous called for Olivia. She left the house around 2 o'clock that afternoon to take Mischievous to the store. Olivia was looking fly and smelling good wearing her new Gucci Envy perfume that I had bought for her. After she left, I got on my computer and worked on my book until I fell asleep. When I woke up I didn't notice how much time had flown by...it was now 8 o'clock at night. I looked at the caller I.D. Olivia hadn't called. I decided to call her, but she didn't answer her phone. I fell back to sleep again, this time I was awakened at 1 o'clock in the morning. "Where in the hell is Olivia?"

I wanted to call her phone again but then I thought, "I want her to think I'm sleep when she comes in." I walked back and forth, looking out the window for Olivia to pull up. At 4 o'clock in the morning I heard her strolling into the house. At the time, I was using the bathroom. When I came out of the bathroom, Olivia was under the covers with her clothes on. Her fresh hairdo looked like do-do. "Olivia where in the hell have you been for the past 15 hours?"

She gave me this dumb look, like I wasn't supposed to question her. We argued and I wasn't backing down until she told me the truth.

Olivia grabbed her keys and purse and said, "I don't have time for this." Before she could exit the house, I snatched her car keys out of her hand and took her purse. She grabbed hold of my tank top and wouldn't let go. We tussled on the floor. I picked Olivia up by her waist and put her out of the house. I told her through the door, "You're not coming back in here unless you tell me where you've been and who you were with!"

Olivia banged on the door repeatedly. She also rang the doorbell incessantly. I went upstairs, laid in the bed and turned on ESPN to drown out the doorbell, the banging and the phone. I ignored all her tactics. I was fed up and couldn't take anymore lies. Olivia rang the phone non-stop, back to back, until her cell phone battery went dead. She woke up a neighbor who allowed her to come in and use the phone. After four hours, I answered the phone, "Olivia are you ready to talk?"

"Yeah," she said, sounding pitiful.

"If you're not going to tell me the truth, you ain't coming in here."

"Dawayne, I'm ready to talk."

Olivia came in the house, took a shower and told me nothing but more lies. She claimed she fell asleep over Mischievous' house. "Olivia, Mischievous has three kids in a two bed room apartment. Why would you fall asleep at her place and not come home to your own bed?" I became very suspicious of Olivia's and Mischievous' relationship. Whenever Mischievous called the house, Olivia broke her neck to take Mischievous wherever she wanted to go. One day Mischievous called and ask Olivia to bring her some cigarettes. Mischievous lives ten minutes away. It took Olivia six hours to come back home. I questioned Olivia about their relationship. I was confused and disturbed to the point that I decided I would ask Olivia if they were gay.

For a month, Olivia hadn't been eating at all. When she came in from work she sat in front of the T.V. If I was in the bedroom she'd be downstairs. She avoided me, thinking I knew what was going on. Olivia sat up all night watching T.V. She had insomnia. Every time I passed by her, she was crying silently in the dark while watching T.V. It didn't matter what time I woke up to either use the bathroom or check on her. She'd be crying her heart out in the dark. I asked her a thousand times, "Olivia what's wrong?"

"Nothing".

I tried to ignore it, but I became deeply worried about her.

I didn't want to pressure Olivia to open up, but this had gone too far. I was beginning to lose my mind because Olivia wouldn't tell me what was bothering her. I never saw Olivia in this state of mind. She looked worried, miserable, pitiful and unhappy. She looked like she was having a nervous breakdown. So, when I asked Olivia if she was gay, it was as if I had turned on a light in a dark room. Her face shined as her smile showed her white teeth. "Olivia you bumping booties with Mischievous ain't chu?"

She just smiled, walked over to the phone, called Mischievous and told her while I was standing there, "Girl he thinks we're gay." Moving her head from side to side like black women do, she laughed and looked relieved of the stress she was under.

After she got off the phone with Mischievous, she left the house and returned two hours later, asking me, "Why do you think I'm gay, Dawayne?"

"Olivia, either you're gay or you have a sport-coat on the side. Which one is it…woman or a man?"

This all could've been simple, but Olivia wanted to make things more difficult than it had to be. She was in complete denial.

"Dawayne, tell me, why do you think I'm gay? Tell me?"

"Well, for one, you made it very obvious that you're cheating. You telling me you have everything you want, including me, and you're still not happy. Just be a women and tell me what's going on?"

Olivia went upstairs, locked herself in Promise's room and wrote me a four-page letter. After writing the letter, she stuck it under the door for me to read. The letter stated that she wasn't gay and I would soon find that out. She also wrote that she wanted a divorce from me. I wasn't surprised by this, the way things were going I knew it wasn't going to last long. At the end of the letter it stated, "I want you out of my house by the end of the month."

I thought she was joking, but she wasn't. I found out that Olivia had taken the money we had saved together in our joint account out of the bank. She paid off some bills, then behind my back, had purchased the house with the rest of the money.

She wasn't lying, I saw a copy of the deed. It was in her name. I never thought she would betray me, not like this. How could she be so vindictive toward me? What on God's green earth caused my wife to be so treacherous and untrustworthy. I told Olivia I wasn't leaving the house until she told me the reason she wanted me to leave. No matter how hard I tried, Olivia stayed in denial about whether she was gay or cheating with another man.

One day, I came home early from work. Roger had talked with his boss and he was able to land me a job at the Maryland National Capitol Park and Planning Commission. My second week of working on the job, we had a company picnic. Normally, I would leave the house at 4:45 AM to be at work on time. But on this day we had my job picnic to attend and Roger and I didn't have to be at the picnic until 8 o'clock. I woke up at 6:30 that morning. Olivia usually gets up at 6:45 to be at work on time. When I rolled out of bed

Olivia woke up and looked at the clock. "Boy you're going to be late for work."

I looked at her and said, "I got some business to take care of today." I didn't want Olivia in my business, knowing I would be home early.

Roger and I left the picnic early, as planned. He dropped me off at 12:45 that afternoon. When I got in the house the phone was ringing. I answered it and guess who was on the other line, Mischievous. She cussed me out for saying she was gay. I wondered how she knew I was home from work. Olivia had to tell her I was home. I checked the caller I.D. Mischievous had been calling all day until I walked in the house.

I couldn't get a word in, so I slammed the phone down. She kept calling until I answered again. When I picked up the phone, I decided to listen to what she had to say. Maybe she would tell me the truth, so I listened to all the cuss words and insults. "Nigga you're not a real man. You don't even like getting your hands dirty. Nigga we like thugs, niggas who smoke weed and drink. You're a church boy. You think you're a pretty boy because you can dress."

I cut her off, "You weren't saying that when you tried to have sex with me."

"What nigga…I don't even like light-skinned men! You know what, I know some niggas that want you anyway! We'll be around there to bury you nigga!"

Then she hung up. I waited outside in front of the house, but she never came.

Chapter 22
Dirty & Ugly

I had kept London out of my marriage, but now I had to break the bad news to her. I needed to move back home. London told me, "You're not coming back here, work things out with your wife."

I tried everything to make the marriage work but Olivia didn't care. "You have to move out of my house." That's what she told me. I finally gave up. I was tired of the fighting, arguing, no sex and all the lies. I moved out just to keep my sanity. I needed to figure out what had just happened to me. On the weekend that I moved out Olivia went away. She checked herself into a hotel to think. I couldn't think at all, I was in a daze. Like a fighter seeing stars, I was punch drunk asking myself, "How did this happen? How could this have happened? What did I do wrong?" And the biggest thing that bothered me was that I didn't know the truth to this ugly and dirty situation.

Now that I was back at London's house, I got Promise for a week and Olivia got her for a week. This continued until I told Olivia's parents what had happened between us. Three months after we separated, I still wanted the truth. I gave Olivia time to think about everything; but she held onto what she wanted to do and that was to divorce me after eight months of marriage.

So, here I was, talking with her parents…telling them the real scoop about our separation. Her father left the house when I got there and he didn't return until I left. I explained everything to her mother. I had nothing to lose, so I unloaded the bomb on her mother. Olivia had told me if I ever told her parents, she would make my life a living hell. I told her mother about the abuse that Olivia experienced when she was young, only because I wanted her to get some help. I felt sorry that she had been abused. I also felt that her abuse affected our marriage and she wasn't in her right state of mind. There were times she used her abuse as an excuse to get out of the house to visit Mischievous. Now that I look back on it, I don't appreciate being played.

A week later, Olivia flattened the tire on my job van. I had driven it home one night and when I came out to go to work the tire was flat. I tried to get a can of fix a flat, but it didn't work. I even tried to drive the van to the gas station to place some air in the tire, that didn't work either. Two days later sheriffs showed up at my door with a temporary protective order, stating that there had been past abuse. It had been four months since Olivia and I separated.

The temporary protective order also stated that I shall not abuse or threaten to abuse Olivia. That the respondent (me) shall not enter Olivia's residence including: yard, grounds, outbuilding, and common areas surrounding dwelling. Stay away from her place of employment. There were six more shall nots included. Number six stated; final protective order hearing will be held on Thursday at 8:45 AM at the Hyattsville Court House on Rhode Island Avenue in Maryland.

When I received the protective order, I thought the sheriffs were going to arrest me. Thursday was only 48 hours away. Olivia wrote: He threatened to hurt me plus take my child away from me. I am scared to go home at night and he has physically abused me in the past, harassing me on the job and at home.

Where it said, "Describe all injuries the respondent has caused the victim and give date," she wrote; "He broke my finger; cuts, plus scrapes and bruises." It hurt me to read that she checked off mental injury to Promise. She knows I love Promise with all my heart and would never do anything to harm my baby.

When Thursday came, I didn't know what I was walking into. I had London with me, and Olivia had one of her girlfriends with her to convince the judge that I was an angry and crazy black man. So she could have custody of Promise, she tried to convince the judge that I abused her. Her lies were very crafty and well planned. The judge was almost deceived by Olivia until it was my turn to state my case. When it was my turn to speak, I stuck with the truth, there was no way I could lie. Olivia had told every lie that could've been told. "Your Honor the reason we're here today is because my wife committed adultery. She has no proof, no evidence, no police report, no doctor records to show that I abused her in the past. We've been separated for four months. Why would she wait four months later to file charges on me? I do not live with her, nor have I been to her house in four months."

The judge asked her when was the last time I had been to her house. Olivia said, "September."

The Judge said, "Well, it's January. Case dismissed, next case."

Not only did Olivia try to have me arrested, but she also had taken Promise out of school. I couldn't understand why she would take Promise out of school when she was attending school for free. She placed Promise with an unlicensed babysitter and asked me to pay the sitter $450 a month. She must have thought I was a fool to pay someone $450 a month. I had to ask her if she was crazy.

For two months, Olivia wouldn't allow me to see or contact Promise. She was finding every way to make my life miserable, and the only way she could do that was by pawning Promise. Olivia changed her cell and home numbers, and found another job where I didn't have the numbers to contact her.

I had no choice but to file a complaint for custody at the courthouse, which cost me $100. A month later, I received a counter complaint for limited divorce and Olivia's complaint for custody. Olivia's lawyer contacted me, wanting me to sign papers that would grant us limited divorce. I told him, "In the state of Maryland, my wife and I have to be separated for one year before a divorce is granted. So, until September comes I'm not signing anything without my lawyer. If Olivia confesses that she committed adultery, then we can get an immediate divorce." That was the end of that conversation.

Shortly after that conversation, Olivia allowed me to keep Promise on the weekends. From March up until we finally got everything settled in court, I sent money, food and gift cards from Giant and Safeway. I even had to purchase clothes, shoes and other necessities that Promise needed for my house because Olivia wouldn't send anything, not even underclothes, when Promise came on the weekends.

Olivia told me that she didn't want to wash clothes when Promise came home. I couldn't believe that she would stoop so low to abuse my daughter to get at me. I understood that she was mad with me, but don't take it out on Promise. Promise is innocent. Olivia did that to get under my skin; she wanted to see me explode but I stood my ground and ignored her games. I knew if I would've hit Olivia it would've been a TKO. When I was around her I felt like choking the life out of her. Every time I would go to pick Promise up I had to pray that I didn't do anything stupid. Thank God I had Roger, J.P. and London to turn to because I was on the verge of snapping many times. Little did Olivia know that they saved her life, because one thing I hate is for someone to mess with my family. If you have a beef with me then keep it between us...don't use my daughter.

I knew I didn't have any money to pay for a lawyer. I was still figuring out how I was going to pay to get my car fixed. The bill on my car started at $4,100, then increased to $6,800. I ended up paying $7,353. Thank God the man at Maaco worked with me until I paid the balance off. It wasn't until June, a year later, when I got my car out of the shop. After two weeks of driving, I knew I had to either sell my car or trade it in for a better one. My car had been hit in the front and it never drove the same.

I traded in my Maxima for a 2005 Dodge Durango. It felt good to buy my first brand new truck. All my other cars were used. It seemed that things were beginning to go my way. A week later, I was approved to move into my apartment. All I had to do was pay my first month's rent and I could move in on July 1, 2005. I was excited to have my truck, and now my own place again. I had been sleeping on the couch for the past ten months.

I started packing my things. Then I received a letter in the mail from the Prince George's court on June 22nd that stated I had to appear in court on August 11th. In the midst of everything that had happened between Olivia and me, I tried to get things settled out of court. All I wanted was visitation rights and the divorce that she so desperately sought.

Olivia told me, "I don't care about settling anything. I'ma get in your pockets nigga." After hearing that, I knew I had to get a lawyer before the court date. I had a hard decision to make. Either I would move into my apartment or pay for a lawyer to defend me in my divorce case. I went with the lawyer. I begun gathering all the information I could find.

Once Olivia knew the court date was near, she did all kinds of things to get under my skin. She tried to provoke me and irritate the hell out of me so she could hold it against me in court. One day she called me so that Promise could speak to me. Promise called me her new man's name. She took advantage of every opportunity to cuss me out, sometimes leaving four and five messages a week on my voice mail.

On our first court date, I thought we'd get everything done; but that's not how the system works. Divorce affects every facet of life, from finances down to the kids. They ordered Olivia and me to take mediation to see if we could work things out. We had to take two mandatory classes that cost another $250 apiece, on top of our lawyers' fees. The next court date was set for October 31st. We got nothing accomplished in mediation because Olivia didn't want me to have visitation rights.

A week before the court date, Olivia's lawyer wanted to settle the case out of court for $10,000. Subtracting the back child support Olivia claimed I owed, it would've left me with $6,848.

I wanted to contest the back child support she claimed I owed. I had checks that I had written and Post Office money orders I had given Olivia for Promise. I didn't take the $10,000 offer to me because I knew I could get more money based on the information I've given to my lawyer about the equity in the house. Olivia said she paid $142,000 for the house, but the truth was she paid $102,000. I had a copy of the deed and proof of purchase for the house, stating that she paid $102, 000, not $142,000.

On October 31, the Master issued Olivia's and my divorce and child support orders. I was obligated by the court to pay $394 a month for Promise, beginning immediately. The Master also ordered joint legal custody, meaning Olivia got physical custody and we both had joint legal custody, in which I got Promise three weekends per month—the 1st, 3rd and 4th weekend of each month. I was also granted four weeks during the summer for vacation with Promise. I was happy that Olivia couldn't keep me from seeing Promise. With the divorce now out of the way and child support taken care of, the Master granted Olivia's lawyer a continuance to pull paperwork on the equity of the house. The next court date was set for December 21st when marital property and back child support would be settled.

Just in case Olivia tried to lie about the equity, I had a buddy of mine who worked for Re/Max Allegiance Realtors pull the information I needed on the property value of the house. There were two properties in Olivia's complex that sold in the past three months. One sold in September for $170,000 and the other property sold in November for $195,000. Now that it was December, I knew there was more equity in the house.

The final court date came on December 21, 2005. I walked into the court building with London and Roger. Olivia's lawyer and my lawyer began discussing the case so we could settle out of court. My lawyer asked me what I wanted out of the house. I wrote down everything I could think of that Olivia kept in her possession that was mine or ours. Number one was the house, wedding pictures, wedding gifts, wedding money that she stole, my couch, ceiling fan and my bed. I estimated the wedding gifts to be $4,000…the money that Olivia took out the account was $4,000. Our lawyers went back and forth on the estimation of the money in the bank account and the wedding gifts. This was becoming a circus… my lawyer believed everything Olivia said. I had to ask him, "Whose side are you on mine or hers? Look, I want $47,000 out of the house and she can keep everything else. If she still wants the back child support then subtract it from the $47,000. I don't have all day to be going back and forth."

My lawyer went over to Olivia's lawyer and they began negotiating again. Olivia's lawyer looked like he was about to blow his wig off once he saw my buy-out price. He went into his briefcase and pulled out documents that showed that the house didn't have $47,000 worth of equity in it. He said there was only $16,000 in equity from the paperwork he produced. Olivia had taken out two equity line loans on the house. She had a first mortgage and a second trust mortgage loan, in which she combined both mortgages into one to get a lower payment. Olivia had to produce the paper showing what she did with the money she had borrowed. She tried to say that we had bills and that she took out the loans to pay them off. My question was, "What did she spend $40,000 on?" I could see were she had spent $12,500, but $27,500 was missing. We didn't have any bills together; the bills she paid off were her personal debt. Olivia couldn't produce anything that had our names. The truth is, she tried to be slick and take all the equity out of the house so I wouldn't get nothing. I found out that she was paying nine percent on the money she borrowed.

Because Olivia's lawyer tried to say there was only $16,000 in the property and my lawyer had the paper saying that the equity was more than $16,000, we decided to let the Master have the final decision on what the equity really was. After we were sworn in, I was called to the witness stand to state my case. While explaining my side of the case, I was rudely and impolitely interrupted by the Master four times. On the last warning given she said, "Mr. Williams, I'm not going to warn you again."

I felt belittled and confused, like a child being told what to say. She wanted me to say, "yes and no." I wasn't able to tell my side of the story. I only got out seventy percent of what I wanted to say. The Master acted as if she had heard my case before. On the cross examination, Olivia's lawyer tried to make it appear as though I didn't support my child. Some men totally abandon their children, but not me; I was there from day one taking full responsibility for my daughter. After I stepped down, my lawyer called London to the stand. The Master cut London off like she did me…she showed no respect and disregarded both our testimonies.

After London stepped down, Olivia was called to the stand by her lawyer. He stuck to the facts in the case. When my lawyer cross examined Olivia, I had written down as many questions as I could for him to ask her.

My lawyer was unprepared. For the money I paid him, I could've represented myself. Black and white don't lie. My lawyer was out to prove that Olivia had planned the divorce and everything that took place between us.

I handed my lawyer our joint account statement, which included how much money was in our account and the proof that Olivia had committed adultery. I studied Olivia's facial expression and her body movements as my lawyer asked her several questions. I stared into her eyes to see how she would lie her way out of this one. My lawyer asked Olivia about the hotels that were charged on our joint account. She looked frightened, her eyes watered and she became speechless. My lawyer repeated the question, "Did you charge a hotel on the joint account? Did your husband know about the charges? Is this your name?" Olivia took a long pause before answering, "Yes I charged a hotel on the account; it was for a friend."

I knew once I had seen our joint account statement that Olivia was cheating with another man. She tried to make it look like she was gay. She disguised her cheating with the help of Mischievous; but I figured it all out. Sportcoat would call Mischievous; then she would call Olivia and act like she needed a favor. But, all the time Olivia was cheating with another man who I called Sportcoat. Olivia would park her car in Mischievous' apartment complex and then leave with Sportcoat in his car to go to the hotel.

After answering that question, Olivia didn't look up and when she did she looked over at her lawyer as if to say, "Save me from answering these questions." Not once was Olivia interrupted, not even when she got emotional. When she stepped down, the verdict was given by the Master.

For everything I had done to be the best man I could be for Olivia and Promise, I was railroaded. The Master didn't care how much love I had for my daughter. She didn't care that I had done my best and given my all to be a father and husband. I didn't think things would turn out that way…from the pawning of my child, the adultery and stealing the money, which Olivia had confessed to. The

Master awarded me nothing, nuffin, na-da. I felt punished. I was another black man who was stereotyped by a system that doesn't care. I also felt that the Master blamed me because my marriage had failed.

The Master did subtract the checks and money orders I had sent to Olivia for Promise. Olivia was awarded back child support, based on the fact that I filed for custody in January 2005. The Master stated that child support starts on the filing date. Before leaving court, I was told I owed $1,991 in arrears. Sixteen dollars was added to my payment per month until my arrears were paid up. So, now I'm paying $410 a month, plus health insurance at $50 along with the doctor bills. All the clothes I bought Promise for my house…shoes, coats, etc…. weren't included in my arrears. I learned the hard way that it's very important to write out a check or money order, because receipts are not accepted in court. They're looked at as gifts.

After the verdict was given, I shook my head in disbelief. As I was walking towards the double doors to exit the courtroom, I heard the Master say to Olivia, "You have two child support cases on file." I couldn't believe it, but knowing Olivia, only she could pull off the greatest show of deception. Promise had been trying to tell me for months that she has a baby sister. I didn't know whether Olivia told her to tell me this to make me mad because I had never seen Olivia pregnant; but I honestly hadn't paid her any attention during our separation.

I went to talk with another lawyer to see if I could do something. A week after the case was over, I wrote to the Master. I wanted her to know that I wasn't making the same amount of money at the time I filed. She denied my request and added on another thousand dollars to my back child support. Now I have to pay back $2,991. The lawyer told me that it wasn't worth going back to court and that I should just pay the money because it would cost me more than a thousand dollars to go back to court and fight.

Some things in life can't be changed.

Chapter 23

Catastrophe

The word catastrophe means a sudden happening that causes great loss, suffering, or damage; terrible disaster.

There's only so much a man can take. One man, one man brought tons of weight that collapsed on my family and neighborhood like the Twin Towers on 9/11. In April of 1998 I recorded this dream and this is how it unfolded.

I tried to stop Omar, Wylie, Martin and Tyson from entering a building with guns. I not only told them not to enter but I begged them, "Please don't go into the building?" But they entered anyway. The police came rushing out of the building and they were arrested. As I stood watching them go down for the crime they committed, my eyes took hold of the sky, there was a helicopter floating over us...shining its light as if they had committed the biggest crime in history. There were news cameras everywhere, the streets were blocked off like the police were on a manhunt. After they were arrested I wondered, "Why wasn't Tyson arrested with them?"

As I turned to walk in the opposite direction, Tyson walked alongside me. In front of us stood London and Eve. They wanted to know what happened. Tyson stopped and told them while I continued walking, knowing I had something important to do. As I passed them, I took one last look back and continued walking. Before me was a gigantic mountain I had to climb. It was a struggle to climb, but I strived with great effort to reach the top. There were rocks, boulders and people in my way, but I made it to the top. When I planted my feet on top of the mountain, I gave praise to the one and only God.

Back in 1985 PCP had a lot of black men and women losing their minds. I've witnessed women taking off all their clothes and running down the street naked. I've seen guys who thought they were Jesus and I've met guys who thought they were professional wrestlers such as Super Fly Snuka and the Junk Yard Dog. I laughed at all of them…it was funny then, because I couldn't understand there frame of mind. The nickname for PCP back then was, Love Boat or Boat. But nowadays, the name is the Dipper. It has caused many men and women to lose their minds, hypnotizing them, making their body unable to resist its magical hallucinogenic power.

In 1999 I witnessed a moment I'll never forget. At the time, I was in the shower running Dove soap all over my body. While washing up, I heard the door in the bathroom open. I knew that Wylie and I were the only ones in the house at the time. I thought to myself, "If this isn't Wylie then someone broke into the house." So, I peeked outside the shower curtain before panicking. After seeing it was him I spoke up, "Wylie what in the hell are you doing coming into the bathroom without knocking on the door first? What are you, a faggot?"

Wylie replied with a, "Shh, shh shhhhh." I opened the shower curtain and saw Wylie standing in front of the mirror dressed in a United States Army camouflage suit with matching hat and black paint under his eyelids. When I looked down at his hands, he had two 9mm's gripped tightly. I thought maybe he was playing, but then I noticed as I talked to him, he said nothing but, "shh."

"Nigga we're not in the forest, ain't no hunting going on around here. We're in South East."

Wylie replied, "Somebody is trying to kill me."

"Who Wylie, who?"

"I don't know shhhhhhhhh."

At that moment I knew he was hallucinating off the dipper. So I immediately got out of the shower without rinsing off. I grabbed some clothes and got the hell out of the house before his mind snapped and he killed me. Before I left the house, I observed Wylie walking from the back of the house to the front, opening and closing the curtains, looking to see if he saw a person he thought wanted to kill him.

This same drug that polluted Wylie's mind also contaminated Omar, Tyson and Martin's minds. One day, Martin got high and told Eve that Omar wanted to kill him, but didn't say why. I wondered if it was the dipper or was it his conscience. Martin knew why he thought Omar wanted to kill him…the truth was Martin had stolen Omar's money. Five years had passed since that took place. Omar took the loss and bounced back. After Martin stole the $20,000, he moved from the minor leagues to the major leagues in the drug game.

Before Tyson came home, Martin, Omar, Wylie and Soprano were all tight. But what I noticed was that the dipper had a different affect on all of them. Martin seemed spaced out, Omar seemed laid back and in control of his high, and Wylie seemed naïve; but the dipper made Tyson do things without a conscience, like a psychopath.

Up to this point in my life, I felt that I had accomplished nothing more than paying bills, child support, and a job that consumed the majority of my time. A job was all I needed to keep me focused. Every day I came home from work, I was in front of my computer working on my memoir.

There were days I would put in twelve to fourteen hours working. I was devoted to completing my memoir. I had to finish because London said to me several times, "Lamont you always start something, but you never finish what you started. Please, for me, your mother, finish something son...finish." So I sacrificed going out, dating and even church on Sundays to get the job done.

I thought by now that my cousins and my brother Wylie would all be tired of the life they were living. They were all stuck, frozen in time...frozen in their adolecent stage of manhood. They were still doing the same things that I had grown out of over the years. But who am I to judge them? I know how easily a man can be drawn back to his destructive tendencies.

It's been a little over ten years since I've left the drug game. I remember the day I stopped selling drugs, I promised God, "If you keep me working a good job, I'll never go back to selling drugs." I've been working ever since. Wylie even gave up the salesman role but still hung out with Martin on the streets.

You would think with all the chances we get in life to change that we would recognize the opportunity and do so. But, some people never change. They pretend by saying, "I'm not the same person I was years ago. I've changed...God is now in my life." I don't care how much a jealous person pretends, their jealousy can't be disguised in love or friendship. Tyson did all he could to convince everyone that he'd changed, but that only lasted a few months after he came home.

Word got back to me that Tyson was a cold serial murderer...every time someone was shot, Tyson's name surfaced as the number one, and only suspect. Yellow tape with the words, Crime Scene covered the streets where Tyson left his trademark and gun shells. He considered himself as the South East Sniper. He thought he was God because he was getting away with it and no one had the guts to turn him in. In several cases, he shot victims and they lived. Most of the people he shot were family and close friends, guys who hung in the neighborhood and who we grew up knowing.

Niggas wanted his head and he knew it…so, he would switch cars. One day he'd be in a truck, the next day in a different color truck or car. That made him hard to find. He was an extortionist—robbing and running up in nigga's houses. He would tell everyone and anyone, even family, "If you don't have my money you're dead." Niggas paid him to keep him from pulling the trigger. He acted as if everybody owed him something.

Tyson believed that niggas in the neighborhood, even Martin, were going to take care of him for life…or, he was going to take care of them. I wondered if jail made Tyson a monster. But, the truth was Tyson has been crying out for help since his mother's death. No matter how much Eve did for him, he wanted more, until more became no more. Word got out that he wanted to kill everyone in our neighborhood. It's been said, "whatever age a person goes to jail, that's the age and level their thinking will be…unless they educate themselves." Tyson went to jail at nineteen for the two bullets he placed in my back in 1993.

No one knew where Tyson was going to strike next. March 1, 2005 two people were shot, one lived and the other was killed. The guy who was killed was Soprano. I wondered, "who in the world killed Soprano?" Soprano was a good friend and the cousin of Rollo. Months after Soprano's murder, I was told that Tyson did it. People started coming to me telling me, "Man you know Tyson shot Razor, Chain, Knox and Spider." I wondered to myself, "Is there a beef I don't know about or has this nigga gone completely crazy?" It was unbelievable to me when I was told Tyson shot Omar too.

When Omar fell on the ground from the impact of being shot in his arm, Tyson stood over him and his gun jammed. Omar escaped death that day because of the police racing to the scene. When Eve heard about Tyson shooting Omar, she stopped living in her own house. Eve would take her kids and stay with other family members to get away from Tyson.

When I heard all this was happening, I had to find out what in the hell was going on. So, I talked with Martin. He told me it was all true. "Martin, has Tyson lost his damn mind?"

"Kojack, I don't know, I really don't? But the nigga keeps pressing me to pay his car note and his car insurance or the snatch man is going to take his car. He's hiding his car right now because they're looking for it. That's what he told me. Kojack, I've given this nigga everything I can give him. I can't give him any more money. When he asks for money he doesn't ask for a little like $20, $50 or $100. He asks for 4, 5 and 10 thousand at time, like I'm Donald Trump."

"Martin tell me the truth, what do you think he's going to do to you when you tell him no? He can't rob anyone else on the block because they're not on the block anymore. Nobody is outside for him to rob. He knows you're the only one with money. That nigga is either going to rob you or try to kill you, then what? He already showed you what he's capable of doing."

"Kojack, I don't know; I don't trust the nigga."

"Martin, I know that's your nephew, but ain't no nigga going to run my mother out of her house. They may run me out, but not my mother. I would die before I let that happen." As we continued talk-ing, I looked at Martin's facial expression. I could see he was deeply worried about something, but he would never tell me what was on his mind.

"Kojack, I'm about to turn my life around. I've been thinking of leaving the streets for good. I'm thinking of taking some real estate classes and moving down to Atlanta. I just want to get away from all this drama and take Wylie with me. I got enough money for us to live off." Little did I know, that would be the last conversation we would have.

Two weeks later on February 28, 2006 at 3:30 AM, Martin was shot several times in the head execution style. When the word got back to me, I knew, like everyone else, that Tyson did it. Twelve hours after Martin was killed, Tyson ran out the house with a gun in front of family members who were grieving over Martin's death. Next thing I heard, a buddy of mine named Radio was killed.

Tyson was on a rampage and he threatened to kill anyone he caught outside, including me. His reason was that we all had something to do with Martin being killed. Tyson tried to switch the weight on Omar, saying that Omar had killed Martin; but we knew Tyson had done it. His reputation convicted him, even though no one witnessed the murder. Eve didn't want to turn Tyson in because Tyson convinced Eve that Omar had killed Martin.

Martin took care of Tyson and his kids. When Tyson came home from jail, Martin had bought him a C-class Benz and gave him a pocket full of money. Tyson's greed for money made him greedy for more. Martin was the man on the block, but Tyson started robbing niggas who bought from Martin, not caring that they still had to pay Martin his money. Tyson didn't care, he blew money like it was growing on trees. He smoked drugs and went to the clubs every night and tricked his money away as fast as he took it.

Omar called me three times telling me Tyson had threatened to kill him, his girlfriend and her daughter. Then he told me Tyson had threatened to kill me. So, I called Tyson to confirm what Omar had told me. Tyson wasn't the type of guy who would tell you what he's going to do. He would sneak up on you and before you know it...BAM, BAM, BAM. When I called Tyson, he was hyped, speaking ignorant and very cocky. "Kojack, I can't get any sleep and I won't until I kill Omar… because I know he was the one who killed Martin."

"Tyson, do you know for sure that it was Omar? Were you there?"

"Nigga, I know he done it. I'm telling you like this, I'm killing everything in my path and everybody on 17th Street. Kojack, I can do what I want to do when I get ready. I got niggas running from me. I'm on top of D.C. Kojack, if I wanted to kill you I could've killed you earlier today when you were over Omar's house. I seen you when you picked him up and I was there when you dropped him off nigga." I got tired of listening to that nigga repeat himself over and over, so I decided to end the conversation. Tyson repeated, "I haven't been to sleep and I can't sleep."

"Tyson I'ma talk to you later, get some sleep. You hear me, get some sleep."

"Alright, Jack."

Then I hung up. After I got off the phone with Tyson, I started praying. His mind was completely gone and there was no way I could talk sense into him. Tyson tried to outslick me but I figured it out. While I was visiting Omar's house Kenny called and that's how he knew that I was over Omar's house earlier that day.

On March 7, 2006 the day of Martin's funeral, Tyson and Omar were told not to come because Eve didn't know which one had killed Martin. Tyson came to prove to everyone that he didn't kill Martin.

I stood outside the church near my truck with J.P., Rollo, Soprano's mother and his sister. Soprano's mother knew Tyson had killed her son. I was surprised to see her. She came to the funeral out of love and respect for Martin and Soprano's friendship. While we stood talking, she realized that Martin and Radio were killed one year after Soprano's death. Tyson was under investigation for Soprano's murder.

As family members pulled up with food for the repast, I helped them carry it into the dining area. As I was walking, Tyson walked over to me and gave me a fake hug, his eyes never connected with mine. Then he walked into the funeral. No one could believe he had the nerve to come. Five minutes later, Tyson had to be carried out of the funeral to get some air. Two men carried him along their shoulders. He looked like he had passed out. He had shortness of breath, his legs dragged on the ground as he was being carried, and saliva flew from his mouth as snot drained from his nose in bubbles. I heard someone say, "This nigga is faking, he should get an Oscar for his performance."

A few minutes later, I saw Omar's girlfriend and I asked her, "Where's Omar?" She told me that he was inside. I was glad he came, but couldn't find him...the funeral was packed from wall to wall.

After Tyson got himself together he rolled out while everyone else went on to the burial site. Tyson didn't come to the burial grounds, neither did Omar. I called Omar to see where he was but he didn't answer his phone.

I knew by now that he should've called me back and said, "I'm okay" or "I'm busy." It wasn't like Omar not to answer his phone. That afternoon around 3:30, a friend told me that Tyson had been killed at 12:00 noon. We were still in church at noon and didn't leave to go to the graveyard until 1 o'clock. I said, "WHAT?" I was in shock. Omar came to my mind immediately, so I called his girl-friends' house and when she answered the phone, I asked her, "Where's Omar? Have you heard from him?"

She said, "Oh my God, Kojack! Omar is on the news!" Then she burst into tears and cried loudly over the phone. That's when I knew Omar had killed Tyson.

Apparently Omar came to the funeral, but when he saw Tyson, he got into a car with two of his comrades and they laid low and watched Tyson's every move. Omar and his comrades, with whom I'm well acquainted, followed Tyson from the funeral around noon, while everyone was still in service at church. They drove alongside

Tyson at a light and fired dozens of rounds into Tyson's car. Tyson jumped out of the car and ran, but collapsed on the front lawn of a vacant house, where he was shot thirty-two times in his face and upper body with high-powered assault weapons. Omar and his comrades had taken the police on a crazy high-speed chase that lasted thirty-seven minutes before the police closed in on them.

The *Washington Post* newspaper wrote: Police quickly spotted the suspects getaway car, and the chase began, authorities said. Eventually, dozens of police cars from the District and Prince George's County, Maryland pursued the car with the help of two police helicopters. The suspects traveled at high speed back and forth between Prince George's and the District before surrendering. The man who was killed was a suspect in two slayings on February 28th. Police said they recovered an assault weapon that was thrown from the suspects' car. As of last night, none of the three men had been charged. Police believe the shooting was in retaliation for the two slain men on February 28th.

A friend of Tyson's was in the car with him, he was also shot, but lived. For two days Tyson's murder was all over the news. The Detective on the news said he never, in his twenty years as a policeman, heard anything happening like this amongst family. ..cousin killing cousin, nephew killing uncle and friends. After I heard that Tyson was killed, I drove around the corner where some of my old friends still hung out and I told them the news...they already knew.

There were at least ten guys out there. Calk Board walked over to my car and said, "I'm glad that nigga is dead. He got what he deserved. All of us were talking about Omar and his comrades gettin' caught. Tyson was shooting everybody and never got caught, but when this nigga gets killed the police catch the niggas that done it. I hope that Omar and them get off, for all that trouble that nigga took this neighborhood through. They done all of us a favor."

There was nothing I could say. I was shocked that all this had taken place. They had peace of mind that Tyson ain't never coming back to terrorize the neighborhood again. It's very sad that one man with nothing to lose caused so many other black men to lose their lives over nothing. Tyson had killed more people than I mentioned. It's been said that he is linked between ten and thirty murders. After he was killed, a lot of victims surfaced to tell me their testimony and how they were victimized by Tyson.

I feel sorry for all the children who will grow up without their fathers. The cycle of fatherless children continues. Deep down in my heart, I look at Tyson's, Omar's, Martin's, Wylie's and my own child. And I wonder how will our kids adapt to what has taken place? How will they function around each other? Will they hate one another? Will they hold grudges? Will there be vengeance for what has taken place? Lord...I hope not.

When Eve found out Omar had killed Tyson, she was convinced that Omar had killed Martin as well. The night before Martin was killed, Wylie and Martin were in the club. Tyson was there also with his sidekick, the guy believed to have been shot in the car with Tyson when he was killed. Tyson walked up to Martin and demanded some money. They exchanged words and Martin left the club hours before it let out, leaving Wylie stranded. Wylie walked the ten miles home in disbelief . This had never happened before. Martin rang our phone until London answered, begging London to see if Wylie was home. London heard fear in Martin's voice; so she got out of the bed to see if Wylie was home. He wasn't.

After that phone call, London couldn't sleep. Something had to have happened to Wylie. She stayed awake until he walked through the door, out of breath from walking the ten miles. Martin knocked on the door at seven in the morning, shortly after Wylie arrived home. One thing about Martin, he was a night owl; he was never up at seven in the morning. Wylie asked Martin, "Why did you leave me at the club? I had to walk all the way home?"

"Wylie, Tyson tried to snatch me at the club last night, I had to leave." The next day Martin was found shot in front of his house execution style.

That same night, Omar was in the hospital with his girlfriend. It's been said that you will never find out the truth until a person is dead. Well, it was clear to me what the motive was and rumor has it that Tyson robbed Martin for a hundred thousand dollars.

Now I understand why Martin gave me a gun before Tyson came home. I believe he knew and feared something like this would happen. If anyone knew Tyson's thoughts, Martin knew because they were cellmates. During the time Martin and Tyson were cellmates, Tyson made a promise to Martin and a few other guys that lived in our neighborhood. He told them, "Because ya'll didn't roll with me on the niggas who stabbed me, I'ma kill all ya'll! 17th Street is dead when I get out." The beef started in jail and ended on the streets.

Four months after Tyson's death, an article was published and it was determined that two more murders took place totaling seven black men killed on one corner. Spider was one of the two victims who were killed in June 2006. The article also stated that Tyson killed his uncle Martin.

I found it strange that Martin never asked for the gun back. I had no need for it and I thought it would be safe to get rid of it to save someone's life, including mine.

I remember a co-worker of mine quoted an African proverb. Marvin Dixon said, "A wolf that travels with a pack will one day surely die, but a wolf that travels alone will outlive them all."

Conclusion
Reputations Fade Away

"This is my time, you understand me.
It don't matter what you tried to do,
you couldn't destroy me. I'm still standing,
I'm still strong and I always will be."
—Words from the motion picture that inspired me to tell my story

Antwone Quenton Fisher, thanks...

Washington, D.C. had the highest number of homicides per capita of any city with a population of 500,000 people or more. During the late 80s and 90s Washington, D.C. was ranked the murder capital of America. Between 1984 and 2005, there have been 6,591 murders of black men on the streets of Washington D.C. *Source: SafeStreetsDC Study of Washington DC Murder Capital*

With so many murders on the streets of Washington D.C. I had to ask God, "What I am I here for?" There were times I wanted to lash out at life, and honestly, I have to say that I wanted to die because that's how I felt at those moments. Nothing mattered to me. I tried to be an animal and have the instincts of a killer. But then I realized the street life wasn't for me. I wonder after witnessing so many shootings and murders in my life, "Why was I spared? Why was I given more than a second chance to get my life right? Why?"

A father's love and physical presence is an essential part of a child's development and character. The statistics don't lie, 70% of America's juveniles and adult inmates have come from fatherless homes. Seventy one percent of all high school dropouts come from fatherless homes. Eighty percent of rapists with displaced anger come from fatherless homes. Eighty-five percent of all children that exhibit behavioral disorders come from fatherless homes. Ninety percent of all homeless and runaway children are from fatherless homes. These statistics translate to mean that children from a fatherless home are: five times more likely to commit suicide; Thirty-two times more likely to run away; twenty times more likely to have behavioral disorders; nine times more likely to drop out of school; ten times more likely to abuse drugs; nine times more likely to end up in a state operated institution; and twenty times more likely to end up in prison. Source: Statistics about 'deadbeat dads' and the effects of absent fathers.

I am the product of a fatherless home, but I won't leave my child unless the Lord says so.

After hearing the verdict in my divorce case, I drove home feeling empty. I never thought I'd leave the courtroom empty handed. I felt like giving up on life that day. The thought of killing or harming myself wasn't an option. That's not what I had in mind. I wanted to have a drink or maybe smoke a joint to blow off some steam.

But I could never go back to what I used to do. I came too far to turn back. I had distanced myself so far from the streets that doing what I used to do would only anchor me deeper. My problems would've never been solved by drinking, smoking and women. Problems don't do anything but create more problems unless solved.

My mind couldn't deal with adding anything else to my plate; so, I decided to go home and grab my writing utensils…my dictionary, my pens and my notebooks. I had to make this day a positive one. Writing helped me regain my perspective and take full control of my destiny. I had to finish what I started. My divorce gave me all the determination and motivation I needed to finish. Nothing stood in my way anymore and I knew at this moment, I had overcome all the obstacles and the people placed in my life. If I didn't die from being stabbed and shot in two separate incidents, then divorce wasn't going to kill me.

Two months after my divorce, I wrote Olivia a letter: Olivia, I didn't want anything from you, nothing. The furniture, the wedding pictures, the gifts and the $47,000 I asked for in court, I didn't want any of it. All I wanted was the truth and I got it out of you. Thanks, It's sad we had to go through court for the truth to come out, but she got what she wanted and I got what I wanted, the truth.

You would think Olivia would be happy, but she's miserable. She got everything and she still tries to make my life miserable. I just pray for her; and now I know that she was just another chapter in my life. Life goes on because one thing I do believe in is the scripture that states; "Be not deceived; God is not mocked: for whatsoever a man sow, that shall he also reap." (Galatians 6:7)

Alicia Keys called it Karma, what goes up must came down. I should've noticed Olivia wasn't right but who really knows a person until you live with them. When you first meet a woman you learn her personality in a couple of weeks, but it takes a lifetime to learn her character.

My life insurance agent, Abraham, gave me the most inspiring words that stuck with me even to this day. I don't know what made him say this to me... I was married at the time and things were okay then. I remember him saying, "Everything in life can be replaced in time, but there are some things that can't be replaced, like body parts and your parents. You can always get another wife and have other kids. Always appreciate the things you have one of, like your mother and your father because once mom is gone you can never get her back." I don't know if he knew whether my marriage would last, but he made me think of the story of Job in the bible. Job lost everything he had, but God gave him double for his trouble in the end.

I can understand and relate to why most black men are giving up on life, especially the ones my age—thirty, and the ones between fifteen and thirty-five. Only a few of us make it off the streets and become successful. Only a few of us can say "Been there, done that, but never again." It's sad that for many of the guys I knew growing up, their first job was selling drugs. Even once some of us grew out of selling drug, they were always there for us to fall back on when times got hard. We never thought about how important a job was until we got older and realized that the street life is a game of roulette. Hey, I may not make the money I used to make on the corners, but I can sleep in peace at night.

I wonder why some black men can't get a job. But then I realize that many other black men, like myself, have wasted too much time getting a street education, chasing dreams of money, clothes, cars, drugs…and most of all, women. This epidemic is widespread and now we're suffering from our personal lack of knowledge because we haven't found our way, our purpose, our calling and our dreams. Out of my old crew, from years back, there're only a few like J.P. and Alvin who have succeeded.

J.P. graduated from college and now owns his own home, which he calls, The Palace.

After Alvin was shot three times, in '97 he gave up the street life and now has two beautiful daughters, his own home and a great job working for Discovery Channel.

Even Roger's life turned out the way he wanted. He's told me stories of his past and how he was determined to succeed. Now, he's living his dream with three kids and another one on the way. I guess I'll be the godfather for the fourth time…I hope it's the girl he and his wife been praying for. They have a very nice house and their own business.

After nearly fourteen years of not speaking to one another, London and my grandmother Theresa broke the ice at my weeding back in 2004. I was happy to see them talking and reminiscing. But shortly after my wedding, Grandma Theresa died in her sleep at the age of eighty.

That was the last time I saw Syrup, at her funeral. Over the years he stopped coming around the family because of the favoritism. It was good to see him, but sad that it had to be that way.

No one cried more than Country at the funeral. For him, that was the beginning of the end. The umbilical cord was cut. After Grandma passed he was kicked out of her house by my aunts. For the first time in Country's life, he's living on his own, facing responsibility. I haven't heard from him, but I did hear he has an apartment out in Greenbelt.

Chicago is still locked up in the Feds in West Virginia. Last time we talked I had to tell 'em about himself. I asked him, "Are you a man or a mouse?" Of course he said he was a man, but after that conversation I don't think he'll be calling me for awhile. He feels I owe him something…I owe him nothing. What he owes me can't be replaced with money, so I told him to keep his money…because nobody can stop me from eating. Chicago inherited some money and he figured he could beat the system…but after thirty years he has to pay.

After serving nine years in jail, Jason came home three years ago. He's working on getting his home improvement license so he can start his own business. He told me while he was in jail he spent time reading, writing and taking classes in carpentry. Jason came home and bought a new Z-71 truck. He was doing well until he violated his parole.

My cousin Kenny is doing very well, working hard and driving a nice car.

After Cee won $62,000 in '96 he was broke two months later. His luck hasn't been the same since. He's currently working driving dump trucks.

Out of all my cousins, the one I have the most love for is Sunnyboy. Sunny changed his life around when he got a nice job working for the post office; he's been there for 15 years. For everything he's done for me, I dedicate the fight I have in me to him. Thanks champ, for every fistfight I won and lost. You were the one who taught me how to fight and I'll never forget those days. I can hear the Rocky anthem playing. I got my guards up because the fight of life ain't over for me, or you; keep fighting. Sunnyboy was diagnosed with diabetes. After hearing that, I got myself checked out fully, AIDS test and all. I've changed my eating habits so I can live longer and healthier.

Omar is the cousin I felt the sorriest for; because of the cards he was dealt. From the outside looking in, Omar's life was the hardest of any my cousins, including me. His father died of AIDS when he was thirteen. His mother had been off and on drugs, and in and out of jail. In Omar's case, he was forced into the street life and dropped out of school to take care of his brothers and sisters who were all split up amongst the family. There were eight of them, including Omar. He's been living from house to house all his life. People have used and abused him. Regardless of his past, regardless of what he's done, my heart goes out to him and the two brothers who sent Tyson to his final resting place. Omar is on twenty-three-hour lock down, with only two visits per week, and currently awaiting his trial date.

Back in 1996, I was in the club, posted up looking cool. I noticed Ned coming towards me. He walked over and shook my hand and gave me a hug. He didn't have to say anything, I already knew. He wanted to say, "I'm sorry." And he did. We never talked about what had happened in the past, but I forgave him and moved on. We all need to realize that forgiveness is a gift handed down from God for us to share with one another. I never got the chance to apologize to Ned's crew for what I had done. But please believe me, I prayed many days and nights for God to deliver forgiveness to my heart. And it came in the form of me forgiving my on cousin, my father and the rest of my family. Be careful what you ask God for, because he will judge you by the same rock you throw at others. Shortly after we saw each other, Ned and a few of his road dogs were arrested for a shooting that involved a police officer.

A person that doesn't plan for the future, dream for tomorrow and hope through hell that there's light at the end of their tunnel, will never accomplish anything worth having or living for. When you have a purpose, a career or a dream, you only focus on that one thing. You become so passionate, so possessed that you don't have time for anything else. Every man and woman should have a purpose, a career and a dream in their life. One of the three should be a life committed to achievement.

Rollo and I still talk…I'm pushing him to find his purpose in life.

Wylie is still dealing with the loss of Martin. They were closer than any of us; that was his hanging partner. I've got faith that he'll come around.

Ever since I've changed, my family changed as well. I have no problem with forgiving, but I could never forget! I can only apologize for the things I've done and said. And I will no longer be enslaved to think like you, act like you, or to be conned, tricked and persuaded to do what you want to me to do. I was always told that blood is thicker than water, but I'm here to tell y'all that reputations really do fade away. If my reputation didn't fade, I wouldn't be playing this game called life unless I was in it to win it. But instead of backing me up, you whip me with tough love .

Many people took my kindness for weakness, and all it did was make me stronger and them weaker. I fought to live and live for what was promised to me. When I was younger, I was laying on the couch asleep in the basement of my house. I was awakened by a voice I heard speaking to me. The basement was dark at the time. I couldn't see anything, but could hear a voice speaking to me. It said, "You're going to write a book." When I heard, "write a book," "I wanted to say, "I can't write and I barely can read." But the voice had overruled my thoughts and I continued to listen. "You're going to go through some trials and tribulations, but you're going to make it." As quickly as I heard the voice, it vanished. At that moment I was given a gift and assignment to carry out. After hearing that voice, I began to dream of mountains. And every mountain that was in my way...somehow, some way I conquered them all. God said in his word; "My grace is sufficient for thee, for my strength is made perfect in weakness." -Corinthians 12:9 Some people get by on faith and others get by because God blinded them of the obstacles ahead to draw them closer to Him. I was a follower to my father, cousin's, friends, women, fancy cars, expensive clothes, to my image and to my reputation. But once I realized my purpose in life, my reputation faded away into my dream...

About the Author

Dawayne Williams, a man of many distinguishing titles, including father, son and brother, now embraces the title writer. His evolutionary work, Reputations Fade Away, not only defies the limitations of reality writing, but it also challenges the limits of the reader's strategic developmental understanding of both Dawayne's matriculating experience and his insight to a relatively dangerous way of living.

Dawayne's journey from the streets and back has undoubtedly been a prophecy that he has led a hazardous lifestyle, confined in an incalculable amount of risky people, and ultimately trekked around chaotic milestones to therefore extend gratuity to God for sparing his life and to further be a living example to any and every disturbed reader who is seeking advice and a positive way out of the streets. He utilizes his gift as a writer as an avenue that both he and his readers can essentially benefit from.

Dawayne now resides in the bitter streets of South East, Washington D.C. where he's pursuing his long-term dream of becoming a comfortably accomplished writer. He's determined to conquer the odds.

Currently, Dawayne is working for Maryland National Capitol Park and Planning as an electrician in the apprenticeship program.

Written by Bennisha Beatrice Lucas

ORDER FORM

Mail Checks or Money Orders to:

Dawayne Williams
C/O Kojack Enterprise
P.O. Box 91733
Washington, DC 20090

Please send _____ copy(ies) of *Reputations Fade Away* to:

Name:_____

Address:_____

City:_____

State:_____Zip:_____

Telephone: (_____)_____

Email:_____

I have enclosed $16.95, plus $4.00 shipping per book for a

Total of $_____.

Sales Tax: Add 5.75% to total book cost for orders shipped to DC addresses.

For Bulk or Wholesale Rates, Call: 202-373-2325

or Email: Kojackkmw@aol.com

Please Visit: www.Reputationsfadeaway.com